The Helena Rubinstein
BEAUTY BOOK

The Helena Rubinstein BEAUTY BOOK

By the experts at Helena Rubinstein
with beauty photographs by John Swannell

COLLINS

First published in 1985
by William Collins Sons & Co Ltd
London· Glasgow· Sydney
Auckland· Johannesburg

Designed and produced by Sackville Design Group Ltd
32-34 Great Titchfield Street, London W1P 7AD
Typeset in Zapf International by Sackville Design Group Ltd

Beauty consultant: Dennise Choa of Helena Rubinstein
Writers: Heather Bampfylde
Jennifer Mulherin
Art Director: Al Rockall
Picture research: Melanie Faldo
Illustrations: Jill and Phil Evans

The Helena Rubinstein Beauty Book.
1 Beauty, Personal
I. Title
646.7'2'088042 RA778

ISBN 0-00-412018-3
Colour origination by Imago Publishing Ltd
Printed in Belgium by Proost International Book Production

CONTENTS

INTRODUCTION

Our perceptions of beauty have changed over the last couple of decades, and there are no longer any standard beauty stereotypes or a particular 'look' that every woman should strive to imitate. Today's woman wants to develop her own personal style and 'look' – one that she is happy with and suits her. She knows that there are no longer any hard and fast rules that must be obeyed at all costs, nor is she the slave of changing fashions although she is aware of new trends and keeps her eyes open to the available beauty options and what is latest and best.

She knows that looking good reflects a basic confidence within herself – that her good looks and sense of style are the external statements of her own self-esteem. The way she moves, holds herself and looks are all dimensions of her beauty. She does not need to have a perfect face with flawless symmetry, but she does need glowing, healthy, youthful-looking skin, glossy well-cared-for hair, a firm body and good colour sense. The odd wrinkle or having too long a nose are of no consequence. She has to develop a skincare and haircare system to suit her individual needs and take her beauty potential into her own hands.

Remember that beauty is not just skin-deep or being a pretty face. It is also conditioned by your personality, your degree of confidence and poise. You need to be in tune with your body, well-nourished with healthy food, fit and active. All this entails a more positive attitude towards yourself and assuming responsibility for your own body. These attitudes go hand in hand with beauty today.

Beauty comes from deep within yourself. It stems from knowing yourself and perhaps even changing the habits and routines of a lifetime as well as your make-up or skincare system. Making the most of make-up and looking after your body can boost your personal prestige as well as enhancing your looks. Feeling beautiful will bring its own benefits, enabling you to change your appearance subtly to meet the demands of different situations and occasions.

This book will help you to fulfil your personal beauty potential. Every woman is unique, and you have to learn how to care for *your* skin type, look after *your* hair, make the most of *your* face, capitalise on *your* best features and find the exercises and diet *you* enjoy most. It does not matter how old you are – so many women in their forties and fifties are now proving that you are never too old to be beautiful. Self-discipline, pampering and hard work go hand in hand with confidence, poise and sophistication for the more mature beauty. The knowledge in this book can help you be better-equipped to deal with the ageing process and even to slow it down by leading a more active, interesting life and keeping fit and healthy. You need to adapt your beauty routines to the ever-changing demands of your age, the seasons and the environment in which we live.

The experts at Helena Rubinstein have evolved a unique seasonal approach to your beauty needs, enabling you to stay beautiful throughout the year and make the most of your individual beauty potential. This way, you can adapt your make-up, skincare and haircare systems to the changing climate and the new trends in cosmetics and fashion.

BEAUTY SELF-ANALYSIS

HOW WELL DO YOU KNOW YOURSELF?

Before you embark on a new beauty programme, you should set aside a little time to analyse your looks and beauty potential – your face, skin, hair, body, figure, level of fitness and lifestyle among other things. Ask yourself some difficult questions and answer them as truthfully as you possibly can to build up a clear picture of yourself. By getting to know your body and tuning in to its beauty needs, you will be better equipped to express yourself and achieve your beauty goals. Positive thinking is vital so that you can recognise your potential and then set out to realise it.

This fresh appreciation of yourself and seeing new possibilities may be a whole new way of looking at yourself as well as your body. If you like what you see, you will feel more confident in your relationships and dealings with other people and even in the way you tackle problems at home and at work. It is important to see beauty as a whole and not in isolation to the way you live. It can be affected by your mood, your state of health, your environment, the climate and many other diverse factors.

When you look in the mirror you will examine different aspects of yourself – your skin, eyes and figure for example – but it is also important that you should have an image of your body in total and not just as a collection of parts which require separate treatments and exercise. All beauty care is inter-related and you cannot concentrate on one aspect without considering the others, too. And looking inside yourself and examining your attitudes and body image is as important as treating the externals. You must analyse the following:

Analyse your face

Although you can improve on nature with skilful make-up to create different colours and illusions, you cannot change your face's basic shape and features (short of having corrective surgery, of course). You have to get to know your face and like what you see – to capitalise on every feature if you want to be beautiful. When you examine it in the mirror, take all the features into account and see what they add up to. Remember above all that your face is a unique statement of you and expresses your personality and your moods. It is infinitely expressive and mobile, reflecting the way you feel, and capable of expressing a wide range of emotions. Decide whether it is round, oval or square; whether your eyes are large and wide, small and narow, deep-set or protruding, wide-spaced or close-set; are you happy with your nose or do you consider it too long, too short, too thin or too broad and is your mouth large and wide, small and pert, thin or broad lipped?

Study all these features and decide on your own self-analysis. The picture you form will be useful when you actually come to follow the advice in later chapters on skincare and make-up.

Analyse your skin

Your skin is the best indicator of your age and health. It is affected by your diet, hormonal changes within your body and the climate as well as by the special care and attention you lavish upon it. You have to *know* your skin if you are to look after it properly and keep it looking young. A regular skincare routine based on twice-daily cleansing, toning and moisturising is all-important. Beautiful, youthful skin is clear, moist, smooth, even-textured and relatively free from lines and wrinkles. Although you should not forget the skin all over your body, the skin on your face is especially important as it is always uncovered and needs protection against extremes of hot and cold, the drying effects of air-conditioning and central heating and pollutants in the air. Look at it in a magnifying mirror and ask yourself the following questions?

1 Is it normal, dry or oily in texture?
2 Is it smooth, rough or coarse?
3 Are there any lines or wrinkles?
Are there any spots, blemishes or enlarged pores?
5 Is your complexion sallow, over-pale or ruddy with broken veins?

Use the chart (overleaf) to help you identify your skin type. You will probably discover that it is a combination of different types – perhaps an oily section down the centre of your face from forehead to chin with dryer patches on the cheeks. Also, bear in mind that it will vary throughout the year and you should repeat this exercise regularly to identify whether any changes have occurred and adapt your skincare routine accordingly.

Analyse your colours

Your skin tone, hair and eye colours will all affect the colours you choose to wear on your face and also your clothes. The colours you use are bound to change

according to the seasons, the time of day, the climate, the occasion and your own personal preferences. All make-up consists of colour and its real purpose is to add colour to your face in such a way as to make it more beautiful and interesting.

You can choose from subtle or bright colours – muddy greens, under-stated browns and greys, warm coppers, dramatic reds, startling yellows and brilliant blues, for instance. They can be matt, shiny, sparkly, glossy or iridescent but they must look right on your face and create a look that you feel happy with and expresses the way you feel about yourself.

You will need a good eye and sense of colour co-ordination to mix and match different shades. Use colour to emphasise your best features and tone down others, to add warmth and definition, shape your face and lift your skin tone. You may use two different sets of colours in each season – one for day and one for evening; or one for work and one for relaxing at home.

You need to have good colour sense to choose the right shades of shadow, liner and mascara to emphasise and beautify your eyes.

Eye shades are determined to a great extent by the colour of your eyes, and you can choose matching, toning or contrasting colours to complement them. For example if you have:

Brown eyes: try dark browns, gold, bronze, green, violet shades and even coral or apricot.

Blue eyes: try different shades of blue, violet, pink, grey and brown.

Green eyes: try green, grey, yellow ochre, bronze, brown and blue.

Grey eyes: try silvery-grey, blue, bright green and pinks. Sometimes you will be able to match your lipstick shade to your eye colour (for example, if you are using pink) but the lip colour you choose should complement your eye colours, hair colour and the shape and size of your mouth. You will probably find a shade that suits

Skin chart – identifying your skin type

Skin type	Characteristics	Its nature	Location
Normal	Moist, smooth and free from blemishes and problems. No dry or excessively oily patches	Although called normal, it is rare and usually the preserve of young women	All over face and neck
Oily	Skin looks shiny and feels greasy, is prone to spots, blackheads and blocked pores, even acne	Found in all ages, especially young. Sebaceous glands over-produce sebum, especially during hormonal changes. Good for older women as cuts down risk of wrinkles	Centre panel of face – nose, forehead, chin, also back and chest
Dry	Dry, flaky and tight. Sensitive and prone to lines and broken veins. May look dull or crêpey	Skin does not produce enough oil and thus its moisture evaporates leaving it dry. Wind, sun, air conditioning, heating and harsh soaps worsen the condition	Cheeks, throat and around eyes
Sensitive	Easily irritated and prone to broken veins and redness. May have flaky patches and be allergic to certain substances	Skin may be dry or oily and reacts adversely to extremes of heat and cold, harsh soaps and detergents	All over face and neck or localised
Combi-nation	Oily patches, especially in central panel, and dry patches, usually on cheeks	Most common skin type which necessitates two different types of skincare – creams for dry *and* oily skin	Cheeks, throat and sides of forehead are dry; nose, chin and middle of forehead oily

you and stick to it — be guided by your colour sense and what you like wearing. Experiment with a wide range of colours to try out different looks – bright fuchsia or scarlet for evenings; bronze or silvery pink for daytime perhaps.

Analyse your hair

Healthy, beautiful hair should be strong, glossy, shining, soft and well-conditioned. Look at your hair carefully and decide whether it measures up to this ideal. If it is lank, dull, oily, thin, dry, badly cut, affected by dandruff or split ends it will need some attention. Regular haircare and visiting the hairdresser will help solve any problems and keep it in tip-top condition. You should look also at the colour and its manageability – does it need highlighting or some richer, warmer tones? Is it flyaway, unruly or unmanageable?

Your hair's condition and cut can affect not only your beauty but also the way you feel – your self-confidence and general well-being. How often have you felt unreasonably depressed just because it feels greasy or looks a mess? Do you rush to wash your hair when you are invited out on a date or to a special function? Do you feel better when your hair is silky, well-cut and sweet-smelling? If your hair does not look and feel right, it does not matter how glamorous your make-up or sensational your clothes may be. So hair is fundamental to beauty and feeling good and happy about yourself, and it is well worth looking after to keep it healthy and shining. This chart will help you to analyse the potential for your hair, and identify your hair type.

Hair type	Characteristics	Problems
Normal	Easy to manage, not too dry not too greasy. Washes well and lasts at least 5 days before further washing required. Adapts to most styles	Encountered only in rare cases when permed or coloured badly
Oily	Lank and dull, prone to dandruff, quickly loses its shape and needs frequent washing with mild shampoo	Dandruff and oiliness, difficult to manage – may be treated by diet as well as regular shampooing
Dry	Fine, flyaway, lacks gloss and lustre and looks dull. Prone to split ends and needs regular deep-conditioning and cutting	Breaking split ends especially when permed or coloured

Analyse your figure

The best test for figure self-analysis is to stand naked in front of a full-length mirror and then turn sideways to either side. Take a good, long look at yourself and decide whether you like what you see. If you decide that you are a little or a lot overweight, then you must resolve to slim down and shape up with a plan of action. The chart will show you the best weight ranges for your height and build so pop on the scales and see how you measure up. Remember that these tables are only guidelines and approximations – they are not gospel. Exercise will help tone up any flabby areas while a reducing diet will help you lose weight.

If you feel happy about the way you look and it seems right for you, then do not worry about what the chart says. Stay the way you are and feel good about it. Also, do not set yourself impossible goals – you will know when you reach your ideal weight at which you can comfortably stick without starving yourself or practising excessive self-sacrifice.

You will have to pay special attention to any flabby areas so identify them now. Even the slimmest women sometimes have heavy thighs, flabby upper arms or too large a bottom. You can work on these specific areas and groups of muscles to tone them up, and firm and strengthen the muscles. Study your posture, too, as you stand in front of the mirror – do your shoulders slope, do you stoop, are you slightly hunched or do your tummy and bottom stick out? Carrying yourself properly, erect with buttocks and stomach tucked well in, will do wonders for your figure, making you look instantly slimmer and taller.

Analyse your lifestyle

Beauty begins with the right attitude and making time, no matter what your lifestyle and how busy it may be. The kind of life you lead – the work you do, your leisure interests and committments – will inevitably dictate the sort of look you wish to achieve. It may be elegant and sophisticated for the office, or natural and sporty for when you feel like relaxing. Perhaps you might combine the two different looks – one for weekdays and the other for weekends. It is most important that you make time for yourself and for pampering your body. Make beauty one of your top priorities and don't regard it just as a luxurious self-indulgence. Your body will not take care of itself without some help from you. At the very least, you must spend time on the basics and do your beauty homework every day – especially developing a skincare routine that suits your skin; having a good haircut and regular conditioning treatments; and perfecting your make-up.

But beauty does not end there – it also stems from the kind of food you eat and how much exercise you take. A healthy wholefoods diet along the lines laid down in this book will be beneficial to your skin, hair and figure as well as your health and energy level. You can fit it into any kind of lifestyle and it need not be more time-consuming or difficult to cook and prepare than convenience foods. Just 30 minutes' exercise three or four times a week will help keep you fit and trim and is well worth doing. Your skin will glow afterwards and you will be rewarded with extra vitality, stamina and the satisfaction of having a firm body. Adapt your beauty routine to your lifestyle. It need not take long each day and the results will make it worthwhile.

Put theory into practice

Having taken a good, long look at yourself, you now know exactly what you have to tackle and probably your goals also. You can set yourself new targets, short-term and long-term, and use the expertise in the following pages to help yourself achieve them. To attain your full beauty potential you will need dedication and self-discipline. Practise can make perfect or nearly so and it is worth perservering.

Your ideal weight chart

Height		Small frame		Medium frame		Large frame	
1.45m	4ft 9in	**42kg**	6st 9lb	**46.5kg**	7st 5lb	**50kg**	7st 12lb
1.47m	4ft 10in	**45.5kg**	7st 2lb	**48kg**	7st 8lb	**51.5kg**	8st 1lb
1.50m	4ft 11in	**47kg**	7st 5lb	**49.5kg**	7st 11lb	**52.5kg**	8st 4lb
1.52m	5ft 0in	**47.5kg**	7st 7lb	**51kg**	8st 0lb	**54kg**	8st 7lb
1.55m	5ft 1in	**49.5kg**	7st 11lb	**52.5kg**	8st 3lb	**55.5kg**	8st 10lb
1.57m	5ft 2in	**51kg**	8st 0lb	**54kg**	8st 7lb	**57kg**	8st 13lb
1.60m	5ft 3in	**52kg**	8st 2lb	**55kg**	8st 9lb	**58kg**	9st 2lb
1.63m	5ft 4in	**53kg**	8st 5lb	**56.5kg**	8st 12lb	**60kg**	9st 6lb
1.65m	5ft 5in	**54kg**	8st 7lb	**57.5kg**	9st 1lb	**62kg**	9st 10lb
1.68m	5ft 6in	**56.5kg**	8st 12lb	**61kg**	9st 8lb	**63.5kg**	10st 0lb
1.70m	5ft 7in	**57.5kg**	9st 1lb	**61.5kg**	9st 9lb	**65kg**	10st 3lb
1.73m	5ft 8in	**59kg**	9st 4lb	**62.5kg**	9st 12lb	**67kg**	10st 7lb
1.75m	5ft 9in	**61kg**	9st 8lb	**64.5kg**	10st 2lb	**68kg**	10st 10lb
1.78m	5ft 10in	**62.5kg**	9st 11lb	**66kg**	10st 5lb	**70.5kg**	11st 1lb
1.80m	5ft 11in	**64kg**	10st 1lb	**68kg**	10st 10lb	**72.5kg**	11st 5lb
1.83m	6ft 0in	**66kg**	10st 5lb	**70kg**	11st 0lb	**74kg**	11st 9lb
1.85m	6ft 1in	**67.5kg**	10st 9lb	**71kg**	11st 2lb	**76kg**	11st 13lb
1.88m	6ft 2in	**69.5kg**	10st 13lb	**74kg**	11st 9lb	**77.5kg**	12st 3lb

SPRING~CLEAN YOUR BODY WITH A NEW BEAUTY PLAN

Spring is the time to brush up on the beauty basics and make them an integral part of your daily life – no matter how busy you are. Looking after your skin and body is one of the best investments that you will ever make so develop a healthy skincare and beauty routine that will stand you in good stead all the year round. This homework is essential if you want to have healthy-looking, glowing skin and shiny hair. However, you must also be aware when to turn to the experts and use *their* products and expertise on *your* body.

This is traditionally the time of year when most women spring-clean their bodies, embark on a slimming diet and try to achieve a new, fresh look as the warmer days of summer approach. In fact, getting summer-ready is an important part of your spring beauty programme. It is the season for reassessing your beauty routines and making resolutions for the coming months as you discover what's new on the beauty scene – the latest and best in make-up, skin and hair products.

After the winter, you will wish to update your make-up with the new spring colours. When you look at the available options, do be aware of the quality of the soft spring light. This tends to dictate a natural-looking make-up with no colour extremes – often soft pastel shades to match the new fashions. The light changes throughout the year and this will determine, to some extent, your seasonal approach to make-up. Bearing this in mind, you may need a lighter-textured foundation than you wore in winter, for instance. Learn to tailor your make-up to the intensity of the light – whether it's a dull grey day in early spring or a bright sunny one full of the promise of summer days to come. Remember that make-up consists in its most basic form only of colour. It is the way in which you use it on your face to look more beautiful that counts – and colour, of course, is made up of light. If you aim for a healthy, relaxed, natural look in your make-up, hairstyle and colour and the clothes you wear, then you will be on the right track this spring.

Haircare is important in spring and you will need to get your hair into tip-top glossy condition after winter neglect, using special nourishing shampoos and deep-action conditioners. To go with your new fashionable look, you may wish to visit the hairdresser for a good cut that is easy to manage and suits you.

You need to extend your new-found attitudes to the rest of your body and your lifestyle, too. Get into shape and prepare for summer with a new exercise regime and a healthy slimming diet that will bring important beauty spin-offs and lay the foundations for future healthy eating and figure maintenance. When you are slimming, aim for your natural shape and optimum weight – do not strive for an impossible ideal that you cannot hope to maintain. You must concentrate on finding the right weight for you – the one at which you feel happiest. Your basic configuration will always remain the same so don't fall into the self-delusion trap. Hand in hand with a healthy reducing diet goes exercise, so you must establish a new activity programme for the months to come. Work-out at home or in the gym, or take up aerobics, running or swimming perhaps – just exercise the available options, and take responsibility for your body *now*.

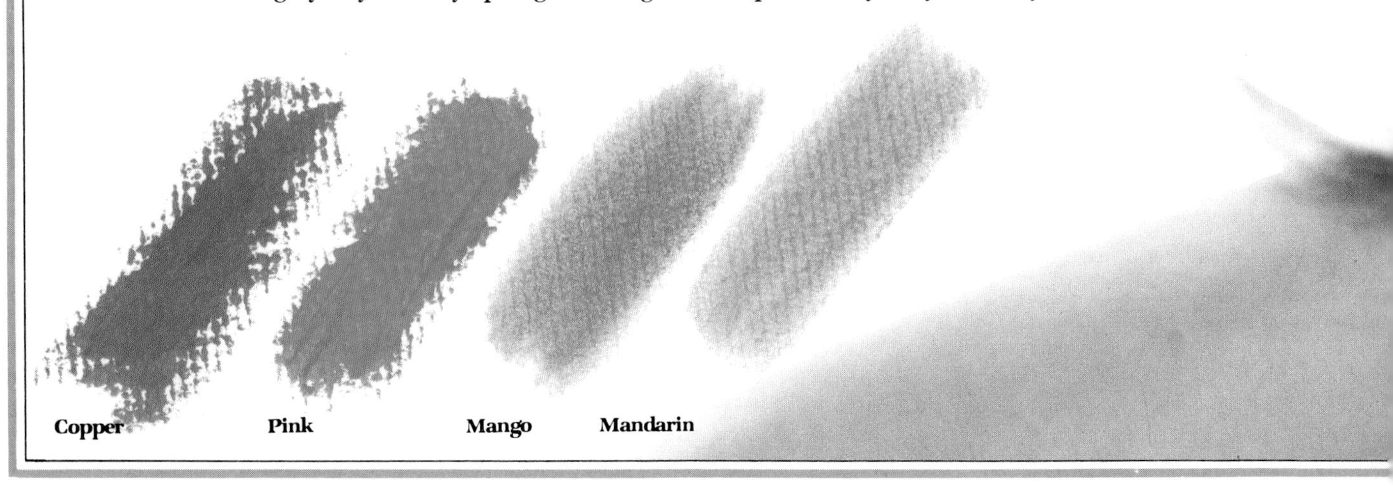

APPLYING SCIENCE TO YOUR TOTAL SKIN PLAN

The skin is a large and complex organ. It weighs about 2.7kg (6 lbs) and occupies a surface area over the body of approximately 1.6 square metres (17 square feet). Because it shows the signs of age and neglect very obviously, it is worth looking after.

The surface of the skin is made up of a fine layer of dead cells which are continually being shed and replaced by new cells from below. It takes about three weeks for a new skin cell to push its way up to the surface (or outer epidermis), although the speed of cell renewal decreases with age. This is why older skin is often dry and coarse in appearance. The epidermis also acts as a protective barrier, helping to seal in the body's moisture and keeping out potentially harmful bacteria and pollutants.

Below the epidermis lies the skin's living tissues and cells, including the sebaceous oil glands, blood vessels, sweat glands, hair follicles, pigmentation cells and, of course, living skin cells. In this layer, called the dermis, all the skin's essential functions are carried out. Blood vessels, for example, supply the skin with food and oxygen while the sebaceous glands produce the oils and moisture necessary for keeping it soft and smooth. The deepest layer, the hypodermis, is made up of fat cells and muscles which give the skin its contour and support structure. Regular exercise helps to keep the muscles firm, strong and supple.

Caring about collagen

A large part of the dermis consists of collagen fibres which give the skin its elasticity and smoothness. It is now known that these tough fibres, made up of protein and elastin, are vital for keeping your skin looking as youthful and as healthy as possible. If these fibres bunch up or 'cross-link', wrinkles and sagging begin to appear, even in relatively young skins. Cross-linking is encouraged by cigarette smoking, too much alcohol, strong sunlight and long bouts of illness. High levels of lead and aluminium in the body, and deficiencies in vitamin C and zinc are also contributory factors.

Your skin's special requirements

No two complexions are the same. Some people are born with beautiful skin, others with less than perfect skin. The best cosmetics in the world cannot alter this natural imbalance because, like eye and hair colour, your basic skin texture and colour, as well as its tendency to be oily, dry or normal, is part of your genetic inheritance. But other factors also affect the skin. These include the physical environment in which you live, the ageing process and, above all, the care and attention you give it. So it is important to take all these factors into account when planning your skincare routine. Moreover, as your lifestyle alters, at different times of the year or as you grow older, you need to be able to adapt your techniques to your skin's changing requirements.

Skin-clean inside

A poor diet is one of the greatest enemies of a good skin and no amount of clever make-up can disguise a sallow or problem skin nurtured on too many fats, sugars and convenience foods – your skin really does reflect what you eat. A wholesome diet is essential and basically this should consist of lots of fresh fruit and vegetables (eaten raw whenever possible); some protein in the form of lean meat, fish, poultry or vegetable protein; and high-fibre foods such as whole grain breads and cereals to help eliminate waste products and improve circulation. Although a well-balanced diet should provide all the nutrients you need for a healthy skin, it is worth remembering that certain vitamins are essential. Vitamin A, found in dairy products, in carrots, spinach, broccoli and watercress and in kidneys and liver, can prevent dryness and wrinkling in the skin. The vitamin B-complex, found in yeast, wholemeal breads and cereals, wheatgerm, leafy green vegetables and liver, is needed to maintain healthy skin; a lack of B vitamins can lead to skin problems. Vitamin C, found in citrus fruits and in vegetables such as broccoli, cabbage, cauliflower and Brussels sprouts, protects collagen fibres and helps keep the skin youthful and supple. Vitamin E is known to help cell reproduction and is thought to slow down the ageing process. Apples, carrots, cabbage, celery, eggs, olive oil, wheatgerm and wholemeal bread and flour are good sources.

Last, but not least, drink plenty of water in order to cleanse your system and keep your skin clear. Some experts recommend no less than eight glasses a day between meals. And for those with a tendency to spots, try water mixed with lemon juice and a little honey first thing in the morning. Mineral water is now an acceptable alternative to alcohol and positively beneficial for the skin. On social occasions, replace at least half of your alcohol or soft drink consumption with refreshing, sparkling mineral water for a clearer skin.

Slimming and your skin

One beauty therapist maintains that one of the main causes of wrinkled skin, after the sun, is fluctuations in weight. When you gain weight quickly, the elastin fibres in the dermis are put under exceptional strain as the skin stretches. When you go on a crash diet and lose weight, the skin does not automatically spring back to its original shape because the elastin fibres have been damaged. The result is the appearance of fine white or silvery lines called stretch marks which, once acquired, cannot be removed.

These rapid weight gains and losses are most common in teenage girls and pregnant women but anyone who attempts to lose weight too quickly can damage their skin. Also important in the skin's appearance are the fat cells in the hypodermis which cushion and support the skin. Loss of much of this fatty tissue through excessive dieting can quickly cause sagging and wrinkled skin.

Spring is traditionally the time for refining and repairing the body and getting into better shape. For your skin's sake, however, diet sensibly and gently massage your body skin with moisturiser as part of your regular skincare routine. Combine your diet with exercises. These do not have to be strenuous but they do need to be done every day. This helps to tone the muscles and to prevent that sagging skin that often appears with even moderate weight losses.

Natural enemies of your skin

Sun, wind and cold are the skin's most obvious enemies. Although winter winds and cold weather may not be quite as damaging as over-exposure to the sun, they take their toll, particularly on dryish and older skins. You do need to take special precautions against wind which on clear spring days can sometimes appear to be deceptively light. It is almost inevitable that winter winds and cold, as well as the minor ailments associated with winter, will have left your skin looking a little tired and out-of-condition. This is the time to pep up your skin with revitalising face masks and exfoliating treatments and to reassess your skincare routine by switching to different beauty products or being more thorough.

Environmental pollution and your skin

Nowadays, your skin has to cope not only with wind, sun and cold but also with environmental pollution. The air in and around major cities and indeed even in the countryside is polluted by chemicals of all kinds. If you consider the rapid erosion in recent years of venerable stone buildings which have survived hundreds, even thousands, of years, you can appreciate how damaging these pollutants are – to your skin. Moisturising and protection help but the increase in skin 'sensitivity' and many skin problems is probably largely due to environmental pollutants. Thorough cleansing and moisturising are the only ways of dealing with this.

Modern living and your skin

Modern living habits have also created new enemies of your skin, and the worst offenders are central heating, air conditioning and detergents. Both central heating and air conditioning are very dehydrating – they ruin your furniture as well as your skin. Although theoretically designed to control the temperature, humidity and circulation of air, many systems are badly made or used inappropriately. The great danger is when the air is so thoroughly dried that the skin loses a great deal of its natural moisture. This can be overcome by installing a humidifier in your home or office or by placing bowls of water near radiators. Take the extra precaution of keeping your skin well moisturised at all times.

Detergents and bleaches are the cause of many skin problems, the most common of which is the loss of skin oils and moisture. Skin irritations and eczema are more serious forms. Get into the habit of wearing rubber gloves when washing dishes and handling household linen. Buy gloves that fit properly and feel comfortable, otherwise you will not use them. Make sure you replace them regularly, particularly if they are of the fine 'surgical' type. Another help is keep a good-quality hand towel and some hand cream near the kitchen sink so that, even after minor kitchen chores, you can wash, dry and moisturise your hands easily.

Your lifestyle and your skin

Lack of sleep, stress, smoking and excessive alcohol all affect your skin, as they do your general health. Lack of sleep produces puffiness, particularly around the eyes. Smoking and excessive alcohol not only affect the colour and texture of your skin but also accelerate the skin's ageing process. Stress, a form of internal weathering, quickly shows itself on the skin as wrinkles, lines and tension marks. In theory, these are all things that we can and should do something about. However, if you cannot radically change your lifestyle or are undergoing a temporarily stressful period in your life, there are some elementary steps to take. Extra vitamins, particularly of the B-complex and C, will help keep the body's defensive system going and may, for a time, delay the external signs of wear and tear on the skin. Regular moisturising and nourishing the skin will also help. These, however, are only short-term measures and are no substitute for a healthier way of life.

Skin colour and skin care

Skin colour is produced by special cells in the epidermis

1

2

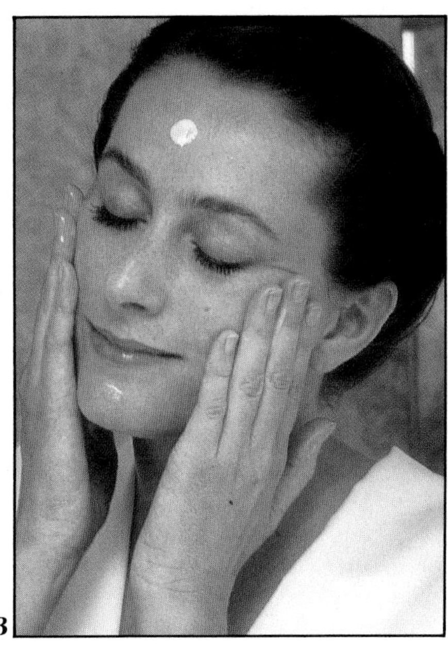
3

The three stages in basic skincare are as follows:
1 *cleansing;* **2** *toning;* **3** *most important of all, moisturising your skin to keep it smooth.*

called melanocytes. Very active melanocytes give the skin a dark brown to black colour, while less active cells produce pale pink or light-coloured skin. Your basic colour is the result of heredity but in general there is little difference in skincare routines. Olive, brown and black skin is usually more oily than very pale or pink skin. Moreover, the darker the colour, the more protection there is from the sun since a greater degree of pigmentation acts as a sun filter. Because of its more oily surface, dark skin ages more slowly than fairer skin and is less damaged by the sun. But dark skin still suffers the effects of dryness caused mainly by harsh winds and cold and also by indoor heating and air conditioning. Bear these small differences in mind when planning your skincare routine.

Basic skincare

Be flexible about skin type

Although it is useful to know what your basic skin type is – that is, whether it is oily, dry or a combination of both – it is important to be flexible about this. Do remember that skin varies from one part of the body to another and that while your facial skin may tend to be greasy, you could well have dryish skin on your legs and arms. The quality of your skin also varies from time to time. The body's monthly hormonal changes often mean that your skin is more oily and prone to spots immediately before and after a period. Many women notice an improvement in their skin when they start taking the contraceptive pill, others say it worsens. Your skin also varies a little from season to season and, obviously, as you grow older. All this means that you should not dwell too long identifying your 'skin type' but rather feel free to adapt your skincare to changing personal and environmental circumstances. In any case, there are certain basic rules which apply to all types of skin and the most important of these is to look after the skin and protect it from unnecessary damage.

If you have been a little careless over winter, spring is the time to remind yourself of the basics of skin care. If you looked after your skin in the winter yet it somehow lacks lustre, you may need to change your skincare routine or change your beauty products. Most skincare routines for the face fall into the well-established pattern of cleansing, toning and moisturising. Looking after body skin and caring for your feet and hands is similar. Your daily face-care routine need take no longer than five minutes and if you acquire the habit morning and evening, it will become as automatic as cleaning your teeth. And it is just as necessary. Always remember that expensive creams, make-up and salon treatments can never repair the damage due to neglect.

Cleansing

Your skin is an organ of elimination through which waste materials from your body are removed. Anything that hinders this process by blocking the skin pores such as dirt, grime and make-up is likely to cause spots, pimples and other skin problems. This is why it is so important to cleanse the skin twice every day, both first thing in the morning and last thing at night.

Soap and water is one of the best and cheapest cleansing agents available and there is no doubt that it leaves the skin feeling absolutely clean and refreshed. It does, however, remove some of the skin's natural oils so moisturising afterwards is essential if you are not to leave the skin dry and taut. Many household soaps also contain harsh detergents which can cause skin irritations. Perfumed soaps can do the same. For cleansing the face, look for a mild soap which is free of additives. Perhaps the most important thing when using ordinary soap and water is to rinse the face thoroughly with not one but two or three splashes of water to get rid of all traces of soap.

Many complexion soaps and cleansing bars now on the market (some are in liquid form) are pH-balanced. This means that they will effectively remove dirt and grime without disturbing the skin's natural acidity and moisture. These soaps and bars are very useful and are particularly suitable for women with dry skin who dislike using cream cleansers.

The traditional way of cleansing the skin and the one still advocated by most beauty experts is to use cleansing milks, lotions or creams. This is undoubtedly the best way to remove oil-based make-up (which is not soluble in water) since the creams melt on the skin and loosen and pick up any dirt and dead cells on the surface. You must use tissues or cotton wool to remove these creams unless they have been specially formulated to be rinsed off with water. One way of making sure that the skin is absolutely clean is to use your cream cleanser, remove it with cotton wool or tissue, and then wash your face with complexion soap.

Medicated cleansing lotions and milks are mostly for oily or problem skins. They are usually applied and removed with damp cotton wool but they can be quite harsh even for oily skins. Do not continue to use them if they leave your skin feeling dry. Cleansing pads, pieces of lint impregnated with cleansing lotion or eye make-up remover, are useful standbys for quick cleansing during the day or when travelling but they are not effective enough for regular use and can be drying. For removing eye make-up, you really do need a cleansing agent especially designed for the job, otherwise traces of mascara can leave dark rings around your eyes. Impregnated pads and clear liquid removers are good for non-waterproof make-up, but the thicker creams and lotions are best for heavier make-up. Try out different types to find the one that suits you best. Whatever you choose, always remove eye make-up very carefully; never rub, pull or stretch the delicate skin around the eyes. One way of avoiding this is to use a damp cotton wool pad, rather than tissues.

Toners, fresheners and astringents

Toners are used to remove all traces of cleanser and to refresh the skin. Many women use them because they leave their skin feeling tingling and clean after using greasy cleansers. Toning should really be the quickest and easiest part of your skincare routine. You can buy either alcohol-free or alcohol-based lotions and astringents. Whereas alcohol-free toners are best for dry and sensitive skins, oily skins will need the moisture stimulating action of alcohol-based products. They tighten the skin temporarily and refine the texture of the skin so that large pores look less obvious. They also improve the circulation of the skin.

Moisturising

Moisturisers are essential for all skins and, whatever your skin type, moisturising is the single most important aspect of regular skincare. Many women do not realise that you cannot *add* moisture to the skin by using special creams. What creams can do is prevent your skin from losing the moisture that is already there. It is very important to remember this basic physiological fact when reading about beauty products. Moisturisers can be divided into two groups. Those in the larger group are oil-based and are known as water-in-oil emulsions. They work by forming a thin, protective layer of oil on the skin surface – this prevents the skin's own moisture from evaporating. They tend to be richer than the oil-in-water kind and are best for dry skins. Those in the other group are water-based emulsions and are more fluid in composition and are ideal for oily skins. Many moisturisers also contain humectants which attract moisture from the atmosphere. These are very effective for women who live in centrally heated or air-conditioned atmospheres.

Most women with dry or normal skins feel happier with water-in-oil solutions and nowadays most of these are light and non-sticky. They serve the additional purpose of creating an invisible lining between your skin and cosmetics. Obviously, the drier your skin and the older you are, the more it needs moisturising. Ideally, you should moisturise several times a day but this is impractical for busy women. Do make sure, though, that you use a highly protective cream and that you adhere strictly to the night and morning moisturising routine.

It is also worth experimenting with different moisturising lotions and creams. Most beauty experts agree that a change of products from time to time benefits the skin. This is because it can become accustomed to one cream and after a while stops responding to it. Spring is the obvious time to look around for a fresh product. For example, you may wish to switch to a lighter moisturiser as the weather gets milder and kinder to your skin.

Night creams and nourishing creams

Special night creams and nourishing creams are always beneficial, especially for women with very dry skin. Any moisturiser that you use for day care may not always be suitable at night. Many night creams and nourishing creams feed the skin with special nutrients, proteins and vitamins. The inner layers of the skin

derive their main nourishment from the blood supply as well as from outside. The cream also helps to slow down moisture loss. and is therefore a very effective moisturiser. Very dry skins and older skins can benefit from some of the rich night or nourishing creams which soften the skin and smooth out surface lines and wrinkles. But alas, although there is no magic ingredient which will permanently remove them once they have appeared, there are special products that can reduce and soften them.

The way in which you use the cream at night is important. You need to use only a little moisturiser or cream and it should be gently smoothed into the face in light upward movements. Take a little more time with this than you do in the morning – and pay particular attention to the neck which becomes easily lined, the forehead and the skin around the eyes and mouth. You can use a special eye cream for delicate tissues around the eyes and lightly tap it in with your ring finger and wipe off any surplus grease with a tissue. Do not apply too much or you may wake up with puffy eyes.

Skin revitalisers

Even good and well-cared-for complexions need pepping up from time to time to stop them from getting sluggish and tired. An ideal time to give your skin a pick-up is at the beginning of each season when you may be changing over to new beauty products and make-up and want your skin looking as glowing as possible for your 'new look'. And in spring it is particularly important to give your skin a stimulating treatment to remove the build-up of dead cells and impurities accumulated over the winter months.

Steam facials

Home facials, face masks and exfoliating treatments are the most common skin revitalisers and they take very little time and effort. A steam facial is so easy that it is surprising that women do not do it more often. Heat helps the pores to push out dirt and impurities and it promotes perspiration and stimulates circulation.

In its simplest form, a steam facial takes about 10 or 15 minutes. Start by getting together all the things you will need. These are: a scarf or bath cap to protect the hair; cleansing cream and tissues to clean the skin before the facial; moisturiser to massage into the skin after the facial; a towel to drape over your head; and finally a large bowl of boiling water. Although they are not essential, a handful of fragrant herbs can be most beneficial. For drier skins, add comfrey, fennel or sage; for greasy skins which may need tightening use mint, camomile or rosemary; and for normal skins try rose petals, elder flower and peppermint. After cleansing your skin, pour boiling water over the herbs, cover your head with a towel and lean over the bowl, steaming your face gently for about 10 minutes. Pat the skin dry, splash with cold water and then dry again. Now lightly smooth on your regular moisturiser to reduce redness and soothe it. Your skin should now feel really fresh, clean and glowing. A word of warning, however – people with very delicate, sensitive skin or broken veins should not steam their faces. Use another revitalising method if you fall into this category.

Face masks

Face masks are particularly good for revitalising the skin, and a great morale booster because their effects, although temporary, are immediately visible. Face masks work by tightening the pores of a greasy skin and by nourishing a dry skin. There are several types and it is important that you choose one that suits your kind of skin. Clay, earth or seaweed-based packs, which are usually rinsed off, are ideal for oily, open-pored skin. These are very effective cleansers since they contain material that sucks out oil and dirt. They also tighten the skin by compressing the pores.

Peel-off masks, which are usually in gel form and contain rubber, wax or some type of plastic, are gentler and more suitable for drier skins. These are less effective as cleansers, although they do remove surface dirt and some dead cells but they are very good for toning and stimulating the skin. Masks that contain menthol or camphor are especially invigorating – and marvellous for the skin before a special occasion or night out. Oily skins will benefit from a face mask at least twice a week and dry and normal skins once a week.

Face mask step-by-step

1 Smooth back the hair from the face and hold back with a wide elasticated headband or scarf.

2 Cleanse and tone the face before applying the mask.

3 Spread the mask evenly over the face and neck leaving a wide circle around the eyes and mouth.

4 Relax, lying down, with cotton wool pads soaked in skin freshener over the eyes, and leave the mask on for the recommended time.

5 Remove all traces of the mask and splash the face and neck with tepid water. Pat dry and moisturise.

Exfoliating the skin

Exfoliation is really a deep cleansing treatment specially designed to remove dead cells and waste matter on the surface of the skin. These often accumulate, forming a barrier of thick, tough, old skin which moisturising creams have difficulty penetrating. This can be removed with a thinning or abrasive agent. Exfoliating products can be lotions, gels or creams, often containing a mass of microscopic granules which lift off the top layer of dead cells and refine and stimulate the layer beneath.

Young skins should not really need exfoliating – scrubbing the face with a complexion brush or with a

rough face cloth is usually sufficient. Older skins require more help using a commercial preparation. The thinned skin will look smoother and more translucent and will have a lighter and more even colour tone. An added bonus is that some of the fine lines and wrinkles on the surface of the skin may disappear for a time.

Establishing a routine

It is very easy to forget about your skincare when you are in a hurry or under pressure at work or at home. Therefore, it is vital that you establish a skincare routine that becomes an automatic part of your life and from which you never deviate. This means that every morning when you get up you cleanse thoroughly to get rid of any grease or impurities that have accumulated in the night while you were sleeping. Then you should freshen your skin with toner and moisturiser before applying your make-up. Repeat this process in the evening to dissolve your make-up and cleanse the skin before going to bed. Apply a heavier, more nourishing moisturiser to do its work while you sleep. After a while, this will become an unbreakable lifelong habit and can only benefit your skin.

In addition to this twice-daily skincare routine, you should set aside an evening once a week or a fortnight, depending on your skin type, to apply an appropriate face mask, exfoliate or steam your skin as described earlier. Use whichever revitalising method is best for you. It is easy to neglect this additional form of skincare but it is important if you want your skin to look its best and really stay soft and glowing with health. Check your skincare products regularly to see if they need replacing. If your usual cleanser or moisturiser does not seem to be doing much for your skin anymore and it is reacting in a lacklustre sort of way, do not be afraid to change it for another product and re-evaluate your skin. It may just need a change to boost its vitality or it may be dryer or oilier than usual and thus your normal skincare product is no longer having the desired effect. What suits your skin now in spring may not be suitable anyway when summer comes with its drying, hot sunny days, or the colder weather of autumn and winter.

IMPROVE ON NATURE WITH THE NEW SPRING COLOURS

Women wear make-up to enhance their image, to help their confidence and to look as attractive as possible to the outside world. It is an aid, not a disguise and is concerned with making the best of your good features and playing down the bad. Make-up can help the way you look but it cannot alter your basic features. It should be as simple and as natural as possible and this is an art which you can master with practice.

Spring-clean your make-up collection

Your make-up collection is probably a jumble of assorted products, some of which were mistake purchases, others once used regularly but now put aside in favour of other colours or products you like better. Take the opportunity at the beginning of spring to go through your make-up and sort out what you really want to keep. Be ruthless – get rid of old lipstick stubs, dried mascara and grease-coated eye shadow. Try to take a fresh look at your face and your current style of make-up. With the beginning of mild weather, your face will probably benefit from a lighter make-up generally with more emphasis on natural colours and tones. Look at beauty and fashion magazines to see which of the season's 'looks' and clothes styles suit you best.

Fortunately, make-up is an area of beauty that does not need a great deal of money. However, whatever amount you spend is more than justified by the boost to your morale that new make-up can give. Don't buy indiscriminately. That really is a waste of money. There are certain basic products that you really need, and others, not so essential, that you feel you can do without.

Your basic make-up kit

Before discussing how to choose make-up, let's look at what you really need. Excluding your skin products, you will need several basic items: one foundation, one blusher, face powder, two or three eyeshadows, mascara, eyeliner or pencil and one or two lip colours (in stick or gloss form). Optional items, necessary for any woman who takes her make-up seriously, are a shader, a concealer (for spots and blemishes), a highlighter, lip gloss and a lip pencil and a brush.

In addition to these, you need good-quality tools with which to apply make-up. Most important are brushes and you should have at least three of these (some are supplied with the products you buy) – one full, soft, flattish brush to apply blusher, a similar but smaller one for highlighting, a large soft, chubby brush to flick away face powder and a flat, wedge-shaped brush for applying eye shadow. You may also want to have a lipstick brush and an eye brow brush (a child's toothbrush will do). Keep all brushes clean by washing them regularly and drying them well away from artificial heat.

Sponges are good for applying foundation evenly and smoothly. Keep left-over ones from finished make-up and make sure they are clean by rinsing out after each application. Tiny ones on sticks are useful for eye shadow. An ordinary pencil sharpener is essential for keeping eye, kohl and lip pencils pointed and sharp; and you will need tweezers for keeping your eyebrows tidy. Tissues, cotton wool and cotton-tipped buds are other necessary items for wiping smudged make-up and blotting lips. Lastly, you need a mirror (get a magnifying one if you are short-sighted), which can be used in natural light or in the evening under bright lights. Special portable make-up mirrors are particularly suitable.

Storage

It really is sensible to store your make-up in a small tool box or fishing tackle case. This is what models do. Left in a jumble on the dressing table or in the bathroom, things can get grubby and broken. You can also neatly carry your make-up and mirror to the best possible light source. Some make-up you will want to carry around with you. Try not to weigh down your handbag with too much unnecessary clutter and keep your portable make-up in a washable make-up bag.

Foundation – the basis of perfect make-up

The purpose of foundation is to give the skin a smooth finish and to make skin tones as even as possible. It also helps to keep moisture in and to protect the skin against pollutants in the air and the drying effects of wind and sun. Lastly, it provides a clear even base onto which make-up goes easily. Not everyone needs to wear a foundation. If you have a very young skin or are one of the fortunate few with a clear, evenly-toned, unblemished skin, then strictly speaking you don't need a foundation. But even in such cases, a very light thin base does help with the application of make-up.

Choosing a foundation

Foundation comes in many different textures and shades and the one you choose depends on your skin type and colour. First decide how much coverage you need. This will vary from season to season. In spring you need somewhat less protection than in winter so change to a lighter-textured foundation which gives a subtle, natural cover. Liquids in bottles and tubes are the most popular and easily used foundation, since they suit nearly every skin type. Some are oil-based for dry skin, others water-based and free of oil for greasy skins, and others are hypo-allergenic for sensitive skins. Cream foundations give medium coverage and are good for dry skins. Older skins should use a light textured foundation, otherwise it may settle in wrinkles. Heavy block foundations and pancake (all-in-one-make-up) are now out of fashion but they are useful for covering deep scars, birthmarks and other blemishes. However, they tend to be rather drying. Gels are very light and ideal for summer but they need a little practice to apply evenly and smoothly.

Which colour?

A foundation should be the colour of your natural skin tone or as close as possible as you can get (no more than either one shade lighter or darker). Most of the major cosmetic manufacturers offer a choice of about eight to ten different colours ranging from pale to dark. These are usually centred on a few tones – ivory, beige, a warmer pinker tone and peach. Study your face carefully and you will be able to identify a natural creaminess, pinkness or beige tone. Compare the colour of your facial skin with the inside of your wrist. It is usually the same, but not always, because you will need to test a little foundation in order to get the right colour when you are buying it.

Delicate blush tones tend to go with blonde hair. A rosy complexion (which accompanies red hair and freckles) can be toned down by a creamy beige. A pale or ivory skin, which often goes with black, dark brown or auburn hair, needs a warm beige. Olive and darker skins should choose golden tones with a hint of warmth.

Beauty counsellors in stores can be helpful but some are not as well-trained as others. Combine your own judgement with their advice. The first time you choose a new shade of foundation, you may be alarmed by the colour as it comes straight from the tube or bottle. Test it on your wrist and try to look at it in daylight outside the shop. It will look different. If in doubt, rub a little of the foundation into your jawline to see that it really matches your skin.

Applying foundation

Most foundations are applied by dotting them on to the face and then smoothing them in with the fingertips or a damp sponge (make sure it is not wet by squeezing in a towel or tissue, otherwise it will simply wipe the make-up off). Do not blend too far into the hairline and smooth under the jaw, fading away into the neck. If you have chosen the right colour, there should be no difference between the skin tones on your face and the natural colour of your neck.

Concealers

Even the best skins may have a few marks, eye circles or blemishes which need covering. Nowadays, there are specially made concealers which can be bought in stick form, in a tube or a small pot. Some are medicated to help with spots and pimples. In general, these should be slightly lighter in colour than your foundation. Dot concealer carefully on shadows under the eyes and on blemishes such as spots, reddish scars or broken veins and blend by patting or pressing into your skin. Make sure you blend in the concealer to match your skin tone; otherwise you can end up with white patches.

Blushers

Blushers are the modern version of rouge and their purpose is to give the cheeks a lively natural glow. When properly used they can add life and colour to your face in a way that no other products can. Too often, however, they are misused by women as a face shaper, resulting in coloured streaks down the cheeks to the jawbone. Once you know how to use blushers, you will see how they enhance the face in a subtle, natural way.

There are four different types of blusher on the market – cream blushers which come as sticks, pencils or compacts; liquids; gels; and powders. Compressed powder blushers are by far the easiest to use and the most popular. Liquids and creams give the skin a healthy sheen and are good for young faces and for very dry skins, but they require a little practice before they can be used effectively.

Choosing the right colour

Choose a colour that is only a shade or two darker than your foundation and will merge naturally with your skin tone. Subtle pink, peach and tawny tones are most suitable for daytime. Remember that blusher should harmonise with your skin tone and also with the clothes or lipstick you are wearing. Above all, avoid bright splashes of colour on each cheek. As with foundation, don't be put off by the colour in the stick or compact. It is difficult finding the best colours without trying them on your face but again spread them lightly on the inside of your wrist if this method of testing has helped you choose a foundation.

Applying blusher
Press your thumb underneath your cheekbone and place your forefinger on the cheekbone. Apply blusher along this line which lies at an angle between the ear and the base of the nose. Blend in carefully just beneath the line so there are no hard edges. Remember blusher should not cover the entire cheek. In addition there is one important rule to remember when applying different types of blusher. Powder blushers are put on after your foundation and face powder; creams and liquids go on before your face powder but after foundation.

Face contouring
With skill you can use make-up to subtly alter the shape of your face or to emphasise your best features and minimise others. Highlighters are always lighter than your skin tone and therefore lighter than your foundation. You can use frosted highlighter which adds shine and is suitable for the evenings, or simply a lighter shade of foundation for a more subtle effect. Usually highlighter is used to emphasise good cheekbones. Apply along the top of the cheekbones above your blusher and towards the outer corner of the eye.

Shaders come in cream, stick or powder form. They are usually darkish and in tones of brown. Powder shaders are by far the easiest to use, or you can use a slightly darker foundation for shading. Success with shading depends on a light touch.

A word of warning: highlighting and shading demand finesse – and time – if your face is not to look unnatural. If you are busy and rushed in the morning, forget about it and confine your efforts to evening make-up. Also bright daylight can often make your shading look slightly brown and grubby on the face. Be cautious and not too ambitious with your face shaping.

Hints for face shaping
1 A double chin can be made less obvious by blending darker foundation or shader under the chin and gently receding it into the neck.
2 A broad nose can be narrowed by shading down the sides from eyebrows to nostrils and by highlighting down the centre.
3 Minimise a large jaw or chin by shading the outer edges with a slightly darker foundation.
4 A long chin can be shortened by darkening the tip with a darker foundation or shader.
5 A small face will look larger with lighter foundation on the outsides of the cheeks and at the temples.
6 Slim down a round face by shading below each cheekbone.

Face powder
Face powder is the finishing touch to a good make-up. Its purpose is to make the face look less shiny and to 'set' the make-up underneath without altering the colouring. Modern face powders are very light in texture and they should be almost invisible on the face. Powders come in two forms – loose and compressed. Beauty experts recommend using loose powder at home and compressed powder for touching up. In practice, a lot of women use compressed powder all the time because they find loose powder messy. Compressed powder can be slightly more oily, so always keep your powder puff or brush applicator scrupulously clean to avoid grease spots forming on the powder.

Buy transparent or colourless powder which barely alters the colour of your underneath make-up. Most modern powders are also translucent, meaning that they have good light-reflecting qualities.

Applying your powder
Apply loose powder by gently patting it onto the skin with a powder puff. Take care not to rub the powder in. Then lightly brush off the excess with a puff or brush. Check that there are no powdery or shiny patches. Ue compressed powder by gently patting it over the face with a brush or powder puff. Make sure that it does not look uneven.

Eyes – focus of your face
The eyes are the face's most vital feature and most women like to emphasise their eyes above all other facial characteristics. Yet it is very easy to get stuck in a rut about eye make-up and be wearing the same type and colour of eye make-up as you were, say, five years ago. You can and should be imaginative with your eye make-up once you have mastered the basic techniques of how to choose and apply it.

Spring is the ideal time to look at your daytime eye make-up. It can be used to complement your clothes and, as you are changing over to lighter fabrics and colours, try more natural or more positive colours, depending on the fashion styles you are following. Remember though that you are co-ordinating, not matching, colours and that your eye make-up is a fashion 'accessory'. But let us first look at your basic needs.

Eye shadows
There are two main types of eye shadow. One is cream-based and comes in pots, sticks, wands, tubes or in gel form; shadow pencils are also cream-based. Powder-based shadow usually comes in miniature compacts or in a palette containing three or four different colours. Both types of eye shadow can be bought with shine, pearl or even glitter in them. Some shiny shadows can be effective as highlighters in daytime but, as a general rule, keep the pearlised and glitter shadows for glamorous evening wear. Powders are the easiest to apply

and are long-lasting. Creams are a bit messy, crease easily and are hard to control since they have a tendency to smear. However, many women with very dry skins prefer them and they are useful for young faces when only a hint of colour is required.

As with blusher, the important rule to remember when applying eye shadow is that cream-based make-up goes on after foundation but before you have powdered your face. Powder eye shadows are applied after face powder.

Choosing the right colours

Nowadays it is fashionable for eyes to have a 'soft' look so, as a general principle, stick to sludgy greens, greys or browns for daytime and keep the bright, shiny colours for evening. You may want to use two shadows in the same tone, one slightly darker than the other for extra definition. Or, alternatively, use a soft pencil in the crease of the eye to add depth to the eye colour. No matter what colour you choose, do not cover the eyelid with the same intensity of colour. Generally, colour is less intense on the lid immediately above the lashes. Blend the colour up and out towards the brow until it fades away. Then smooth the deeper tone into the crease of the eye.

Using eyeliners and pencils

Eyeliners for defining the shape of the eye usually come in three forms – as pencils, wands or in a cake which is applied wet with a fine brush. All are fairly easy to apply. Almost no one wears a harsh, stark eyeliner these days so avoid black unless your eyes are very dark. Choose a soft colour which matches your eye shadow and smudge it to produce a hazy edge close to the upper lashes and underneath the lower lashes.

Mascara

Every woman should wear mascara and it comes in wand, cake or tablet form. Waterproof mascara is essential if you enjoy swimming or active sports. There are also special conditioning mascaras that stop the lashes turning brittle. Special mascara with 'building' agents which coat and lengthen the lashes should be avoided by women who wear contact lenses as they may irritate the eyes.

Unless you are very dark, choose a brown or blue mascara – the heavy, black, spiky look may look too harsh. Remember, mascara's purpose is to supply a natural-looking improvement on your own lashes.

Always apply two coats of mascara, allowing each to dry thoroughly, otherwise it may smudge. Do use it on both the upper and lower lashes. This gives the eye an attractive 'open' look. One important point: remove all traces of mascara when cleansing the face, preferably with special eye make-up remover cream. Stale mascara can be damaging for both the eyelashes and the sensitive skin around the eyes.

Eyelash curlers

Many women still like to use eyelash curlers and they can certainly make the eyes look open and bright. They can be difficult to use but the important thing is not to pull at the eyelashes when curling and to use the 'scissors' gently.

Eye disguises

Small eyes Blend darker shadow outwards from the centre of the lid, leaving the inner lid paler to enlarge the eye. Blend a smudge of darker colour under the bottom lashes from the outer corner to about the middle of the eye.

Protruding eyes Never use pale or bright colours or frosted shadows. Apply dark shadow close to the lashes and blend to a less intense colour above and across.

Hooded eyes Shade all the lid, extending colour upwards at the outer edge. Highlight the browbones and draw a fine line from the centre of the top lid extending slightly upwards where the droop begins.

Close-set eyes Apply shadow and eyeliner from the centre outwards and a little beyond the eyes. Blend a lighter shade or highlighter into the inner corners of the eye. Use mascara only on the outer lashes.

Deep-set eyes Use a lighter shadow on the lids and a darker shade above. Highlight the brows.

Round eyes Apply shadow rather heavily at the outer corners and blend upwards and outwards towards the brows. Highlight the centre and inner corners of the lid and do not use eyeliner beneath the lower lashes.

Lips

Your mouth is perhaps the most expressive part of your face and is often seen as an indication of your mood or personality. Women have emphasised their lips for hundreds of years and there have been endless fashions in both lip colour and shape. The lip colour you choose can enhance or disguise the natural shape of your mouth. It can also complement your skin, hair and eye colouring and, like eye make-up, it can be used as a fashion accessory to pick up or blend with the clothes you are wearing.

Types of lipstick

Conventional stick lipsticks are the most common type. But lipstick also comes in compacts, often with its own brush, as lip gloss (with a glycerine or petroleum jelly base), in long tubes with wands or in pots. Lip pencils – soft, wax-based crayons – come in two thicknesses, one for outlining the lips, the other thicker for filling in colour. The type of lipstick you choose is a matter of personal preference. Do, however, experiment with lipstick types as well as colours. If you have always

Making-up eyes is quite easy when you have the right equipment – brushes and applicators.

used a stick, try a compact lipstick or a crayon for a change. They certainly make it easier to shape the lips.

Lip colours

The range of lip colours is huge yet most women have their favourite colours which they buy time after time. This is somewhat adventurous. Every woman should have a little wardrobe of colours and types with which she is constantly experimenting. Buying a new lipstick is not expensive yet it is a marvellous morale booster and, as a fashion accessory, your lip colours should change from season to season just as your clothes do.

Most women know instinctively which colours suit them, and you can get different effects by varying the tones and textures of a range of colours. Be daring occasionally and choose a bright pink, a soft red or a raspberry shade if they seem to suit you. For conventional spring daytime wear, look at new shades in the soft pinks, light browns and earthy colours. You may want to choose a coloured lip gloss for a change, or simply add colourless lip gloss to a new lip colour.

Applying lip colour

Learn to outline the lips with a pencil or brush. Even with a natural look, the lips need definition. Make sure the pencil has a sharp point to get a clear-edged outline. Fill in with matching colour from a stick or compact. then blot the lips with a tissue and reapply. For more shine, apply a thin coat of lip gloss to the centre of the upper and lower lips. If your lipstick tends to 'bleed', you can apply a special cream around your mouth before using lipstick.

Hints for altering lip shapes

Thin lips Outline slightly just outside your natural lip with a special brush,keeping to the exact shape. Fill in with a slightly deeper tone.

Full lips Outline just inside your natural lipline. Fill in with matt colour in the same shade. Always avoid bright, shiny or heavy colours.

Fatter lower lip Use a slightly lighter shade of lipstick on the top lip, with a darker tone on the lower lip. This change in colour tone needs to be very subtle, otherwise it will look odd.

Spring make-up – fresh and pretty

With all the new colours and fashions arriving in the shops, spring is a good time to ring the changes in your make-up and change your 'look'. Study the glossy magazines to find what is best for you – your colouring, skin tone, eye colour, hair, style of dressing and basic wardrobe. If you have been wearing the same old make-up for years, now is a good opportunity to update it. But do not choose something really dramatic or outrageous unless you are very socially outgoing and this suits your image – better to change it gradually by degree and find a look with which you feel comfortable.

Pastel shades and soft, muted colours often look good in spring – pretty pinks, lilacs, powder blues, soft greens, peach and apricot. You must experiment to see which colours suit you and the best way to apply them. If you are naturally fair-skinned and blonde, then a light honey coloured foundation is very flattering. Neutral colours may be best for eyes — soft browns, greys and greens – while pale pink blusher will define cheekbones and lips can be pink or apricot shining with gloss.

Dark blondes should take care with their daytime make-up as although strong, bright colours may be suitable for evening wear under harsh lights, they may look washed out or over-made-up if worn during the day. Opt for a light foundation near to your natural skin tone, and smoky muted eye shadows. For a splash of colour, choose a bright lipstick in pink or red.

Brunettes with a darker skin tone can get away with darker, earthy tones of foundation and blusher and more dramatic make-up. They can use dark kohl crayons or pencils to outline their eyes and on the inner rims, with bronze, brown, green, gold and blue shadow. Lips can be coloured pink, red, orange, copper, wine or earth shades for a flattering finish.

Black women may find it best to aim for a glossy transparent effect on their skin which emphasises its smoothness and polish. Iridescent colours are most effective for eyes with lashings of mascara, while bright vivid lipsticks are fun and add a touch of glamour.

Experiment with the available make-up, testing it on the inside of your wrist or hand to see what you like.

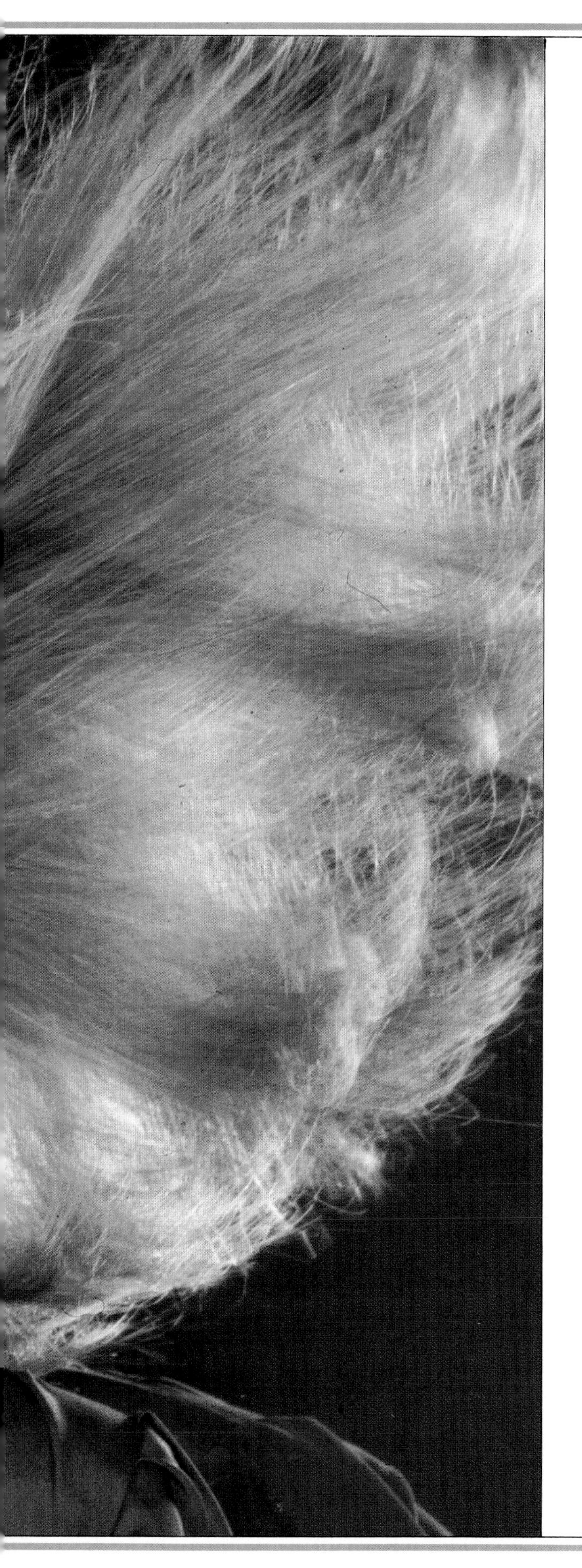

SPRING HAIRCARE

BRUSH UP ON THE BASICS

Your hair is your most important beauty 'accessory'. Its condition and style can affect your general appearance in a most obvious way. If it is poorly styled or in a bad condition, no amount of clever make-up or fashionable clothes can detract attention from it. Your hair is the frame for your face, and its colour and style should suit your skin and enhance your facial features. How to 'wear' your hair and how best to look after it are determined by a number of factors. These include the texture (fine, normal or coarse), its moisture content (dry, normal or greasy), its movement (wavy, curly or straight) and its natural colour. Like skin, these are basically part of your genetic inheritance. However, with skill and care you can modify or change some (but not all) of these factors, at least on a temporary basis.

Spring reassessment

Spring is the time to remind yourself of the basics of hair care, taking into account your particular hair type. Give dull hair a revitalising conditioning treatment after winter and reassess your hairstyle. One that is natural and easy to manage is best in spring, particularly if you have worn elaborate party styles over winter. Look to what is fashionable but always adapt it to suit your face and your particular hair type.

Healthy hair

Like the fur coat of an animal, the condition of your hair reflects your general health. Strong and glossy hair is healthy hair whether it is curly or straight and whatever its colour. Usually hair is not in peak condition at the end of winter, simply because most people are less healthy during colder months. Now is the time when you should naturally be altering your eating habits and taking more exercise. Make a positive effort to eat more fresh fruit and vegetables and to improve your general physical condition. It really will be reflected in your hair and can be more effective than any number of artificial aids.

Some hair facts

Like skin, hair is a complex living organism. Basically, each strand of hair consists of three layers. The outer layer or cuticle protects the inner layers; the inner cortex, made up of long, thin cells, gives the hair its elasticity and contains the pigments for colouring; the central medulla is spongy tissue.

Nourishment

The root of every hair is encased in a follicle and at the base of this is a tiny nodule, a papilla, which contains protein cells to nourish the hair. Blood vessels and sebaceous glands supply the hair with further nutrients and lubricating oils. As with the skin, the activity of the sebaceous glands determines the degree of dryness or oiliness in your hair.

Texture and movement

Whether your hair is wavy, curly or straight depends on heredity, as does the texture of your hair. Most people have between 90,000 to 150,000 hairs on their head (fine-haired blondes have the most, coarse-haired brunettes and redheads have the least) and on average you lose about 100 to 200 hairs a day, which are continually replaced by new hairs. Physical or hormonal changes in the body, and illness, shock or stress can increase hair loss but in most cases this is temporary.

Growth

Your hair grows at the rate of about 13mm (½in) per month but this varies not only according to season (hair grows faster in warmer weather) but also according to age (growth slows down as we get older) and your general state of health and fitness. Contrary to popular belief, cutting the hair does not encourage hair growth although it does make the hair look healthier simply because it gets rid of split or impoverished ends.

Colour

Your hair colour is determined by three pigments – black, red and yellow – which are present in the cortex. Blonde hair has yellow pigment with traces of red; red hair is mostly red pigment with traces of yellow and black; dark brown and black hair are both concentrations of black; and lighter brown hair shows traces of red. Hair goes grey when the cortex stops producing any pigment at all. The age at which this occurs is largely a matter of heredity, although emotional shock and stress, serious mineral or vitamin deficiences, especially of vitamin B, or a thyroid condition can produce prematurely grey hair.

Know your hair type

You can identify the texture of your hair by examining two or three individual hairs. Fine hair is like a silken thread and it is soft and slippery. Generally, it lacks fullness and body and is often difficult to set and keep in a certain style. Women with fine hair should stick to a natural, easily managed style that shows off the shine and texture of the hair. Coarse hair, usually dark brown or black in colour, is thick and often wiry. It generally takes well to setting but is best suited to simple or dramatic styles.

Your hair's natural tendency

Your hair may be wavy, curly or straight and it will be easier to manage if you take advantage of its natural tendency. If your hair is curly, get your hairdresser to follow the line of the curl or layer it (straightening curly hair is not generally successful and can be very damaging to the hair). Wavy hair tends to fall in a certain way and you should try to follow this natural waving shape. After setting or straightening, it tends to quickly revert to its own style. Straight hair usually hangs and swings well but many women get bored with it. It can generally be permed successfully.

Every woman needs to alter her hairstyle from time to time but do study your particular hair type carefully before adopting a currently fashionable or radically different style. Remember there is nothing that can alter the texture or thickness of your hair although you can curl it or colour it. Capitalise on your hair's natural advantages if you want hair care to be easy.

HAIR CARE

The condition of your hair – whether it is healthy, clean and undamaged – is largely up to you. Beautifully well-conditioned hair is easy to achieve but it requires regular (although not time-consuming) attention.

Shampooing

Your hair needs to be kept clean and this means washing it at *least* once a week. If your hair is greasy, you may need to wash it more often – some women wash their hair every day. The best guide is to wash your hair when it starts to look and feel dirty, greasy and dull. Your choice of shampoo is all-important. Detergent shampoos, which often come in jumbo-sized 'family' bottles, are drying and harmful for all types of hair, including greasy hair. Most shampoos are now formulated for dry, normal and greasy hair; others treat tinted, coloured, lightened, bleached and straightened hair. Many shampoos are pH-balanced and enriched with a bewildering range of ingredients such as herbs, fruits, balsam, oil, egg, lemon and so on. Since all shampoo must be thoroughly rinsed out of the hair, it is uncertain how beneficial these ingredients are.

As a general guide, herbal ingredients in shampoos and conditioners are said to enliven the hair; balsam adds thickness and body; lemon is good for oiliness; camomile lightens hair; and protein and egg-based products thicken and protect dry and damaged hair.

Hair in spring should be glossy, soft and very healthy. It needs regular deep-conditioning.

Establishing a regular haircare routine to suit your hair type will be really beneficial.

With so many products on the market, the best thing is to experiment with shampoos until you find one that suits you. Buy one that is pH balanced and suits your hair type, but buy a sachet or small bottle so that if it does not suit you, you have not wasted too much money. Some beauticians recommend baby shampoos – they have the advantage of being mild, gentle and cleansing (a plus if you need to wash your hair frequently), but they are not much use for problem hair.

How to shampoo

The way you shampoo your hair is as important as your choice of shampoo. Follow this step-by-step guide for the best results.

1 Bend forward so your hair falls over your face and brush your hair gently from base to tips to remove dead hairs, dirt and grime.

2 Before shampooing, massage your scalp gently, rotating your fingers to remove any dead particles.

3 Wet the hair thoroughly with warm (not hot) water. A shower attachment is most convenient for this.

4 Work a small quantity of shampoo into your hair and massage the scalp with gentle kneading motions. Then rinse thoroughly in warm water. Your hair should not need another application of shampoo unless it is particularly greasy or dirty. If so, repeat the lathering and rinsing process.

5 Rinse the hair thoroughly (two or three times) until it feels clean and squeaky. It is important that all traces of shampoo are removed, otherwise you will leave the hair feeling dull and sticky. Finish with a rinse of cool or cold water to close the pores.

6 Squeeze your hair gently to remove excess water and dry lightly with a towel.

7 Do try to let your hair dry naturally for as long as possible before using a hair dryer. Hair is at its weakest when wet and is more easily damaged by heat.

Conditioning your hair.

Most hair, but by no means all hair, needs regular conditioning to repair the damage caused by constant brushing and combing and by using heated hair dryers, rollers and tongs. If your hair has been tinted, dyed, permed, straightened or bleached, a conditioning treatment is essential to restore it to its natural condition.

Types of conditioners

Cream rinses, which are used on a regular basis by most women, are like fabric softeners. They coat the surface of the hair with a fine wax-like film that makes the hair silky, manageable, tangle-free and more capable of holding its style. Some are formulated to counteract dryness or dandruff. Choose one that matches your shampoo but do use these in moderation, and only a little at a time. Used in excess, they make the hair greasy and sticky – if you find you are washing your hair more often than normal, leave off the cream rinse for a couple of shampoos.

Women with greasy hair do not need conditioners, and women with naturally healthy, undamaged hair need conditioners less regularly. Perversely, they can make healthy hair fly-away and unmanageable. Be guided by your hair. If it feels out of condition, use a conditioner; if it doesn't, don't.

Deep conditioners are rich in creams and oils and are good for very dry or damaged hair. After winter, most hair is naturally a little unhealthy. At the beginning of spring, you may need a deep conditioner. It will probably be the case if your hair has been tinted, damaged or bleached. Central heating can also make the hair dry and brittle. Have you been regularly teasing your hair into elaborate styles with heated rollers, tongs or crimpers? Look at your hair carefully. If it is frayed and frizzled like an old piece of rope, give yourself a proper conditioning treatment and then keep your hair healthy throughout the season with regular cream rinses.

Protein and moisturising treatments are massaged into the hair and left on for about 10 to 20 minutes. These strengthen the protein structure of the hair and are good for brittle, dry hair. Some are used before, some after, shampooing. Follow the instructions carefully. Treatment packs are richer and more nourishing. Like a face pack, they need to be left on for about 30 minutes or more, and usually the head is wrapped in a towel or polythene hood to help heat reach the follicles. Again follow the instructions carefully. These packs are particularly suitable for badly damaged or bleached hair.

For a do-it-yourself treatment, gently massage warm olive, almond or castor oil into the scalp. Cover the head with a towel wrung out in warm water and as it cools, repeat the process once or twice. Finally shampoo the hair and rinse thoroughly. Unless your hair is really badly damaged, you should only need one such treatment to keep your hair in good condition until the summer, but if necessary, repeat every three or four weeks.

Your spring hairstyle

The beginning of the season is a good time to consider your hairstyle. Does it suit you and your face? Is it easy to manage? Are you bored wih it? How fashionable is it? Think about these things carefully, and if you decide on a re-style think along natural easy to care for lines in preparation for the summer ahead. Firstly remind yourself of the general styles which suit different face shapes.

Face shapes and styles

Long face Long straight hair or hair piled on top of the head does not suit your face. Keep your hair full at ear level and fluff it out with waves or curls. A fringe often helps to make it look rounder.

Round face Avoid fluffing out your hair at the sides and don't have it too flat on top of the head. Keep the hair to jawline length and no shorter, and keep it flat at the sides covering the cheeks.

Square face Leave the forehead clear and cover the jawline with curls or waves.

Heart-shaped face Hair should be full over the cheeks, either with fluffy waves or curls, or straight hair can be well cut to give extra volume.

Low forehead Have a deep fringe which starts far back on the crown of the head.

Prominent nose Emphasise the crown with an upswept style. A long fringe also helps.

Your hairstyle and fashion

Be cautious about following the very latest trends in hairstyle fashion. Think first about whether the style would suit your face, your figure and your general style of dress. Secondly, is it a style that your hair type will take? It is no use, for example, yearning for a classic bob if your hair is wavy or curly. Nor is it practical, if you are a busy woman, to have a style that needs constant attention with rollers and tongs to look good. Remember that once you have adopted a particular hairstyle (usually achieved by cutting, colouring or curling) it is with you for some time. Unlike a hat which doesn't suit you, it cannot be discarded.

This is not to suggest that you ignore fashion – nothing is more ageing than a hairstyle you may have chosen years ago, unless it is a very classic style. Rather you should adapt fashion to suit you. Fortunately, hairstyling nowadays is aimed at healthy naturalness and the secret of that lies in the perfect cut for your type of hair.

You and your hairdresser

If you have a regular hairdresser whom you trust, seek his or her opinion about a new hairstyle. Talk the style through – will it suit your hair type, will it need a lot of attention? If your hairdresser suggests something you feel uneasy about, say so and don't be rushed into decisions particularly about cutting long hair to short or even medium-length. Don't make spur-of-the-moment decisions about permanent curling or colouring either. You could regret it. However, a good hairdresser will pick up your individual fashion looks and recommend a hairstyle to match. A good stylist will explain why he or she thinks a fringe or body perm will suit you and it is wise to listen to such advice even if you don't act on it immediately. If you are not sure about the look you want to achieve, then aim to get there gradually in two or three cuts.

Needless to say, it is foolish to have a major re-styling job on your first visit to a new hairdresser, however fashionable or well-recommended. A good stylist needs time to get to know how your hair responds and moves.

The perfect cut

A good cut is essential to your hairstyle, whether it is long, medium-length or short, and this can only be achieved by a professional. All hair should be cut about every six weeks, more often for a very short cut. If you leave hair to grow long it will be straggly with split ends. In other words, it will look unkempt. A good cut means that the hair is styled to swing or curl in a naturally attractive way.

There are two basic methods of cutting. Hair can be cut to all one length, although it can be shorter or longer in some sections. If, for example, your hair is to be turned under, the layer underneath is often cut shorter. This style suits thin, fine hair since it gives it fullness and it is good for long, straight hair. Hair can also be layer-cut to different lengths all over the head. This is usually best suited to thicker wavy or curly hair. These cutting styles can be used alone or in combination to create a wide variety of styles.

Short hair Hair cut in short styles is the easiest to look after. Whatever the style, it must be cut really well and trimmed often, otherwise it will look straggly. Curly and thin hair are usually better cut short.

Medium-length hair This is probably the most flattering length for most women but such styles require more attention than either short or long hair. This is because they tend to lose their setting or shape more quickly unless they are cut to follow the hair's natural movement, wave or curl. Wavy and thick hair is good at this length.

Long hair This is generally easy to look after, depending on the style you choose. Swathed effects take time and practice to get right but simple, free styles which show off the sheen and quality of the hair require little attention. Long hair can take a wide variety of styles but few long-haired women experiment with more than one or two. If you do not want a major re-styling in spring, ask your hairdresser to suggest a few new ways to wear your hair which will suit you.

Drying and setting your hair

Most women use an electric dryer to do this job. The heat helps mould the protein keratin in your hair into different shapes, and thus blow-drying wet hair will enable you to set it in your desired style. Heated rollers and curling tongs are also used for setting hair. Which is the best method?

Blow-drying: this method is very effective but can be too drying and damaging to hair if you use it every day – twice a week is the maximum if you want to have healthy hair. Never use on a very hot setting. Although it speeds up the drying process, it also damages the ends, scorching them or leaving them brittle and dry. Use a dryer with a blow-wave nozzle and a full hairbrush with all-round bristles to get the shape you want. For controlled styling you will need a low wattage, but if you just randomly blow the hair dry, then a higher wattage is suitable. Never hold the dryer nearer than 15cm/6inches away from your hair and keep it moving — don't concentrate the heat for too long in one place. For added volume, it is best to dry *underneath* the hair first and then the top, starting with the back and sides and drying the fringe or front last. Blow-drying may be a difficult art to master initially. You need good coordination to wind the hair around the brush in one hand and dry with the other. It always looks so easy when your hairdresser does it, but it is more tricky in practice. Angle the dryer so that the hot air is directed along the length of the hair away from the scalp. This will help smooth down the ends. For more detailed information on blow-drying, turn to Winter hair on page 130.

If you want to straighten wavy hair, you should try to dry it close to the roots, working outwards and brushing each section straight. To give hair extra body and make it look fuller, roll the sections of hair around the brush and dry one at a time.

Heated rollers: this is a good way of setting your hair if you want quite a firm hold. They are used on dry hair to give it extra curl and bounce. Used too often, however, they will make your hair brittle and dry. To help avoid this happening, you should wrap each roller in tissue paper before rolling the hair around it. It will look strange but it will afford some valuable protection. Never be tempted to use them on wet hair – they will not work and, moreover, it is dangerous.

Rollers: you can use ordinary rollers on wet hair. For a loose, wavy effect, use only a few large rollers, whereas if you want a tight, curled look which will last longer, use more smaller rollers. You can use setting lotion or a special gel or mousse to make the hair easier to handle and increase the hold.

Curling tongs: these are good for quick repair jobs and are easy to use. The plastic or Teflon coated ones are best as they are not so likely to scorch your hair as ordinary metal ones. Use only for a few seconds – never leave them on the hair for too long, and dip the ends in setting lotion for added protection. Use on dry rather than wet hair, just to reset any strands which have wandered out of place.

SPRING BODY

WORK-OUT AND SHAPE-UP FOR THE SUMMER

In the spring, your thoughts will turn naturally to getting in trim after the winter and slimming down for your summer holiday and the sunnier, warmer days ahead when you can wear less clothes and reveal your figure better. This is the time of year when most women resolve to embark on an exercise programme or take up a new sport to get fit and firm. Daily exercise will tone up muscles, making you feel more supple, too. Being fit and super-slim is an important adjunct to beauty. You cannot be beautiful if you feel overweight, dull and lacking in energy. What's more, a fitness exercise plan can have important beauty spin-offs. Your skin will glow and look clearer and more radiant – it will benefit from the boost to your circulation, and you can attack ugly patches of cellulite on hips and thighs.

If you never take any exercise, or have not done so since your schooldays, then it might be a bit of a shock to your system at first. But it can be fun and it will help you to shed weight and feel more alive. It will complement your slimming diet and tone up any stubbornly flabby areas. Your present level of fitness will determine to some extent how well you get on and what you can achieve, but the more unfit you are, the more you stand to gain. If you have problems performing simple exercises like touching your toes or running upstairs, then you cannot rush it, and you must start off slowly, progressing gradually with gentle stretching exercises and a gradual build-up aerobic programme.

Do not be disappointed if you feel exhausted or stiff after your first work-out or jog. Real fitness cannot be achieved overnight and you have to work at it. Our gentle home work-out as shown in the following pages will not over-tax you, and you can increase the repetitions and stretch even further as you become more proficient. You can spend extra time concentrating on any stubborn areas which need special attention like a spare tyre or heavy thighs. If you practise the work-out regularly you will soon feel stronger and more supple

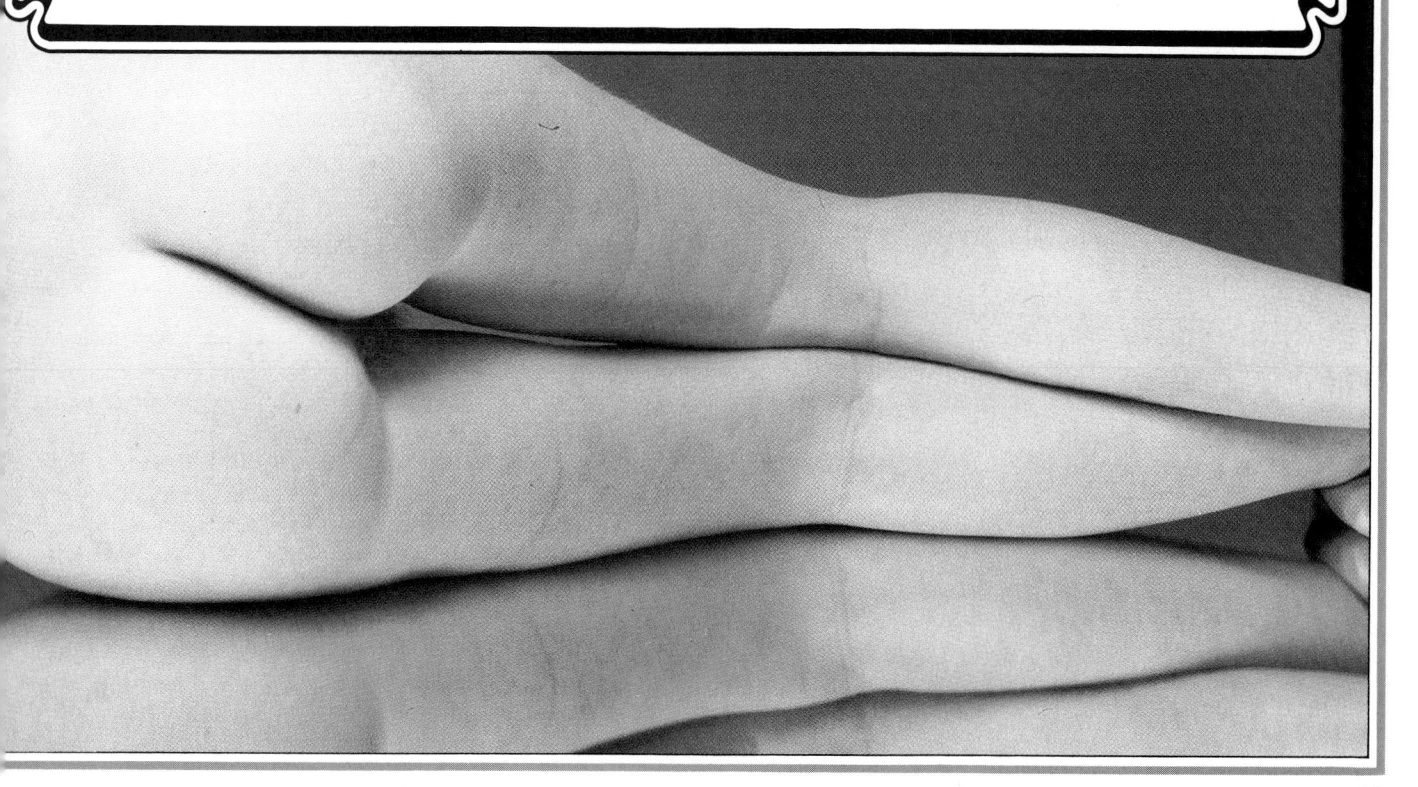

and you will look slimmer, too. It is not so strenuous as some routines and is an enjoyable, gentle way to exercise. However, it will bring fitness and beauty benefits if you carry it out at least three times a week. You will use every part of your body from your shoulders and arms right down to your calf and ankle muscles. Not only will it make you look and feel better, but it will also strengthen your heart, boost your circulation and improve your cardiovascular (heart-lungs) endurance.

You will need to be dedicated and self-disciplined to work-out regularly at home. To make sure you don't shirk, put aside a regular time for your exercises and stick to it. If it makes it easier, you might like to put on some music with a strong rhythmic beat to help you concentrate on what you are doing. Choose a room where you can be alone and uninterrupted, take the phone off the hook and spread out a mat or towel on the floor in readiness for any floor exercises. Make sure it is warm and draught-free. There should be enough room to jump up and swing your arms above your head and to either side of you without knocking into anything.

Work-out rules and guidelines

1 Always warm-up before you start the work-out proper (or any other exercise for that matter) with a few stretches or a short comfortable jog.

2 Wear loose comfortable clothing such as a tracksuit, leotard, tights and leg-warmers (to prevent muscles becoming cold and stiff or injured), or shorts and T-shirt. *Don't* wear tight jeans or anything which will restrict your movement.

3 Don't exercise immediately after eating a meal. Wait at least an hour.

4 Don't exercise if you feel ill, especially if you have a fever. Wait until you feel better.

5 If you have a history of heart disease, high blood pressure or some other serious medical disorder, go to your doctor for a check-up before you embark on any exercise programme.

6 Work evenly on both sides of your body or you may produce uneven results.

7 Remember to train, *don't* strain. Build up gradually and don't rush your exercises. Listen to your body and always aim for quality *not* quantity. As you get fitter and stronger you can work-out faster with more repetitions. But until then it is better to perform a few exercises slowly and well rather than skimp on them and perform them badly. This may lead to injury.

8 Always stretch smoothly and gracefully without any jerky movements.

9 Do the exercises in the sequence given.

10 If an exercise gets painful, stop at once. It should be enjoyable and do you good. If it is hurting you, stop and stretch gently to ease out your muscles. Don't be tempted to 'go for the burn'. Likewise, if you feel giddy or faint, stop exercising immediately and rest.

11 It is important to breathe correctly while you work-out – deeply and rhythmically. Exhale during effort or contraction, and inhale with recovery or expansion. Breathe right from your abdomen – not in short shallow gasps – in through your nose and out through your mouth. Steady regular breathing will maintain a regular flow of oxygen to work your muscles.

12 After exercise, always have a warm bath or shower to ease the tension out of tired and aching muscles and prevent any post-exercise stiffness.

Aerobic exercise

Remember that you only get out of exercise what you put into it. To enjoy the benefits, you have to make it a regular feature in your life. If you really want to get fit and slim, you should try a combination of different exercises – as well as your stretching (isotonics) exercises do some aerobics to develop strength and endurance.

Running, swimming and cycling are the most popular aerobic exercises. They speed up your heart rate as you exercise so that oxygen is supplied faster to the muscles. If you are exercising properly you should not get out of breath, your heart and lungs will get stronger and you will develop more stamina. In fact, your whole body will move in a steady, sustained rhythmical way. Although oxygen is supplied to your muscles for energy at the same rate at which it is used, at first you are bound to feel a little breathless because your body will not be accustomed to the new strains you are placing on it. Aerobic fitness comes only gradually as a result of practice but if you do it regularly you will get stronger and build up your own protection against strain and stress on the heart. To start off you must try some gentle running or jogging/walking, cycling or swimming, say, three times a week for about thirty minutes on each occasion. Whichever you choose, try to do it in a relaxed, comfortable way, stopping to rest when it becomes too much for you. If you don't enjoy it, then try one of the other sports. Here are some hints on how to get started:

Running

This is best of all because you can do it anywhere, anytime, at any age, with a friend or on your own and, what's more, it's inexpensive and you do not need any special facilities. Run wherever you like – in the park, country, city streets, on the beach or an open road. Be sure to wear comfortable clothing – a tracksuit is best – and proper running shoes to cushion your feet, protect your legs and spine and prevent injuries. The best way to get going is to run on grass which is less jarring to your spine than road-running. Warm-up before you run to ease out muscles with a few simple stretching exercises and then set out of your front door. Just keep going for half of the specified time and then turn round and run back. It does not matter if you have to stop and walk when you get breathless. When your breathing feels easier and less laboured, start jogging again. As you build up your sessions, you will find yourself gradually running more and walking less. Here's a basic programme for you to try:

Weeks 1-4
Run/walk for 15 minutes, 3 times a week, until you can run non-stop for 15 minutes.

Weeks 5-8
Run/walk for 20 minutes, 3 times a week, with a longer run of 30 minutes at the weekend, until you can run non-stop for at least 20 minutes.

Weeks 9-12
Run steadily for 20-30 minutes 4 times a week with a longer run/walk of 45 minutes at weekends.

Beauty tips: wear minimum make-up and a good moisturer to form a protective layer between your skin and the wind. In warm, sunny weather, wear a protective sun-cream to prevent burning.

Swimming

This is probably the safest aerobic sport of all and is great for people who are overweight or suffer from backache. If you swim regularly, three or four times a week, you will gradually reshape and streamline your whole body. It is a marvellous way of toning up and firming slack musles. You can use any stroke you wish – breast stroke, backstroke or crawl. By varying the strokes you will use different sets of muscles and develop better all-over fitness. Swim as many lengths of the pool as you can for at least 20 minutes, resting when necessary. As you get fitter, you can gradually build up the amount of time you spend swimming.

Beauty tips: wear a cap to protect your hair from the drying effects of the chlorine in the water. And rub in plenty of moisturising cream afterwards to keep your skin soft and supple. If you wear make-up, make sure that you wear waterproof mascara so that it will not run and does not get streaked.

Cycling

If you do not fancy running or swimming, then cycling may be an enjoyable way to exercise aerobically for you. It is more practical than other sports as you can use it as a means of transport to get to the shops or to work. Cycling hard burns up 650 calories an hour so it is a good way to get slim as well as fit. Start off by cycling on alternate days for about 30 minutes per session. You can gradually increase your time out and the distance covered as you become more proficient. Before you set out, always check the tyre pressures, brakes and saddle height. Take a repair kit and pump with you.

Beauty tips: the same advice applies as above under *Running*. Wear a good moisturiser to prevent chapping in cold weather, and a suncream in summer.

Tennis — get in on the racket

If you enjoy ballgames, tennis might be the right sport for you, especially in the summer months, or even all-the-year-round if you have an indoor court near your home. Whatever your level of fitness, you can still enjoy this exciting game. If you are a complete beginner or have not played for many years and need some brushing-up, then you can enrol for a course of lessons on service, footwork and basic strokes. Individual coaching will help improve your game and make you more proficient.

It is important to know how to play the game properly in order to avoid injury, too. Stretching wildly for the ball can cause damage, and you should learn how to play safely. Once you know the basics, you can practise them until they become automatic. With technique and speed, you can think about joining a club.

If you want to take up tennis seriously, you should play at least two or three times a week to derive any lasting fitness benefits. Once weekly is not enough, especially if you do no other form of supplementary exercise. Instead of getting fitter, you are more likely to over-strain muscles. Invest in a decent racket, one with a standard or midsize head if you are a beginner. Cheap rackets with unfamilar names are not a good buy as they often shatter or may jar your elbow. You will also need proper tennis shoes to safeguard your feet and legs, especially if you are playing on a hard synthetic court. Grass is the easiest and kindest surface. Your shoes should be comfortable to wear and capable of withstanding and absorbing a lot of shock as you move around the court.

Watersports

Although these are not truly aerobic, apart from swimming, they are an enjoyable way to exercise, especially if you live close to the coast or even a large lake or reservoir. Surfing and wind-surfing are becoming more popular, especially among women. Both help you to build up strength and power and firm your body as they use different groups of muscles. You have to be in tune with the wind and waves and have a great degree of flexibility and suppleness to succeed. You need to be a good swimmer in case you take a tumble and should supplement these sports with running, swimming or some aerobic exercise to build up overall fitness and stamina.

If you decide to take up wind-surfing (or boardsailing), you can get professional lessons from a special school to learn about technique and safety. Start off on a lake or estuary before you progress to the open sea where winds and currents can be far more unpredictable and potentially hazardous.

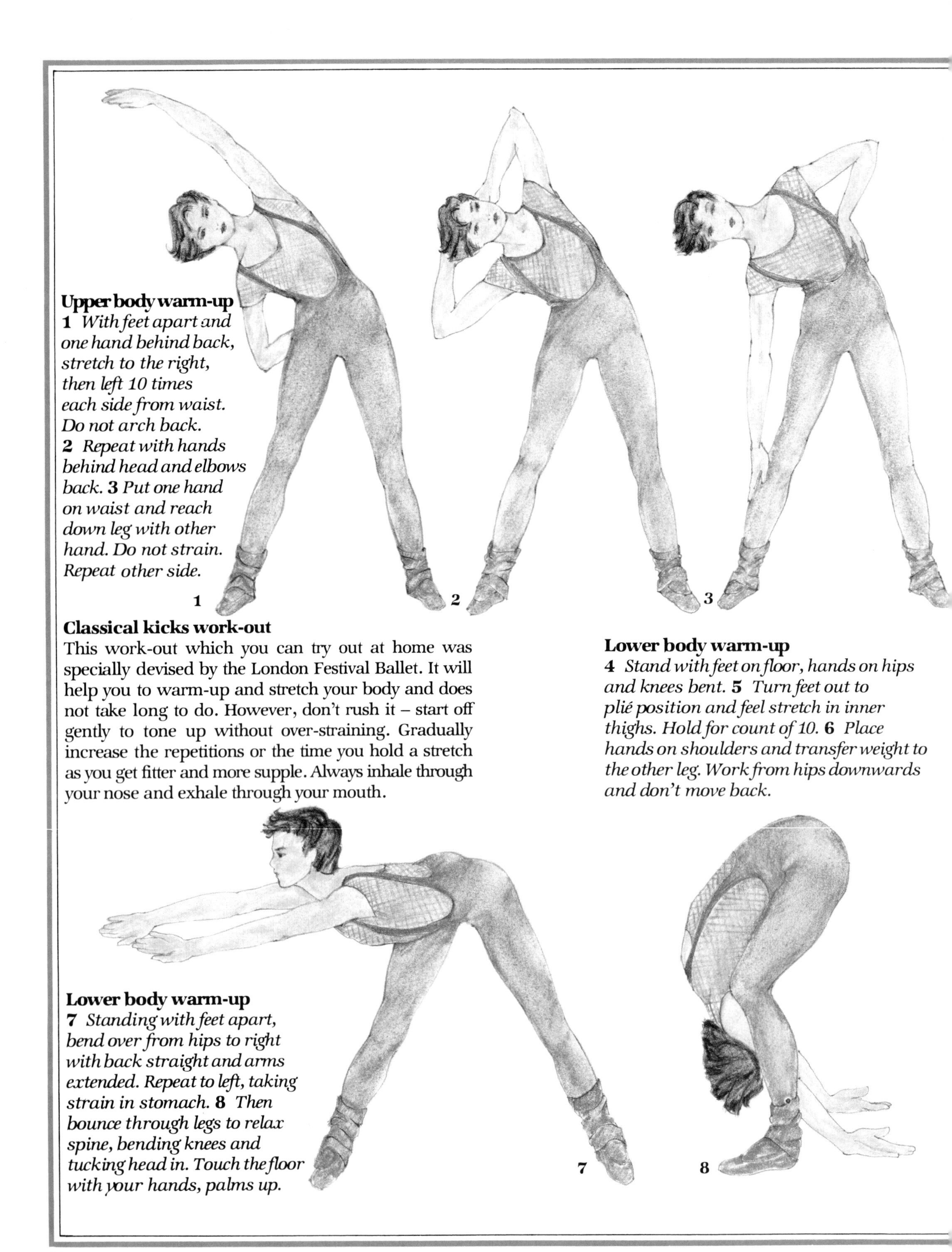

Upper body warm-up

1 *With feet apart and one hand behind back, stretch to the right, then left 10 times each side from waist. Do not arch back.*
2 *Repeat with hands behind head and elbows back.* **3** *Put one hand on waist and reach down leg with other hand. Do not strain. Repeat other side.*

Classical kicks work-out

This work-out which you can try out at home was specially devised by the London Festival Ballet. It will help you to warm-up and stretch your body and does not take long to do. However, don't rush it – start off gently to tone up without over-straining. Gradually increase the repetitions or the time you hold a stretch as you get fitter and more supple. Always inhale through your nose and exhale through your mouth.

Lower body warm-up

4 *Stand with feet on floor, hands on hips and knees bent.* **5** *Turn feet out to plié position and feel stretch in inner thighs. Hold for count of 10.* **6** *Place hands on shoulders and transfer weight to the other leg. Work from hips downwards and don't move back.*

Lower body warm-up

7 *Standing with feet apart, bend over from hips to right with back straight and arms extended. Repeat to left, taking strain in stomach.* **8** *Then bounce through legs to relax spine, bending knees and tucking head in. Touch the floor with your hands, palms up.*

Lower body warm-up
9 *Lean over from waist, twisting upper body and place left hand on floor by right foot, right arm above you. Look up at right arm. Repeat to other side.* **10** *Warm-up arms by extending to either side slightly behind body and hands flexed. Rotate gently.*

Work-out rules
You should do these exercises in the sequence shown, working different areas of the body in turn. If you feel any strain or pain, stop and stretch gently until it eases. If you are worried, consult your doctor. Wear a leotard and tights or loose, comfortable clothing, and have a bath or shower afterwards to cool down and feel refreshed. Wear the minimum of make-up while you work-out, or cleanse thoroughly first and apply a good toner and moisturiser. Cleanse again afterwards and apply your usual make-up. Wearing heavy make-up while you exercise may go cakey and even streak if you get hot from all this physical exertion and start to perspire. If you want to wear make-up, choose a light tinted moisturiser or extra-light foundation.

Classical kick
11 *Standing with one foot flat on floor, kick other leg in opposite direction to top half of body. Keep the supporting leg straight, and direct arms in opposite direction to upraised bent leg.*

Abdominal control
12 *Lie with feet hip distance apart, arms extended with bent elbows. Raise body off floor by tilting pelvis and lifting one vertebra at time. Hold for 10.* **13** *With base of spine on floor and head raised, clutch one knee and raise leg.*

Abdominal control
14 *Head and shoulders raised, extend legs upwards and reach for feet. Exhale and hold in tummy muscles.* **15** *With knees bent and feet apart, raise body off floor and reach through legs with alternate arms. Keep in line with back, looking up at ceiling.*

Leg control
16 *Lie on side, supporting upper body with arms, palms flat on floor and raised hip slightly forwards. Flex your foot and raise and lower your leg without bending back. Reverse legs and repeat to other side.*

Relaxation stretch
17 *Kneel on floor and stretch forwards with arms extended and chin on floor. Hold.* **18** *Lie on front, raise upper body, arms bent. Tense buttocks and lift legs.*

SPRING DIET

YOUR HEALTHY EATING PLAN FOR A SLIM NEW YOU

Spring is traditionally the best time of year for embarking on a slimming diet and spring-cleaning your body with fresh foods, especially fruit and vegetables which are marvellous cleansing agents and help eliminate any toxic wastes. With warmer summer days and a holiday on the beach ahead of you, you should be thinking about shaping up to lighter summer clothes and a swimsuit. We have devised two healthy slimming regimes that *work* to cleanse your body on the inside and make it look more slender on the outside, too. They both revolve around healthy wholefoods and are nutritious as well as slimming. Because they are high in fibre, you get plenty to eat and need not feel hungry.

If you tend to eat a highly refined diet, these healthy diets will represent a radical change in your eating habits – for the better. Even after you reach your target weight and come off the diet, you should try to continue eating healthy foods along the guidelines laid down and you will receive health and beauty benefits. You may be surprised to learn that nutrition plays an important role in beauty. Good high-quality foods are the fuel for your body to make beauty work for you. They help preserve your looks, prevent premature ageing and give you youthful, clear skin and healthy, shiny hair. If you feel out of shape, unfit and lacking in energy, your skin looks dull and your hair lifeless, then your diet may be at fault. Our healthy slimming and eating programme may help you improve your looks from within yourself.

Spring-clean diet

Start off by spring-cleaning your body and detoxifying your system. This will help eliminate any poisonous substances from your tissues and your bloodstream. As a result, your skin will look smoother, less puffy and water-logged. Bad eating habits and over-refined, additive-enriched convenience foods all take their toll on your body and it is important to get rid of any pollutants before you embark on a slimming or healthy maintenance diet.

Raw foods, especially fresh fruit, vegetables and juices, are the spring-cleaning tools you must use. High in nutrients, especially vitamins and minerals, they will rapidly eliminate the poisonous residues of junk food, smoking and alcohol from your system and make you feel more energetic and alive. You should follow the raw food regime for at least one week, preferably two, if you really want a thorough body spring-clean. It may sound daunting at first but it is really quite pleasant when you get accustomed to the change in your eating pattern and the increased fibre in your diet.

You will probably find that you feel full up even though you are eating less food than normal because you have to chew raw food more to break down its fibre. And although it sounds restrictive, there are lots of interesting fruit and vegetables to choose from in addition to raw cereal foods, yoghurt, juices, herbal teas, nuts and seeds. On warmer spring days, salads and cold meals make a refreshing change after the heavier food of winter.

If you have been ill or are feeling under the weather, it may be wise to wait until you feel really strong before embarking on the diet. If you have any doubts about your level of health and fitness, consult your doctor. Here is a menu guideline for you to follow each day. Choose from the following:

On waking: 1 glass freshly squeezed lemon juice in mineral water.

Breakfast: 1 small portion muesli soaked overnight in mineral water or fruit juice with chopped fresh or dried fruit, nuts and seeds (sesame, pumpkin or sunflower).
1 glass freshly squeezed citrus or vegetable juice.
1 cup herbal tea (no milk or sugar).

Lunch: 1 large salad of mixed vegetables, fruit, nuts, seeds and sprouted grains with oil and lemon or yoghurt dressing.
Fresh fruit of your choice.
Mineral water or 1 cup herbal tea.

Mid-afternoon: 1 glass fruit or vegetable juice or piece fresh fruit.

Dinner: 1 large salad of mixed vegetables, fruit, nuts, seeds, sprouted grains with oil and lemon or yoghurt dressing.
Small portion natural yoghurt with fresh fruit.
Mineral water or herbal tea.

Snacks: freshly squeezed fruit and vegetable juices, mineral water, fresh fruit and sticks of raw vegetables (carrot, celery, peppers).

Herbed kebabs (see recipe on page 48)

You should find that this strict vegetarian regime is quite satisfying for a short period, but you should not stay on the diet for longer than two weeks. It is only intended as a short-term measure to cleanse your system before you embark on the more varied gradual weight reduction diet. The diet rules are as follows:

1 Don't drink any alcohol, soft fizzy drinks, tea or coffee.

2 Don't smoke.

3 Don't eat any cooked foods.

4 Don't eat any sugar or use artificial sweeteners. If you really do have an impossible sweet tooth, then try a little honey or some soaked dried fruits as a more natural and healthy way of sweetening dishes.

5 Don't use sweetened juice. For the best vitamin and mineral content, squeeze the fruit and vegetables yourself. This is easily done if you have a juice extractor.

Healthy slimming diet

Now that you feel thoroughly cleansed and are starting to receive the health and beauty benefits of your spring-clean, it is time to embark on a more long-term healthy eating regime. This is *the* diet for today's figure-conscious beautiful woman who has a healthy, active lifestyle. You are probably looking and feeling better already but you have to learn how to keep these benefits through healthy eating, and not reverting back to your old bad habits.

Although you may think that your usual diet is quite healthy anyway and that you are already well-nourished, it is a sad fact of life that most people eat predominantly unhealthy food, and that many are malnourished although they have plenty to eat. The average Western diet is singularly unhealthy – it contains too much salt, saturated fat and sugar and too little fibre and unrefined foods. Such a diet leads inevitably to being overweight, feeling tired and lethargic and not looking one's best.

Most women admit to being a little overweight and want to lose a few pounds (kilos), especially in the spring when holidays are looming in the coming summer months and there is added incentive to look good in a swimsuit. A healthy wholefood diet will help you to lose weight, especially if you usually eat convenience foods, white bread, a lot of saturated fat and sugar. It will also establish healthy new habits that will last a lifetime and keep you looking slimmer, younger and more beautiful. Even after you reach your ideal weight, you can continue following the diet guidelines. Obviously, you may be tempted to indulge in a chocolate bar or creamy dessert occasionally, but these little lapses won't make any difference in the long run if you eat a generally healthy diet most of the time.

This diet need not cause you any expense or inconvenience. You can buy most of the wholefood ingredients in your local supermarket or health food store. Organically grown fruit and vegetables are harder to find and cost a great deal more than the usual sort. Unless you are prepared to pay high prices or grow your own, you should buy fresh produce and wash or scrub it carefully to remove all traces of chemical sprays. As far as good food is concerned, quality does not always go hand in hand with expense. Low-fat soft cheeses, eggs, poultry and cheap white fish fillets are just as nutritious as expensive steaks. And it is just as quick to grill a fish cutlet or make a delicious salad as to heat up a convenience meal.

Diet guidelines

1 Eat less salt. We get quite enough sodium from the food we eat without salting it as well. Make more use of fresh herbs and ground spices to season and flavour food. Too much salt upsets our natural water balance and may cause fluid retention and water-logged tissues. And in the long run, a high salt diet may predispose you to high blood pressure, heart disease and stroke.

2 Cut out sugar. Keep it in mind that sugar consists only of empty calories. Even raw cane brown sugar has little nutritional goodness. The only things sugar can do for you are to pander to your sweet tooth, put on unwanted weight and rot your teeth – you are better off without it. You can use dried fruit, fresh fruit purées or a little honey to sweeten yoghurt, desserts and cakes.

3 Eat less fat, especially the saturated animal fats (butter, hard margarine, lard, fat on meat, hard cheese, full-fat milk and cream). These not only make you fat – they make you a future target for heart disease, too. Eat polyunsaturated fats instead – fish oils (in herrings, mackerel, salmon, tuna), sunflower and safflower oils and soft vegetable margarine.

4 Have more fibre. This is the indigestible cellular substance that makes up plant walls. The average refined Western diet is low in fibre and this leads to many health problems, including constipation, varicose veins, diverticular disease and colitis. By eating more fresh fruit and vegetables and 100 per cent wholemeal bread, brown rice and wholewheat pasta, baked potatoes and muesli, you can increase the fibre in your diet. This brings many beauty benefits, too. It helps you to stay slim with glowing skin because fibre absorbs water and toxic wastes in your body and helps eliminate them. Because it is so chewy and filling, you eat less and don't have to fill up on unhealthy fattening snack foods. You will notice that on a high-fibre diet your skin and hair will look less lacklustre and more alive, any spots will start to clear up, black rings under the eyes will be less noticeable and stubborn areas of cellulite on hips and thighs will improve.

5 Eat more fresh fruit and vegetables, especially in their raw state. These are a rich source of vitamins, minerals and trace elements, all essential for beauty and good health. Your skin and hair reflect your inner state of health and the manner in which you fuel your body. High-nutrient good food cleanses you inside and supplies all the the substances you need to build and repair healthy cells, remove waste matter, provide energy and vitality and keep you looking youthful. Just as the condition of a dog's fur coat tells you something about its health, your skin is the best external indicator of your inner wellbeing. To keep it looking its best, smooth, soft, translucent and wrinkle-and blemish-free, you have to feed it from within as well as plying it with creams and moisturisers. The good skin diet includes:

Vitamin A for smooth, even-textured skin. Lack of it leads to scaliness, dryness, enlarged pores and spots, and premature ageing. It can help correct over-oily skin and fight off acne. You can obtain it from fish liver oils, dark green leafy vegetables (cabbage, kale, spinach), yellow fruits and vegetables (carrots, apricots), eggs and liver.

Vitamin B-complex for carrying oxygen to skin cells, preventing tiny lines, and cracked skin around the mouth, and fighting acne, whiteheads and blackheads. You can get it from whole-grain cereals and bread, liver, fresh green vegetables, dried beans and pulses, fish, milk, eggs and cheese.

Vitamin C for helping to build healthy strong collagen in your skin, protecting it from wrinkling and broken veins and premature ageing. To ensure a regular supply of vitamin C you should eat daily some citrus fruit (lemons, oranges, tangerines, limes), blackcurrants, tomatoes, peppers, potatoes, leafy green vegetables and strawberries.

Vitamin E for reviving tired skin, avoiding dryness and stretch marks, stimulating circulation and slowing down the skin's natural ageing process. You can get it from leafy dark green vegetables, whole-grain bread and cereals, avocado, seeds, wheat germ and cold-pressed vegetable oils.

Eating a healthy diet along the lines laid down here will supply all the vitamins and minerals you need. Perhaps the most important mineral is zinc – it helps keep your skin strong and elastic, and lack of it may lead to sagging, wrinkles and stretch marks.

Courgette and carrot salad (see recipe on page 48)

6 Cut down on alcohol, tea and coffee. These are all the enemies of good health and a good, clear skin. Such stimulants will cause your skin to age prematurely and make your complexion appear rather coarse and uneven in texture and colour.

Get set go

Now for the diet itself. Use it to lose weight initially and then to maintain your new slim shape. Weight loss will be slow but steady – probably in the region of about 2lb/1kg per week (maybe more if you have a lot of weight to lose and are exercising as well). Crash diets are all very well but they rarely supply all the nutrients your body needs to keep it in optimal health, and the more rapidly you lose the weight the more likely you are to quickly regain it afterwards. The beauty of this diet is that it will help to teach you new healthy eating habits that will last a lifetime and actually keep you slim in the years to come. It supplies all the essential nutrients you need and will help make you more beautiful. It is fairly flexible and there are lots of food choices so that you need not eat any foods you dislike.

Before you start, weigh yourself and fix a target weight which is not unreasonable. Check your weight once every week, remembering to weigh yourself at roughly the same time either naked or wearing the same clothes. Your weight loss will probably be more rapid in the first week or so and then will gradually slow down as your body grows accustomed to its new regime. Don't be impatient if it takes time – remember that this is the sensible longterm way to lose weight and keep it off for good.

Design your weight loss or healthy eating programme around seasonal fruit and vegetables. Unfortunately, many of the summer salad stuff, soft fruit and more exotic vegetables will not be in the shops yet. There may be expensive glasshouse-grown varieties or imported exotica, but you can always use more bargain-priced home-grown spring produce – especially raw grated root vegetables, shredded spring greens, leeks, sprouting broccoli, mushrooms, watercress, chicory, oranges, apples, grapes and peas.

Note: the amount of weight you lose will depend to a great extent on how much you weigh at the beginning of the diet and how overweight you are. Most people will lose only about 3.5kg/7lb but anyone who is very overweight may see more dramatic results and even lose 7kg/14lb over, say, three to four weeks. It is perfectly safe to stay on this diet for a month as it provides all the nutrients you need and sufficient calories to keep you going throughout the day without feeling tired.

Vary the dishes you choose each day so that boredom does not set in, and even when you achieve your target weight try to keep eating a really healthy diet along the guidelines set out above.

On this diet, you have a wide range of choices for each meal so there is less chance of getting bored and neglecting the healthy food. The degree of variety means that it will suit you, no matter what your personal preferences, likes and dislikes. Although you should try to resist snacks between meals and discipline yourself to only three meals a day, there are some slimming, low-calorie suggestions if you cannot resist them. You may choose one suggestion from each of the following meals:

Breakfast

1 Small bowl dried fruit (peaches, apricots, prunes, pears, apple rings, figs) soaked overnight in water and lemon juice *plus* spoonful of natural yoghurt.

2 One egg, poached or boiled, with one slice wholemeal bread/toast and scraping of low-fat spread or vegetable margarine.

3 Small helping unsweetened muesli soaked overnight in fruit juice with chopped nuts, natural yoghurt and fruit of your choice.

4 Half a grapefruit (no sugar) with one slice wholemeal bread/toast and scraping of low-fat spread or vegetable margarine.

5 100ml/4floz natural yoghurt with 5ml/1 teaspoon each of bran and wheatgerm and chopped fresh fruit.

6 100ml/4floz natural yoghurt whirled in blender with 1 banana *or* 1 slice of fresh pineapple, brewers yeast powder, 2 drops vanilla essence and enough skimmed milk to thin.

7 100ml/4floz natural yoghurt blended with 15ml/1 tablespoon tomato concentrate, 5ml/1 teaspoon each of wheatgerm and brewers yeast and ground almonds, 1 egg yolk, juice of 1 orange, chopped parsley and enough skimmed milk to thin.

8 Fresh fruit salad of orange and grapefruit segments in their own juice with a spoonful of natural yoghurt *plus* 1 slice of wholemeal bread/toast.

9 Small bowl California raisin compôte (*see* recipe) with yoghurt.

Drink: either 1 glass unsweetened fruit or vegetable juice *or* 1 glass hot water with juice of ½ lemon *or* 1 cup unsweetened lemon tea, herbal tea or decaffeinated coffee.

Lunch:

1 Salad of raw vegetables, fruit and herbs (lettuce, Chinese leaves, chicory, red and green peppers, radicchio, fennel, cucumber, cauliflower florets, mushrooms, grated carrot, sliced courgettes, spinach, watercress, mustard and cress, curly endive, radishes, tomatoes, onions, celery, sprouted seeds, beansprouts, alfalfa, chopped herbs *with* a yoghurt dressing (*see* recipe).

plus 1 slice wholemeal bread *plus* 50g/2oz low-fat cheese (ricotta, quark or cottage) *or* 75g/3oz lean chicken (no skin) or fish or prawns.

2 Omelette made with 2 small eggs cooked in 2.5ml/½ teaspoon oil and filled with 1 sliced tomato, fresh herbs, cooked leaf spinach or a few shrimps.

Note: do not have omelette if you had an egg for breakfast.

3 1 small jacket-baked potato topped with 15ml/1 tablespoon grated cheese *or* low-fat soft cheese and herbs *or* natural yoghurt and chopped chives *with* a small portion of salad.

4 One portion of liquidiser soup with a small salad. Choose from:

cucumber – blended with natural yoghurt, lemon juice, fresh mint, coriander, garlic and black pepper.

gazpacho – tomatoes (skinned) blended with green pepper, onion, cucumber, lemon juice, garlic, herbs and black pepper and iced water.

fresh tomato – skinned tomatoes sweated in a tiny amount of oil in a pan with onion and garlic. Add some chicken stock, fresh basil and parsley and black pepper. Blend with natural yoghurt and chill.

Dessert: fresh fruit of your choice.

Dinner:

1 75g/3oz white fish or chicken, grilled or poached.

2 Grilled kebabs of chicken livers *or* kidney *or* scallops *or* white fish *or* chicken with mushrooms, peppers, cherry tomatoes and quartered onions *or* Herbed kebabs (*see* recipe).

3 Poached or grilled scallops with lemon juice and herbs.

4 One green or red pepper stuffed with a mixture of fresh herbs, tomato, onion, mushroom and yoghurt, and baked in a moderate oven.

5 Small salmon steak or white fish fillet baked in foil with lemon juice and herbs and shrimps (optional).

6 Bean and vegetable casserole (mixed beans and vegetables baked in a sauce.)

Plus:

Small fresh vegetable salad *or* steamed green vegetables or carrots *or* Courgette and carrot salad (*see* recipe).

Plus:

1 slice wholemeal bread *or* 1 small portion brown rice.

Dessert: fresh fruit *or* low-fat cheese with celery *or* small portion natural yoghurt *or* California raisin compôte (*see* recipe) *or* Spring fruit salad (*see* recipe).
Drink: mineral water *or* fruit or vegetable juice *or* herbal or lemon tea *or* decaffeinated coffee.

Snacks: these are not to be encouraged but if you really need something between meals, try one of the following:
1 Sunflower, sesame or pumpkin seeds.
2 Fresh fruit in moderation.
3 Raw vegetable sticks – carrot, celery, peppers dipped in yoghurt.
4 Trail mix (*see* recipe).
5 Crunchy granola bar (*see* recipe).

Diet recipes

Crunchy granola bars
25g/1oz flaked almonds, chopped
25g/1oz hazelnuts, chopped
75g/3oz California raisins
100g/4oz porridge oats
25g/1oz sesame seeds
60ml/4 tablespoons sunflower oil
60ml/4 tablespoons honey

Grease a shallow baking tin. Mix all the ingredients together in a bowl and press the mixture lightly into the tin. Bake at 180°C, 350°F, gas 4 for 25 minutes until golden. Cool in the tin for 5 minutes and then mark into squares with a sharp knife. Cool for 10 minutes and remove to a cooling rack.

Fruity muesli
225g/8oz porridge oats
100g/4oz California raisins
50g/2oz wheat germ
50g/2oz sesame seeds
50g/2oz sunflower seeds
75g/3oz toasted hazelnuts, chopped
50g/2oz dried apricots, chopped

Mix all the ingredients and store in a screwtop jar. To eat, soak overnight in water or fruit juice and serve with fresh chopped fruit and natural unsweetened yoghurt.

California raisin compôte
100g/4oz California raisins
100g/4oz dried figs
100g/4oz dried apricots
thin strip of orange rind
2.5cm/1in cinnamon stick
5ml/1 teaspoon honey (optional)

Soak the dried fruit overnight in water. Place in a pan with the orange rind, cinnamon and honey. Simmer gently until tender and cooked. The liquid should reduce and thicken a little. Serve warm or cold. This makes enough compôte for three breakfasts so keep it fresh in an airtight container in the refrigerator.

Trail mix
175g/6oz California raisins
100g/4oz sunflower seeds
100g/4oz banana chips
50g/2oz toasted coconut flakes
50g/2oz glacé pineapple, chopped
100g/4oz dried apricots, chopped

Mix all the ingredients together and store in an airtight jar for up to three weeks.

Yoghurt salad dressing
100ml/4floz natural yoghurt
juice of ½ lemon
15ml/1 tablespoon finely chopped onion
salt and pepper
chopped fresh chives or parsley

Beat all the ingredients together until smooth.

Oil and lemon dressing
100ml/4floz olive or sunflower oil
juice of ½ lemon
2.5ml/½ teaspoon French (Dijon) mustard (optional)
salt and pepper

Blend all the ingredients until smooth, store in a screw-top jar in the refrigerator.

Omelette
2 medium eggs
10ml/2 teaspoons cold water
salt and pepper
dot butter or margarine

Beat the eggs, water and seasoning lightly with a fork. Melt the butter in an non-stick omelette pan and, when sizzling, add the egg mixture. Draw the runny mixture in from the sides towards the centre until the omelette is set lightly. Add the filling of your choice. Cook gently until golden underneath and set and creamy on top. Fold over and slide onto a plate.
Filling:
1 *30ml/2 tablespoons chopped fresh herbs*
2 *30ml/2 tablespoons grated cheese and herbs*
3 *30ml/2 tablespoons grated cheese and 1 tomato*

4 *25g/1oz low-fat soft cheese and 25g/1oz shrimps*
5 *25g/1oz chopped ham or chicken or flaked smoked mackerel*

Home-made yoghurt
You will need a yoghurt maker for this recipe.
550ml/1pint skimmed low-fat milk
15ml/1 tablespoon skimmed milk powder
60ml/4 tablespoons natural live yoghurt

Heat the milk to boiling point. Remove from the heat and cool to 43°C/110-112°F; use a sugar thermometer to get an accurate reading. Mix the skimmed milk powder with the natural yoghurt 'starter'. Stir into the warm milk and pour into warmed jars in the yoghurt maker. Cover with the lids to seal. Replace the cover over the jars and leave for at least 4 hours with the machine switched on. Check whether the yoghurt is set before removing. If should be set, thick and custardy in texture. Transfer to the refrigerator and leave for at least 12 hours. It should taste pleasantly tart. Mix with muesli or fresh fruit and nuts, or use as a topping for fruit and in salad dressings.

Slimming kebabs
75g/3oz chicken livers, kidneys, scallops, white fish or chicken
3 button mushrooms
2 chunks red pepper
2 chunks green pepper
1 small onion, quartered
2 sherry tomatoes
1 bay leaf
5ml/1 teaspoon oil
squeeze of lemon juice
salt and pepper

Cut the offal, fish or chicken into chunks. Thread onto kebab skewers with the vegetables and bay leaf alternately. Brush with oil and lemon and season. Place under a hot preheated grill, turning occasionally until cooked all over.

Herbed kebabs
1 small avocado, peeled and stoned
1 grapefruit, cut into segments
¼ cucumber, sliced and halved
squeezed juice of 1 grapefruit
chopped fresh basil or mint
basil or mint leaves for garnish

Cut the avocado into small chunks and assemble on kebab skewers alternately with the grapefruit and cucumber. Arrange on a serving dish, pour over the grapefruit juice (this will help prevent the avocado discolouring) and sprinkle with chopped herbs. Garnish with basil or mint.

Courgette and carrot salad
50g/2oz grated carrot
75g/3oz coarsely grated courgettes
iced water
juice of 1 lemon
juice of 1 orange
salt and pepper

Place the grated carrot and courgette in a bowl and cover with iced water for 20 minutes. Drain and spin dry. Mix with the orange and lemon juice and season to taste. Toss well and serve immediately.

Spring fruit salad
225-350g/8-12oz melon flesh, eg. honeydew, ogen, galia melons and watermelon
few green seedless grapes
4 fresh dates, stoned
orange juice

Use a vegetable baller to shape the melon into small balls, or cut into cubes. Chill well. Mix with the grapes and dates and pour over enough orange juice to cover. Add a few drops of orange liqueur if wished. Chill well before serving with yoghurt if wished.

Baked salmon
1 salmon cutlet
50g/2oz shrimps or prawns
juice of ½ lemon
a little oil
fresh chopped thyme and basil
15ml/1 tablespoon chopped spring onion

Place the salmon on an oiled piece of cooking foil. Arrange the shrimps on top and add the remaining ingredients. Fold the foil over to make a neat parcel, taking care to seal the ends securely so that no cooking juices can escape and keep the salmon moist. Place on a baking sheet and cook in a preheated oven at 180°C, 350°F, gas 4 for about 15-20 minutes.

Baked stuffed pepper
1 red or green pepper
½ small onion, chopped
3-4 button mushrooms, thinly sliced
5ml/1 teaspoon oil
1 tomato, skinned and chopped
chopped basil, oregano or parsley
45ml/3 tablespoons yoghurt
salt and pepper
5ml/1 teaspoon grated Parmesan

Spring fruit salad (recipe on page 48). Fresh fruit juice (water-melon or tomato) makes a healthy drink.

Slice the top of the pepper and retain for a lid. Scoop out the seeds and pith. If the pepper does not stand securely on its end, level the base. Sauté the onion and mushrooms in the oil until soft. Add the tomato and herbs and sauté for 2-3 more minutes. Mix in the yoghurt and season and fill the pepper with this mixture. Sprinkle with cheese and replace the lid. Stand in a baking tray filled with a little water and bake in a preheated oven at 180°C, 350°F, gas 4 for 1 hour.

Quick wholemeal bread

550g/1lb 4oz 100 per cent wholemeal flour
10ml/2 teaspoons sea salt
1 packet easy blend dried yeast
30ml/2 tablespoons oil
300ml/½pint water at blood heat
30ml/2 tablespoons molasses
50g/2oz cracked wheat
50g/2oz chopped walnuts
milk or egg for glazing

Make in the food processor, using the plastic dough blades. Mix the flour, salt and yeast. With the machine on, pour the oil, water and molasses through the feed tube with the cracked wheat and walnuts. Process for about 2 minutes, or until the dough is smooth and elastic and leaves the sides of the processor bowl clean.

Shape into a round and place in an oiled bowl inside a sealed polythene bag. Leave in a warm place for 1 hour or until doubled in size. Knock back into shape on a lightly floured board and leave in a warm place to prove, covered with a cloth. When the dough rised to the top of the tins, glaze and bake in a hot oven at 230°C, 450°F, gas 8 for 25 minutes or until well-risen, crisp and brown. Cool on wire trays.

Chicken and peach salad

1 cold roast chicken breast, skinned and boned
1 fresh peach, stoned and sliced
few crisp lettuce leaves
50ml/2floz natural yoghurt
10ml/2 teaspoons mayonnaise
2.5ml/½ teaspoon mustard

Dice the chicken and place in a bowl with the peach and lettuce leaves. Mix the yoghurt, mayonnaise, any peach juice and mustard. Toss the salad.

GET FIT AND READY FOR THE SUMMER SUN

When summer arrives, you will have to adapt your beauty routines – skincare, haircare and make-up – to the longer, hotter days. Do not make the mistake of leaving them to take care of themselves just because you feel and look better already. You cannot hide behind a sun tan either – for the summer sun is the worst enemy of your skin and hair and can cause them irreparable damage if you do not protect them adequately from its powerful rays.

In order to get summer-ready you have to find the best look for you, which is vital, healthy and natural. Make time for yourself this summer by spending it on the basics – developing new hair- and skincare systems and a healthy eating plan which is based on nutritious seasonal, refreshing salads.

Skin and make-up look more natural and golden in summer but they do not just happen. Your skin changes from season to season and you will need to adapt your skincare system accordingly to its new requirements. Suncare is vital if you are to protect your skin from becoming dry and wrinkled. There are scientifically tested products to help you – sunscreens and sunblocks, that form an invisible protective cover-up. Then you can feel confident about baring your body to the sun – whether it's on a holiday beach or in your own back garden. Capitalise on the beauty lessons of spring to achieve a sporty, outdoors look. You can contrive your make-up to be subtle and understated but stunning nevertheless. Learn the secrets of sun beauty – whether it's on the beach by day, or sundown glamour for romantic summer evenings. The trick is to achieve maximum results with the minimum of make-up while still protecting your skin and keeping the moisture in.

Your body will be under close scrutiny so don't abandon your spring exercise regime – keep it in good shape with regular work-outs and sport. Pay special attention to the details – to smooth, hairless legs, beautifully soft and manicured hands and feet, and a dazzling summer smile. There is extra emphasis on health and fitness now, and exercise has never been easier or more enjoyable. It is a great way to get outside in the sun and cultivate your tan. The wonderful range of fresh fruit and vegetables available at this time of year will also help maintain a slim silhouette.

Heat is your hair's worst enemy so you will have to protect it from humidity as well as the drying, damaging effects of the sun. Salt water and chlorinated pools also take their toll so it is just as well to know how to look after holiday hair and keep it in top condition. A short manageable cut is easily looked after, takes little time to dry and is cool on a hot day.

Lastly, fragrance is an integral part of summer – just think of the heavy scent of flowers hanging in the still heat of a hot day. You need to know which scents to wear and when to wear them. The sun can play tricks with perfume so it is best to save it for glamorous evenings out when you want to feel alluring and not to wear it on the beach on a very hot day. Whether you choose a light floral fragrance or a heavier spicy scent, it will add the finishing touches to your overall beauty.

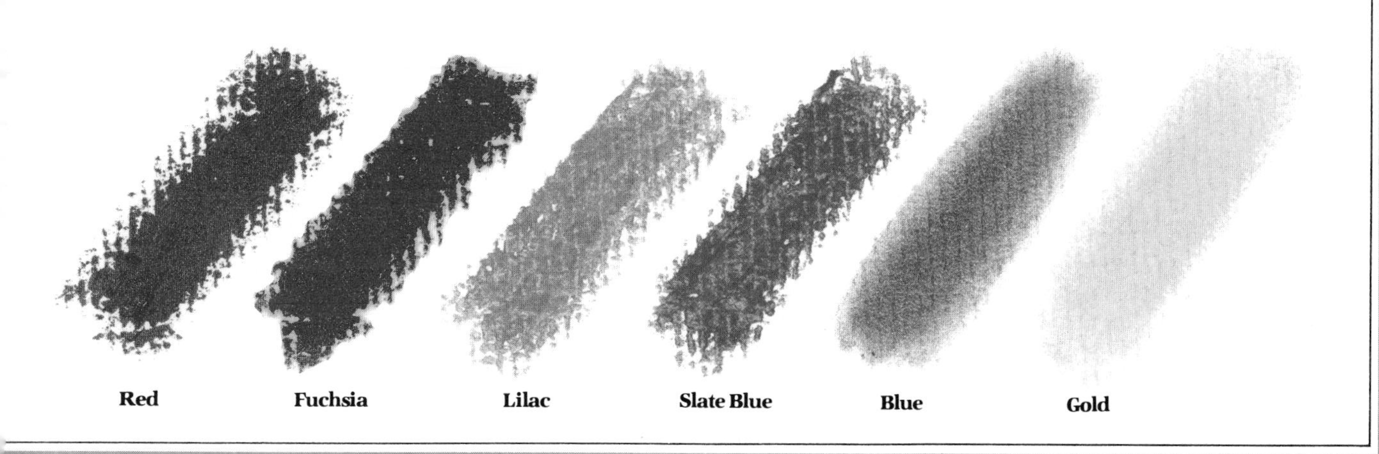

Red Fuchsia Lilac Slate Blue Blue Gold

SCREEN YOUR SKIN FROM THE PENETRATING SUN

Everyone wants a holiday-looking golden tan when summer arrives but did you know that sun is your skin's worst enemy? Although a lovely bronze colour can make you look youthful and bursting with health, it also accelerates the normal ageing process in your skin and can irreparably damage skin cells, making it appear wrinkled. If you want to look tanned, you must take sensible precautions to protect your skin from sun-damage and that means wearing a sunscreen at all times – not just when you are lying on a hot beach but also in sunlit city streets.

The tanning process and your skin

Sunlight contains tanning ultraviolet-A rays (UVA) and burning ultraviolet-B rays (UVB). When your skin is unprotected, both these sorts of ultraviolet light penetrate the epidermis and break down the extensive network of collagen fibres in the underlying dermis. They cause the protein therein to grow thick and hard and eventually the collagen fibres themselves 'cross-link' and twist together so that your skin loses its elasticity and starts to sag and wrinkle. Fine lines appear around your eyes and mouth.

Obviously this process takes time and one short sunny holiday will not make too much difference to your skin, but the cumulative effect of years of sunshine and deep summer tans will take their toll on your skin eventually and it will gradually lose its elasticity and youthfulness.

A tan is really your skin's way of protecting itself from the sun's burning rays. Deep in your skin are some cells called melanocytes which contain a brown pigment – melanin. When your skin is exposed to ultraviolet light, these cells travel upwards to the epidermis to act as a protective shield and absorb the UV rays. They help prevent burning and give your skin a light golden colour. As you increase your exposure to sunlight your tan will become deeper and darker.

The degree to which you tan depends on your genetic inheritance to a great extent. This influences the way that melanin is distributed throughout your skin and the amount you produce. If it is evenly distributed you will get a uniform tan, but if it is concentrated in some areas and sparse in others you will acquire freckles or a blotchy-looking tan. This is the experience of some fair-skinned Northern European women who never tan successfully. Darker olive-skinned Mediterranean people produce more melanin than traditionally fair English 'roses' and tan more easily. So no amount of expensive creams and tanning preparations can alter your melanin allocation and distribution, and if you are inclined to burn easily or sprout freckles in the sun, you may be better off using a fake tanning cream for your skin's sake.

There are other factors, too, which affect your tan. These include:

1 Where you tan: the sun's rays are most powerful and their angle more acute the nearer you go to the Equator. Therefore your chances of tanning – and burning – are greater in this region and you should take special care, especially if you are naturally fair-skinned.

2 The time of year: in the northern hemisphere, the sun's rays are strongest around the time of the summer solstice, June 21st, whereas in the southern hemisphere they are most powerful in mid-December. You should take special protective measures to look after your skin during these months.

3 The time of day: the most dangerous time to be out in the sun is around noon when the UV rays are at their strongest. They are less intense before 11am and after 3pm. If you are quite pale and do not have a good base tan you should limit your sunbathing in the middle of the day and if possible restrict it to the early morning and late afternoon. When your tan darkens, you can venture out at midday but only if you are well-protected with an effective sunscreen. Remember that 65 per cent of the sun's daily radiation reaches us in those dangerous four hours in the middle of the day.

4 The reflection of the sun's rays: the ultraviolet rays bounce off the ground, buildings and other surfaces onto your skin, and they are reflected by white or shiny surfaces. Thus you stand a greater chance of getting burned if you are lying on a pale sandy beach or skiing across white powdery snow. Reflectors, mirrors and foil mats have the same effect. Whereas white surfaces reflect the rays, black ones absorb them. So wearing a black dress in the hot sun will protect any sunburnt areas of your body but will make you feel hotter than you would with a white dress.

A freshwater shower after sun-bathing or swimming is refreshing and also washes out any salt from your hair which may make it feel dry and coarse.

Speedo

How sunscreens work

A successful painless tan is the result not only of careful, gradual sunbathing but also of choosing the right sunscreen for your skin. Its effect is to filter out the harmful burning UV-B rays and allow the gentler UV-A rays to gradually penetrate your skin and tan you. If you want your skin to stay moist, smooth and young, you should not aim for a deep bronzed colour. This extreme form of tan can fundamentally alter the genetic make-up of its cells and make your skin dry, flaky and leathery, both in appearance and texture. A light golden tan is just as flattering and far less damaging. Some women regard a deep tan as a sort of status symbol and think their holiday a failure unless they return home really dark and bronzed. However, your skin will be the loser in the long run if you do this too many years running. Aim for gold instead and make use of the sun's benefits – it relaxes you, helps promote the formation of vitamin D in your skin and boosts circulation.

Your choice of sunscreen will depend on your personal preference for oils, creams, lotions, gels or foams, and your skin type. Lotions and creams are easily absorbed by the skin and leave you feeling dry and silky smooth. However, they do need frequent application to be really protective. Oils and gels feel greasier and are more messy to wear – tiny grains of sand tend to stick to your body. But they stay on your skin longer and make it gleam and glisten in bright sunshine, making you look very attractive on the beach. Most sunscreens are perfumed and smell fragrantly of coconut, lemon or some other delicious aroma. If your skin is very sensitive or tends to develop allergic rashes, you would be well advised to look for a specially formulated product which is irritant-free.

Sunscreens usually contain chemicals such as benzophenones, salicylates and a substance known as PABA (para-amino-benzoic-acid) which is the best sunscreen ingredient of all and filters out virtually all burning rays. Look for PABA on the label when you compare the different suncare products. A substance to avoid is oil of bergamot which enhances your tan but has been linked to some skin problems and disorders. For this reason, most manufacturers and cosmetic houses no longer put it in their sunscreens.

It is a common misapprehension that sunscreens and sunblocks are the same thing, but they are not. Whereas sunscreens filter out most of the harmful burning rays of ultraviolet light, sunblocks are even more protective. This form of absolute barrier is ideal for sunburnt patches of skin, ultra-sensitive areas and people with very fair, delicate skins. You have probably seen men and women on the beach with a mysterious white substance smeared thickly on their noses or lips – this is zinc oxide, a powerful sunblock which blocks out everything.

The sun protection factor number system

To help you find the right sunscreen for your skin, they are graded on a scale of sun protection factor numbers (SPFs), the highest being for highly delicate skins down to the lowest for dark oily skins. Developed by a Viennese professor, Franz Greiter, this system will enable you to tan successfully. However, the major beauty houses have developed their own individual codes using different scales, so you should ask the beautician for advice on which SPF number to choose for your skin, based on her professional expertise and your past experience of sunbathing. When you buy a suncare product, do not be tempted to cheat on your skin and pretend that it is darker or more sun-resistant than it really is. Protection is the name of the game, and if you quickly go beetroot and sore in intense sunshine even after a short exposure time, you should choose a sunscreen with a high SPF rating. As your tan processes and deepens, you can change to a lower number which will allow more tanning rays to filter through and penetrate the skin.

You may find that you use different numbered sunscreens at the same time. For instance, you may protect your face and particularly vulnerable areas like your shoulder blades, breasts, stomach, knees and elbows with a higher SPF sunscreen than you use on your arms and legs.

Helena Rubenstein sun protection index

	Skin type	Suncare
Numbers 10-6	Pale, sensitive inclined to burn easily	Start off with a high number and gradually work down as your tan deepens. Maximum time in the sun wearing sunscreen is 3½ hours
Numbers 6-4	Normal, balanced skins which tan gradually but may burn first and need some sun protection	Apply sunscreen regularly perhaps with a higher number on your face and other sensitive areas. Maximum time in sun wearing sunscreen is 2½ hours
Numbers 4-2	Dark, olive skin that tans easily and rarely burns but needs maximum protection	Use higher number on your face and don't skimp on sunscreens – your dark skin will not protect you from sun damage although you can stay in the sun longer

This table will help you choose the right SPF for your particular type of skin. Remember that in order to tan safely it is essential to choose the right numbered products or you will end up with a bad case of sunburn.

Applying the sunscreen

When and how you apply the sunscreen is also important. For an even all-over tan, you should rub it in generously and uniformly. Don't skimp on it and apply it too thinly or you may not get maximum protection. Massage it gently but thoroughly into your skin, paying special attention to any sensitive areas where you know from experience that you are inclined to burn – your feet, backs of knees, shoulder blades and even between your toes! As stated earlier, use a higher SPF number on these spots, and especially on your nose and face.

Check the instructions on the bottle, tube or can to see when and how often the sunscreen should be applied. To be at their most effective, some have to be rubbed into the skin long before you even venture out into the sun – back at the hotel, say, before you even hit the beach. On holiday, this is a good time and place to put on a sunscreen as your hands are clean and dry and you can be especially careful. Many products will not be absorbed so well into moist skin which is damp from seawater and perspiration.

Most sunscreens have to be reapplied regularly – at specific intervals of several hours. You cannot put it on in the morning and expect it to last right through the hottest day. Sea-bathing and normal perspiration will also help to wash it away, and therefore you should massage in some more after swimming or any exercise or strenuous activity such as a cycle ride, a jog, a game of tennis or even some brisk walking.

You are not safe from the sun even while you are swimming, and you should wear a special waterproof sunscreen for extra protection. Ultraviolet rays can penetrate the water and still give you a nasty burn two or three feet below the surface of the pool or sea.

Likewise, you should protect your skin on hazy overcast days which appear safe but when you are still potentially at risk. The ultraviolet rays can penetrate light cloud cover, and a light sea breeze may fool you into thinking that it is cooler and less hazardous than it really is so that you could end up with windburn as well as sunburn if you do not apply a sunscreen. Take care if you are walking outside, especially on the coast, as the wind can intensify the effect of the sun and you will end up burnt with dry, flaky skin. As an additional precaution, moisturise your skin well before setting out and afterwards when you take a bath or shower or just wash your face.

Building up a tan gradually

Too many women rush outside on the first hot day of summer or when they arrive at their holiday destination and spend as much time as possible sunning themselves. But even with the added protection of a sunscreen, this is bad for your skin. If you live in a climate where sunny days bring some welcome relief after the cold dull days of winter and a wet spring, this is obviously a great temptation but you must resist it. If you want to tan the easy painless way without ending up as a burnt offering to the great sun god, you should limit the amount of time you spend in the sun each day. Build it up gradually, exposing yourself for longer periods as your tan deepens and you are less inclined to burn. Here is a chart to guide you:

Tanning chart

	Fair skin	Normal skin	Dark skin
Day 1	15 minutes	20 minutes	30 minutes
Day 2	30 minutes	35 minutes	40 minutes
Day 3	45 minutes	50 minutes	55 minutes
Day 4	2 hours	2 hours	2¼ hours
Day 5	no limit	no limit	no limit
Day 6	no limit	no limit	no limit
Day 7	no limit	no limit	no limit

These times are rough approximations and not gospel, and obviously they may change according to the intensity of the sun, the extent of your tan and the SPF of the sunscreen you wear. Another way of calculating safe exposure time is to multiply the product's SPF by the number of minutes you could expose your skin to the UV-rays *without* burning. For example, if you could safely sunbathe unprotected for 20 minutes in the hottest part of the day and wear a sunscreen with an SPF rating of 8, you could go in the sun protected for two hours and forty minutes. Of course, you should reapply the sunscreen regularly for maximum protection.

Tanning and problem skins

The sun affects different skins in a variety of ways and although it can be damaging if it is not treated with respect and care, it can be positively beneficial to some women who suffer from problem skin, while it makes some skin disorders worse.

Acne: The sun helps unblock pores, dries particularly oily skin and sloughs off the top layers to clear the spots. However, although it brings this temporary relief in the case of many people, the acne may erupt again worse than ever when your tan starts to fade. Using a sunlamp to prolong your tan many help but obviously this could prove damaging to your skin in the future.

Freckles: these are caused by the uneven distribution of melanin in your skin and are most common in very fair-skinned people and redheads. Although they tend to get darker in the sun, the surrounding skin may be

inclined to burn, so you should take care to wear a high numbered sunscreen. And if you have been using some sort of bleach recently to lighten them (probably with ineffective results) you should stay *out* of the sun altogether or wear a sunblock. Sun-freckled skin can look very attractive, so wear your freckles with pride instead of trying to cover them up – just be sure to always apply your sunscreen.

Liver spots: these disfiguring brown marks which appear on hands and faces may be caused by a combination of factors – years of exposure to the sun and wind combined with your skin's natural ageing process. If you take a contraceptive pill or have a B-complex vitamin deficiency, you may be more likely to develop them. There is little you can do to remove them once they appear, although some dermatologists have treated them successfully with bleaching creams, whereas nutritionists recommend a healthy wholefoods diet which is particularly high in vitamin B. Wearing scent or a sun product containing oil of bergamot may also predispose you to liver spots. If you see any signs of their appearance on your skin, the best thing you can do is to get out of the sun straight away.

Cloaca: these are the dark pigmented blotches which may appear on your face and stomach if you sunbathe during pregnancy. These are caused by the increased hormonal activity in your body. Freckles and birthmarks may darken, too. Although many expectant mothers develop a lovely golden tan without encountering these problems they should always wear a good sunscreen. If cloaca do appear, use a protective sunblock to prevent them getting worse. On the other hand, most women tan more easily during pregnancy and there is a body of scientific evidence to suggest that regular exposure to sunlight helps prevent stretch marks.

Perfume: it is always best not to wear any scent when you go out in the sun. Some of the ingredients contained in perfumes and toilet water may cause an unpleasant burn if they come into contact with strong ultraviolet rays. As they can also attract unwelcome visitors like mosquitoes and flies, perfumes are best saved for the evening *after* sunset.

Dermatitis: the sun usually aggravates this distressing condition, so if your skin is affected, you should take care to protect yourself adequately and preferably to stay out of the sun altogether.

Sunburn

Of course, sometimes, despite all your precautions, you may underestimate the intensity of the sun and your ability to withstand it, and the result is a bad case of sunburn. Some women seem to think that they have to endure the discomfort of burning first in order to tan later, but this is not true. Sunburn will not tan you any faster and it is not the painful price you have to pay for ending up with beautiful bronzed skin. In fact, it has the opposite effect and actually slows down the tanning process as it dehydrates your skin in such a way that the top layers of skin cells slough off making you peel and blister, opposing and prolonging the tanning process.

Sunburn actually occurs when the epidermal cells are bombarded by burning UV-B rays, causing the enzyme capsules within to burst, destroying the cells and releasing an irritating substance into the surrounding tissue. The other effect of these powerful rays is to dilate the tiny blood vessels which lie just below the skin's surface. As more blood is pumped through them, their walls break down and leak serum and blood toxins, leading in turn to external redness, then swelling, and possibly blisters and localised pain.

When it comes to sunburn, prevention is better than cure, so how do you know that you are in danger of burning? What are the warning signs that you should look out for? This may all seem pretty obvious to you, but many women lie happily on the beach all day in a cooling sea breeze or under a hazy sky quite oblivious of the sunburn they are cultivating. Knowing your skin and how well it can tolerate the sun is a good starting point, and the wisdom of experience is always a help. Try to evaluate the sun's intensity, whether it is hiding behind the breeze or some thin cloud cover, and take into account your latitude in relation to the Equator and also the time of day.

Now examine your skin. Does it look slightly red or feel sore and tender to a light touch? If it displays either of these tell-tale signs, get out of the sun immediately before you damage it further. If you are wearing a sunscreen and these symptoms still appear, it may be due to one of two reasons. Either you are wearing too low an SPF number to protect your skin adequately, or you are exposing your skin for too long and should limit your sunbathing to early in the morning and late in the afternoon when the sun is less intense.

If you burn, your skin will get very dehydrated and you should try to replace some of the lost moisture immediately. Splash some cold water onto the affected area to take the burn out of your skin. Or, if the burn is more extensive, have a cool bath and add a few drops of soothing oil. Relax in it for about 10 minutes or so – not too long. Do not rub yourself vigorously dry with a towel – obviously this would be very painful and may aggravate your burns. Gently pat yourself dry with a *soft* towel and then massage in a soothing, moisturising after-sun lotion or a special medicated sunburn treatment. The medicated aerosol sprays that you can buy in most chemists and drugstores offer some instant relief. Otherwise, you can make up a paste of equal parts of bicarbonate of soda (baking soda) and cold water and apply it to any burnt areas of skin with a soft cloth or some cotton wool. Another way of relieving sunburn is to keep applying cold wet compresses at regular intervals. Many people swear by an aloe-based lotion or calamine, but although calamine lotion is certainly soothing it is also very drying which is the last thing your skin needs. If you do not have any specially formulated sunburn products handy, then use some petroleum jelly, baby lotion, aloe cream or a good moisturising lotion – they are all more hydrating than calamine and good second-best options.

Diet can also help in speeding up your skin's recovery and you should try to take multi-vitamin tablets and a zinc supplement every day in addition to eating whole-foods and at least one salad. Keep on moisturising – your skin cannot get enough water at a time like this – and for goodness sake, stay out of the sun. If you go out walking, cover up any sunburnt areas and protect yourself with a sunblock for good measure. You may experience problems sleeping at night. Every time you turn in your sleep you will awaken feeling sore and burning. Sleeping in the nude and powdering the sheets generously with talcum powder may help relieve any discomfort and make the bedclothes feel softer and more comfortable against your skin.

After-sun care

The way you look after your skin after a day out in the sun is equally important as the sunscreen you wear to protect it against burning. Even if you do not burn, you still need to moisturise your skin after sunning yourself. Throughout the summer, you should apply a good moisturiser every day to your face and body to keep the skin smooth, supple and moist. This really is a good habit to adopt as regular moisturising before, during and after sunbathing not only helps keep in your skin's own supply but also puts back some of the lost moisture.

An important aspect of after-sun care is bathing. Run a warm or tepid bath and make sure that the water is not too hot or it will help open up the pores in your skin and cause you to perspire and lose much-needed moisture through evaporation. Add a few drops of fragrant bath gel or aromatic oil to help seal in your skin's moisture — add it while the bath is filling up with water to create plenty of relaxing bubbles. Many soaps are very drying so choose one that contains a high percentage of oil.

Gently dry yourself and moisturise immediately before contact with the air causes your skin to start dehydrating. A moisturiser will form an effective barrier between your skin and the air, making it soft and supple and preventing dryness.

The sun can be very tiring, especially if you are enjoying a holiday on the coast. The combination of intense heat and bracing sea air may be quite a shock to your system initially so try to relax in the evenings after a day on the beach and take it easy.

Prolonging your tan

A holiday tan, however deep a shade of gold or bronze, will soon fade away if you do not take measures to protect and keep it. Even when the autumn comes, you need to continue moisturising every day, especially after bathing, to stop your skin drying out and flaking. Your skin is continually renewing itself from below as new cells come to the surface and die. Thus it is forever shedding its outer layers, and as a tan is barely skin deep it will not last forever. Using less soap in the bath or shower, patting dry very gently to prevent rubbing away any flaky skin, and regular moisturising will all help you stay tanned.

The best way to keep your tanned look throughout the coming winter months, of course, is to top it up regularly with a course of sun-bed treatments. But you should treat these artificial tanning sunlamps with respect – although many of the new models will not burn you, they can still age your skin. Used regularly over a long period, your skin may gradually lose its youthful bloom and elasticity, so it really is better to enjoy your tan in the summer only and not to attempt to keep it throughout the year by artificial means. Ultra-violet rays, whether they come from the sun or out of a lamp, are still damaging.

Protecting your lips

Because your lips do not contain any protective melanin granules or oil glands, unlike your skin, they need extra-protection in the sun. Intense sunshine causes them to dehydrate, crack, burn and blister. You may even develop a nasty lipsore which could take several days at least to clear up. However, there is no need to suffer as you can protect them with a special lipscreen with its own built-in sunblock. These come in handy swivel cases and will block out all ultraviolet rays. They should be applied frequently before and during sunbathing sessions.

If you are caught short without a lipscreen, you can make do with an ordinary glossy lipstick, which will seal in moisture and afford some measure of protection. Many good-quality lipsticks contain PABA nowadays and are thus quite effective at filtering out harmful rays. If you do not mind looking bizarre, zinc oxide paste will form a white impenetrable barrier. Remember that strong winds can chap or burn your lips too, so always protect them when out walking.

Shade your eyes with dark lenses

Good-quality sunglasses are a *must* to protect your eyes from bright sunshine and glare which can not only make you squint and cause fine lines around your eyes, but may also lead to eye strain, giddiness and headaches. They are especially important when you are sitting, walking or lying in the sun, or driving. When choosing

a pair of sunglasses, you need to look for effective lenses in fashionable frames which will flatter your face. And although there is a wide range of attractive products on the market, not all of them are dark enough to be really effective and fulfill their purpose.

The best sunglasses eliminate at least 70 per cent of ultraviolet light. You can test them out quite simply by trying on a pair and looking at your reflection in a mirror. If you can still see your eyes through the lenses they are not dark enough. This is the case with many pretty pinks, blues, oranges and yellows which allow too much light to penetrate them. Dark colours are the most effective and you should look for browns, greys and greens. These natural colours absorb light well and transmit the colour spectrum with minimum distortion.

You should also test the lenses for distortion and quality. Do this by holding the glasses at arm's length.

It is worth investing in a pair of attractive sun-glasses with fashionable frames to protect your eyes from the sun and cut out glare. Make sure that they do the job effectively and feel comfortable.

Now focus on a long, thin vertical object such as a pencil. Move the glasses slowly up and down and the image should remain the same. If it appears to move, try on another pair and repeat the test.

A good pair of sunglasses should feel comfortable to wear, so unobtrusive in fact that you should not really be aware that you have got them on. Test them out for comfort as well as quality. Do they sit comfortably on your nose, without feeling too heavy or pressing too hard? Do they stay on or slide off too easily? Are they a good fit against the sides of your head and do they rub against the skin behind your ears? Take all these factors into consideration.

Polarised and photochromatic lenses are very popular and you should make sure that you understand the distinction between the two:

Polarised lenses: these are banded in seven layers so as to totally eliminate any glare or, indeed, reflected glare. They also have the advantage of being shatterproof and shock-resistant — worth considering if you have an unfortunate habit of dropping your glasses, sitting on them or popping them into your handbag and forgetting where you put them.

Photochromatic lenses: these are responsive to light in such a way that they darken accordingly in bright sunshine and grow lighter in subdued light. Although this may seem advantageous, they do take time to change colour and thus they may not be very effective in dazzling sunlight for several minutes. This makes them unsuitable for driving, especially as a car windscreen absorbs ultraviolet rays anyway so that the lenses may not darken to the right extent. Also, most lenses of this type tend to transmit about 45 per cent of sunlight so although they are often very attractive they may not prove a good buy.

Mirror-coated lenses: these reflect heat as well as light and thus they are cool to wear, even on the hottest days. They effectively eliminate glare, cutting out about 90 per cent of light. However, other people may find them rather alarming when they talk to you and see only their own mirror image reflected in the lenses rather than your eyes!

Another factor to take into consideration is whether the sunglasses have shatterproof safety glass or plastic lenses. Although the latter are lighter than glass, they do scratch easily and you need to take special care to keep them scratch-free. Always replace them in their case or a soft cloth bag after use – don't throw them into your pocket or the depths of a handbag along with keys, coins and other sharp objects which could damage the lenses irreparably. Glass lenses tend to be more scratch-resistant and are usually more effective at blocking out glare and ultraviolet light.

To summarise, look for a pair of sunglasses that will:

1 Protect your eyes.
2 Are comfortable to wear.
3 Are easy to keep in good condition.
4 Will not break easily.
5 Will flatter your face and enhance your beauty.
6 Will match your wardrobe and accessories such as bags, belts and shoes.

After-sun eye care

After a day in the sun, your eyes may feel tired, tight and dry. You can revive them before a night out on the town with soothing pads soaked in toner or skin freshener. Lie down and relax and place a pad over each eye. Alternatively, you can use ordinary squeezed out cold tea bags or slices of cucumber but this is a bit messy. Rest for 10 to 15 minutes, then wash your face and freshen up with some skin toner before reapplying your eye make-up for the evening.

Holiday packing list

Last of all, if you are planning a holiday in the sun, make sure that you include all the beauty items you will need when you pack your suitcase. It is surprisingly easy to forget things and leave them behind, and they may be impossible to buy when you arrive at your holiday resort and discover the loss. Forgetting your favourite lipstick or special blue mascara, for instance, will not start your holiday off on the right footing, especially if you cannot even find a good substitute. To be on the safe side, you can use this handy checklist and tick off the items as you go along.

Make-up: zip-up waterpoof, leakproof bag containing foundation, translucent powder, concealer, blushers, tinted moisturiser, highlighters and face-shapers for evenings, eye liner or crayon pencils, eye shadows and glosses, mascara, lipstick and lipgloss, brushes, sponges, applicators and tissues, face mask pack.

Sponge bag: cleanser or complexion soap, toner, moisturiser, eye make-up remover pads or lotion, body lotion, bath oil, talcum powder, massage glove or mit, toothbrush and toothpaste, dental floss, flannel or sponge, emery boards, nail varnish and cuticle remover, antiperspirant, razor, nail scissors, hand cream, shower cap, hair removal cream.

Haircare: shampoo, conditioner, setting gel, mousse or lotion, finishing rinse, hair-in-the-sun protective lotion or cream, clips, rubber hands, styling brush and comb, rollers, hair dryer (dual voltage with special adaptor), heated styling brush with gas cylinder attachment, ornate combs.

Suncare: sunscreen, sunblock, zinc oxide, special lipscreen, sunglasses, after-sun soothing creams and lotions, medicated treatment for burns, petroleum jelly, bicarbonate of soda.

General: pain-killers, travel sickness pills, antacid or indigestion tablets, antiseptic cream, plasters.

Remember when packing that all liquids and creams should be in leakproof, unbreakable jars or bottles, preferably plastic ones, with the tops screwed on securely so that nothing can escape in transit and ruin your clothes. As an extra precaution, seal the containers in plastic or polythene bags. Do not pack hair spray, antiperspirant spray, perfume atomisers or any other pressured containers in your case.

BEAUTY ON THE BEACH AND SUNDOWN GLAMOUR

The growing sophistication of life in holiday resorts means that you need to look good not only when you are sipping your midday drink at the poolside bar or in the evening disco, but also when you are swimming or sunbathing on the beach. You will want make-up that is versatile but natural-looking and quick and easy to adapt from a daytime look to evening glamour.

Swimming and sunbathing
Wear the minimum of make-up on the beach, in the sea or pool, or wherever you expect to get lots of sun. Your aim is to acquire a suntan – and, of course, you must always apply a sunscreen to suit your skin type and give you adequate protection *before* you go out in the sun. Sun products come in the form of oils, gels, lotions, creams and milks, and some are lightly tinted to enhance your tan. Creams and lotions with built-in moisturisers are best for dry skins while light gels and non-oily lotions suit women with oily skin.

The problem with most make-up on the beach is that certain products such as blushers and highlighters can partially block tanning rays in such a way as to leave you with an odd and incomplete tan. Moreover, unless your make-up is truly waterproof, it will smudge or run in the heat of the sun and when you swim. It must be said, though, that waterproof mascara is an invaluable asset on the beach – it enables you to emerge from the water still looking glamorous. An alternative, if you want to go to the trouble, is to have your eyelashes dyed before you go on holiday. The dye looks completely natural, is waterproof and lasts about six weeks. Apart from mascara, wear lipstick on the beach. It is an excellent sunblock for lips which you don't want to burn. Choose a glossy, natural colour, perhaps a copper or russet tone which goes naturally with a tan, or even a pale silvery pink. Keep the rest of your make-up for wearing indoors or in the shade and vary your look for the evening.

Your summer face
Once out of direct sunlight you will probably bathe and cleanse your face. Many women prefer to use soap and water in summer rather than cleansing creams. Choose a mild pH-balanced soap especially if your skin is dry. If you prefer to use a cream, one way of getting rid of the slightly cloying effect they can have in summer, is to use a refreshing skin toner on your face after cleansing. It is both cooling and invigorating. Moisturise your face immediately after cleansing. You may think you don't need to do this in hot sticky weather when the skin feels moist, but remember that you have been exposed to the notoriously drying effects of the sun. Although the damage is not apparent now, you really must use a moisturiser to protect you from the drying effects of the sun and help preserve soothing moisture on the skin's surface.

Daytime make-up
Never use a heavy foundation in summer. In fact, once you have acquired a tan, you may not need a foundation at all. Tans tend to clear up the complexion and get rid of minor blemishes, and they give skin a glowing, even tone which can look most attractive. However, a light foundation does help if your tan or skin tone is not quite even. Make sure it matches the colour of your tanned face or is just a shade darker. Anything too dark can look rather theatrical. If you have simply acquired a light tan, try using a transparent bronze-tinted gel as an alternative to foundation. Although these can look alarmingly brown in the tube, they are transparent on the face and give a clear, golden tone to the skin. Some are waterproof and can be used when you are swimming. When you choose a gel, do check its sun protection factor number. You still need protection if you are walking outdoors or swimming, and not only when sunning yourself on the beach. There is no need to use a powder on top of a gel, although if there is too much shine on the tip of your nose or on your forehead, dab with a little translucent powder.

To complement your glowing face and enhance your tan, you may wish to switch to glossy blushers and eyeshadows. Try a copper or bronzed-toned blusher on the cheeks, or a natural summer tint with a hint of rose if this suits your skin tone. For indoors, you can use a little highlighter on the top of the cheeks and under the brows if you wish, but strong sunlight picks out its own highlights so dispense with this out of doors.

Sunglasses are a must on the beach. They protect your eyes and help you not to squint so much. This is important since every time you screw up your face you

are inviting new wrinkles. These show up particularly around the outer corners of the eyes. However, if you wear glasses all the time you are likely to end up with panda patches around the eyes. These can be covered with foundation or gel but it is more sensible to leave the glasses off from time to time so that your tan will be more even and natural.

For eye make-up, use eye glosses, pearlised gels or powders. Cream shadow may crease into any fine lines during hot weather. Slightly pearlised shadows give a soft, light-reflecting colour to the lids which is ideal for a natural, summer look. However, shiny colours do tend to show up wrinkles so avoid these if your skin is older and use soft-textured eye crayons instead which are easy to blend in and are long-lasting. Go for soft eye colours which tone with your blusher. Harsh, strong colours are likely to detract from your natural look so try colours like cinnamon, ginger, brick or bronze which are more suitable with a healthy-looking tan.

Eyeliner isn't strictly necessary on a summer face but if you decide to use it, try a soft crayon in a light brown or copper shade. Avoid water-based paint-on eyeliners as they will run or smudge in the heat and above all, avoid harsh colours, especially black, for a natural summer look. Finish off your eye make-up by curling your lashes (especially effective for a wide-eyed, open look) and then apply two coats of waterproof mascara, separating the lashes with a brush so they do not look heavy or spiky. As a final touch, you may even wish to apply a little sheen to your eyebrows with some vaseline or petroleum jelly.

Do wear lipstick all the time in summer as a protection for the lips against sunlight and also dehydration. Choose glossy-looking lipsticks in the clear transparent colours which, for the most natural look, tone with your blusher and eye colour. Bronze and russet or brick colours look good with a tan but bright fuchsias, orange tones and scarlet are also very flattering and complement your sunny holiday mood. They are well suited to the bright, dazzling sunlight. Use tinted lip gloss, or coat your chosen shade with transparent lip gloss. Lip colour tends to disappear quickly in the heat so reapply regularly not merely for cosmetic purposes but for protection as well.

Evening make-up

Artificial light tends to drain colour from the face so for summer evenings you need to apply your colour with a slightly heavier hand. Work with your tan, not against it. Don't be tempted to wear pearly pinks and mauves on your cheeks, and vivid blues and greens on your eyes as you would for winter evenings. Your skin tone is quite different at this time of the year, even with a light tan, and it is best to stick with your natural look – intensified to look a little more dramatic for informal summer evenings.

Use the same tones on your face as for daytime but apply the colour in more depth. Evenings provide the occasion to use highlighters. A little gold brushed across the top of the cheekbones can really lift the face. Apply it as well on the browbones for a starry, wide-eyed look and try it on the hairline and temples and, for a special effect, along the collarbones and tops of the shoulders. Keep to coppery, brownish shades in shiny or pearlised finishes and again apply with more intensity. Use a soft, brown pencil to define the eyes, smudging the outline to achieve a natural look.

In the evenings, wear a more dramatic shade of lip colour if you wish. Soft and even bright reds, corals and burgundies can look wonderful if they match your skin tone and can add that exotic touch for a special summer occasion. Use plenty of lip gloss on top of your colour. Some women may find the pale, pearlised pinks you might wear on a winter evening are flattering but they sometimes look odd on a bronzed skin.

Holiday glamour

If you go away on holiday, you will want to look really glamorous in the evenings if you are dining out or going dancing. This is one time when you can really sparkle and shine and try out some new make-up and beauty techniques that you might not use at home. Your skin will probably be very tanned, and pearly and iridescent eye colours, frosted lipsticks and glosses will all look good. Before you leave for your holidays, invest in some new cosmetics in some exotic shades and colours to try out in the evenings. You will feel a million dollars, relaxed and tanned after a day on the beach.

But don't go for harsh colours which are too dark and over-dramatic – make your make-up match your mood and the occasion. The 'look' you might choose for a quiet candlelit dinner for two may be quite different from what you might wear to a disco, for example, where you can carry off bright, glittering colours which are very striking. As a general rule, you need to emphasise your eyes and lips with shiny colours that add some evening sparkle.

After a day in the sun, you will probably want to cleanse, tone and moisturise your skin thoroughly before applying fresh make-up. Make the most of your tan and don't cover it up. Use a bronze tinted light foundation or moisturiser or some shiny gel or gloss – just enough to even out your skin tone and enhance your natural colour. Now apply some shiny blusher, perhaps in an earthy brown or copper shade which will blend into your tan. Concentrate on your eyes, aiming to make them the focal point of your face. Pearlised browns, golds, bronzes, coppers and silvers all look good. Use eye liner or smoky eye pencils to outline

them, and lots of mascara. If you have tinted lashes you may not need it. You can have your lashes dyed in a beauty salon or do it yourself at home. Black, brown and blue are the usual colours, and they do help avoid streaked and smudged eye make-up.

Sports make-up

If you lead a very active outdoor life in the summer months and want to look beautiful while you exercise, you will need some form of sports make-up. An active lifestyle brings with it a new set of beauty needs as your skin will need extra protection, and make-up must be light and colourfast.

A light foundation or tinted moisturiser with built-in sunscreen has several functions on a practical level – it protects your skin against sunburn and windburn and the drying effects of wind and sun. It also acts as a barrier against pollution and prevents dry skin and chapping. These are all very ageing to the skin, and if you want it to stay looking youthful, fresh and glowing, you should always wear some form of protective make-up when you exercise, especially outdoors.

Before and after every run, work-out or other form of exercises, you should moisturise your skin. If it is sunny, cover all the exposed areas of your body with a sunscreen. If you like to exercise bare-legged and your legs are rather white and puny-looking after the winter cover-up, you can always fake a tan with self-tanning lotions and preparations. They are easy to apply and look very natural indeed, and will give you the confidence of lovely brown legs.

Thick make-up is never a good idea when you are exercising – it will streak or get cakey, especially when you start to perspire. Choose a light natural-looking foundation which is near to your skin tone and smooth gently over your face and neck. Or, if you like an even lighter more transparent effect, a tinted moisturiser is very effective. Remember that regular exercise may affect the appearance and condition of your skin. it will be pink and glowing immediately afterwards and its general circulation will improve. Because it will become more active, you must take special care with your daily skincare routine, especially when you bathe or shower after a work-out or run. Cleanse really deeply and thoroughly to get rid of dirt, perspiration and pollution; then tone and moisturise before reapplying your usual make-up.

Don't forget your lips, hair and eyes when you exercise. A glossy lipstick will help keep lips moist and protect them from sun and wind, or you can use a sunblock on hot days.Carry it in your pocket if you are out running or playing tennis and reapply regularly. When you exercise hard, your hair may get dry or even greasy if you tend to get very hot. You may find that you are washing it more often than usual. If so, use a mild shampoo and be rigorous about regular conditioning treatments. Even if you are not swimming, waterproof mascara is a good idea as it will not streak if you get very hot and sticky.

It is good for your general morale and self-confidence to look good while you exercise and may spur you on to even better times and performances, especially if you are competitive. Unfortunately, active, sporty women tend to be perceived as unattractive and unglamorous in the public mind. But thousands of women are now disproving this myth and showing that fit and strong are beautiful and that they can look glamorous even when they return from a long run or cycle ride.

Summer and perfume

Perfume is a beauty aid which has been used for thousands of years and every woman has a few favourite scents that she wears all or most of the time. Give some thought to the perfume you wear in summer. Climate can change the fragrance of a perfume; in a warm, humid summer, perfume evaporates more quickly but it also tends to be heavier and sweeter. Oriental fragrances and many floral scents such as violet and jasmine can simply be overpowering in a warm summer or in a sun resort, although they can be spectacular in winter.

Choose a perfume that is fresh, light and cooling and that suits your skin and your holiday mood. Remember that perfumes react differently on individual skins so what smells wonderful on your best friend may not suit you. Don't rely on the smell in the bottle but always test on your skin and leave for an hour or so. In general, light floral or mossy, herbal scents are ideal for summer. Beware, however, of citrus-scented fragrances when you are outside in the sun even though sharp, lemony perfumes may seem especially appropriate at this time of the year. Oil of bergamot is a common ingredient in these and some other perfumes – and it is potentially dangerous. At worst, natural bergamot oil can cause dark, blotchy patches on the skin when it is exposed to the sun which can only be removed by skin peeling. In rare cases, such patches can even lead to skin cancer. It is also very sensitive to the skin and if used while you are sunbathing can cause you to burn quite quickly. Since most perfumes rarely include a list of ingredients on their container, it is wise to avoid wearing *all* perfumes when sunbathing. If you must wear perfume on the beach, scent a cotton wool ball and hide it in your bathing costume, away from the sun's rays. Alternatively scent the brim of your hat or beach towel for a more subtle aroma.

Many floral perfumes also attract bees and wasps. This is because you smell like the pungent flowers they feed on, so again it is wise to keep your perfumes for indoors or evenings to avoid insect bites.

PROTECT YOUR HAIR FROM THE SUMMER SUN

The beginning of summer before the onset of holidays is the time to think about your hair condition and style in the light of the holidays you have planned or are planning. Most people take a vacation in the sun and your hair, like your skin, needs particular care and attention when it is exposed to heat and sun. For this reason, it needs to be in peak condition. Deep-condition the hair if it is damaged and needs such a treatment and deal with any hair problems before you depart for your sunshine holiday.

Dandruff

Dandruff is the most common of all hair problems and there are few women who have not suffered from it from time to time. It is an unhealthy condition which can be either mild or more persistent. Essentially dandruff is dead tissue from the scalp and it shows up as white flakes near the root of the hair. It can affect both dry and oily scalps. If you have dandruff, do not use a brush or comb vigorously and never scratch the scalp however irritable it may be. These can leave tender, exposed areas on the head which can become sore and even infected.

There is no single cause of dandruff, but your diet certainly affects it. Too much sugar, starch and fat encourage it. If you have not reduced your intake of these, you really should, not merely for your hair's sake but in order to have a trimmer and healthier body for your summer holiday. Physical and emotional stress and strain are also contributory factors and it has been suggested that hormones and heredity play some part in determining whenever you are likely to suffer from dandruff.

There is no quick way to cure dandruff but it is essential to keep the scalp clean. Wash the hair frequently with a mild shampoo. Do not use a medicated shampoo unless you really have to – that is, if the scalp is infected. Some of the so-called dandruff shampoos are too harsh to be used regularly on your hair. Climate also seems to affect dandruff and it is more common among people who live in colder regions. Once you are in the sun – and take the usual precautions about summer hair care – the condition may clear up.

Damaged hair

Straightening or bleaching your hair are among the worst things you can do to it. Straightening is far more damaging than perming since it can stretch the hair, destroying its elasticity. This, combined with the use of heated rollers and tongs, can lead to brittle, dry and broken hair. Strong bleaching weakens the hair and scalp and can give it an unhealthy straw-like quality. If you must straighten or bleach your hair, have conditioning treatments regularly. It is particularly important to get your hair in as good a condition as possible at the beginning of summer. Once you are outside in the sun, the hair is subjected to potentially even more damaging conditions unless you take special precautions to protect it.

Holiday hair care

During summer and particularly when you are holidaying in a sun resort, your hair is exposed to relatively unfamiliar environmental conditions. Sun, heat and water are generally what the holidaymaker seeks and, in small doses, these are good for your morale, your health and your hair.

One way to give the hair a natural sunny look is to have it streaked before you go on holiday. This must be done by your hairdresser and ask his or her advice about what will suit you. Fortunately, streaking does not need frequent touching up and if it is done subtly and well, the colour of your streaks should not be greatly affected by the sun. If you decide to treat your hair this way, do look after it on holiday. Ty to keep the hair covered with a pretty scarf in the sun or a large straw sunhat, and remember to condition it often, otherwise it can become dull and dry. If your hair is quite fair anyway, it will probably go even more blonde and you may get an attractive sunstreaked effect.

Sun and heat These dry out the hair and can cause split ends. While the sun can lighten fairish hair in a very attractive way, it can have disastrous effects on tinted or bleached hair by altering the colour. Do protect your hair with a hat and, as you will probably be washing your hair frequently, use a mild shampoo and a cream rinse conditioner if your hair is naturally dry. When you are outside in the sun relaxing on the beach, you should make sure that you protect your hair adequately, either with one of the special hair-in-the-sun preparations that you can buy in most good

You can tie or clip long hair back off your face in summer for an attractive look and to stay cool.

A short, fashionable hair-cut is ideal for hot climates: cool to wear and easy to wash and set.

chemists, or you can just smear some sunscreen lotion over your hair. After swimming and at the end of the day, rinse your hair out well with fresh water to remove any saltiness, sand or traces of chlorine if you have been in the pool. Then wash with a mild shampoo and condition.

Water Salt and chlorinated water dry and bleach the hair. Combined with exposure to sun, the hair can become brittle very quickly. Always rinse the hair in fresh water after swimming in the sea or a chlorinated pool, even if you don't shampoo it. Again use a cream rinse after shampooing if your hair tends to be dry. Remember too that water (humidity) in the atmosphere affects the hair. Curly hair becomes curlier, straight hair straighter, and set hair loses its shape very quickly. This is one of the reasons why it is impractical to have anything other than a very easy-to-manage, natural style for your summer holiday.

Your hair is responsive to its environment and if the atmosphere is very humid in hot, muggy weather, it will suck moisture into the hair shafts. This plumping up of the shafts will make your hair look thicker and fuller – a bonus for women with very fine, thin hair. However, if your hair is naturally curly or wavy, it will look even more curly – you have probably noticed this when you have been walking in light rain or drizzle. You need to protect your hair from water if it is permed and artificially waved, as it may cause the curl to fall out and the hair will look straight and dull. Humidity creates problems in good hair management: flyaway or wavy hair may get completely uncontrollable and will curl in the wrong direction and fail to hold its style. There is little you can do about this unless you put your hair up under a scarf or hat to protect it. If you suffer from this syndrome, at least you have the consolation of knowing that all this extra moisture is doing your hair good and making it more supple and glossy.

Swimming: whether you are swimming in the sea, a freshwater lake or the chlorinated water of a swimming pool, your hair will be under attack as these all have a drying effect and actually dehydrate the hair. This may seem surprising after learning that atmospheric moisture is actually beneficial for your hair, but there is a very good reason for this. After swimming, your hair dries by a process of evaporation and this tends to remove natural moisture which was in the hair before you went for a dip. Drying your hair naturally in the sun or using a hand-held dryer will exaggerate this effect and make it dryer still.

Chlorine is often added to swimming pools and this chemical is especially dehydrating to hair, made worse if you are bathing in an outdoor pool in the sunshine. To protect your hair, you should wear a snug-fitting swimming cap – there are some quite fashionable styles to choose from. Some women even tuck their hair up under a straw hat with a ribbon under the chin and swim in this! The situation is exacerbated if you are blonde, as frequent swimming in chlorinated water may eventually lead to your hair looking slightly green! Many pools are now filtrated in such a way that chlorine is not necessary – if you swim in this type, you need have no worries.

Like chlorine, sea-water is also drying, and the salt will leave your hair feeling unpleasantly sticky and tasting salty. After swimming, always rinse your hair out with some fresh water, either under a beach shower, or take a bottle of water with you for this purpose and just tip the contents over your head and rub vigorously until all the salt has worked out and the hair feels clean.

Protect your hair in the sun — summary

The sun can damage and dry out hair, bleaching and giving it a straw-like quality. If you don't want to cover it up all the time, you will have to take special measures to protect it. In addition to regular conscientious conditioning treatments you should take note of the following tips and advice. Use this handy checklist for reference:

1 Wash with a mild shampoo which will not dry the hair too much. There is nothing wrong with frequent washing if your hair can take it. If you are on holiday or live in a very hot climate you may need to wash it every day to keep it in top condition and feeling good. Forget what you have been told about too-frequent washing being bad for hair. You are the best judge of what is right for your hair.

2 Use a hair conditioner to seal in the hair's natural moisture against the drying effects of sea, sun and wind. In addition to your normal creme rinse, you should use a deep-action conditioner at least once a month throughout the summer. You can apply it at home – the oil and henna wax treatments are especially good for restoring shine.

3 Avoid using electric blow-dryers if possible – they are drying and damaging to hair and a major cause of brittle, split ends. They literally can burn away the cuticle of the hair and cause the shaft's inner layers to unravel. Allow your hair to dry naturally, but in the house and not outside in the sun which can also be drying and bleaching.

4 Cover your hair up in sea breezes or its natural moisture will be encouraged to evaporate and it will feel very dry – likewise, in the hot sun and when swimming. Wind a colourful scarf around your head, wear a sunhat or swimcap. If you really don't like covering your hair, then smear it with plenty of sun-screen lotion, or buy and apply one of the special hair-in-the-sun preparations.

5 The sun may lighten or streak your hair especially if you are naturally fair or blonde. If your hair is chemically tinted or coloured or you have a permanent wave, you should take extra care in strong sunlight as it may exacerbate the drying effect and even cause odd things to happen to coloured hair!

6 Opt for a short hair cut which is easy to care for, quick to dry, requires no special setting and will keep you cool in summer. There are many fashionable styles that you can choose from – one of them is bound to suit your face and 'look'. If you have long hair, pin it up with combs or clips – never rubber bands which can damage the hair. It should stay neat and tidy all day and look glamorous, too. Or tie it back in a simple pony tail or plaits.

7 If you have been swimming and your hair is still wet, towel-dry it gently and comb it out with a wide-toothed comb. Never pull or force the comb through tangles – it will damage your hair. Work on one section at a time, gently separating the strands of hair. Nor should you use a nylon or natural bristle brush when your hair is wet. You can dislodge hairs and split the ends. The best method of all is to finger-dry it just by rubbing out any excess moisture and then running your fingers through your hair to quick-set it. Your hair will fall in the right direction and you will be surprised how nice it looks for so little effort.

8 At the end of the summer after a holiday in the sun, your hair will be more porous than usual. If you are considering colouring or streaking it, do a test first on a few strands to see how the colour takes. You may find that the chemical dyes penetrate too efficiently and the effect is brighter than you anticipated. Warn your hairdresser about this.

Summer styles

No sensible woman on holiday wants to spend a lot of time setting and styling her hair. Generally, it is a waste of time. In humid conditions, your style will not hold its shape and, of course, if you swim a lot, your wet hair will constantly need attention.

Choose a short style which will dry quickly and naturally. It should need no more effort than shaping and fluffing with your fingers. Leave your hair dryer behind and let the sun's warmth dry your hair – it is much less damaging. If you must take rollers and curling tongs, only use them to style your hair in the evenings when you are going out. Even then, stick to simple styles. Elaborate coiffures are inappropriate for informal summer evenings.

Long hair is just as easy to manage. Allow it to dry

naturally (after rinsing out any chlorine or salt water) before you put it up in a knot for coolness or tie it back in a casual pony tail (never use elastic bands on the hair – they tear and break it). Plaits can also look marvellous with simple, unfussy beachwear and a lightly tanned skin. You can use pretty tortoise shell or plastic combs in different colours to keep your hair back off your face.

If you decide to braid your hair it looks very effective if plaited while it is still wet straight after a shower. Just gather all the hair into one plait, starting high up on the head and secure with beads or ribbon for a pretty finish. Your hair will then dry naturally without any bother, and when you brush it out later it will look crinkly and attractive as it cascades onto your shoulders.

Another style that you can try out on wet hair, either in the evening or on the beach after a dip in the pool, is to tie your hair back into a loose chignon. Twist each side of hair into a coil shape after combing back smoothly from the forehead. Pin the coils at the back and then roll any loose hair at the back around the coil and pin to secure.

If you get bored with a straightforward pony tail secured centrally at the back of the head, why not ring the changes and tie it at the side instead so that the hair hangs forward over one side? This is more modern and glamorous, especially for beachwear, and you can use brightly coloured beads threaded onto elastic to make it prettier, or fix a bright flower or bow in your hair to cover the band. You could even try two pony tails, one on each side of the head. It looks trendy and keeps you cool when the sun is beating down relentlessly on your shoulders.

Heavy thick hair can be gathered up loosely at the crown of the head and twisted into a casual-looking bun and pinned in place. A few loose strands hanging down look attractive and prevent this style from becoming too severe. Again, you can soften the effect with a ribbon or a real or imitation flower (don't forget to take it out when you go swimming, though).

FOCUS ON YOUR LEGS, HANDS AND FEET

During the summer you tend to uncover your body more, and therefore every curve, hair and exposed area of skin must be able to stand up to close scrutiny. The things that you could neglect and get away with during the colder spring and winter months cannot be tolerated now. The first way to get summer-ready is to remove all unwanted hair – nothing looks so ugly as hairy bare legs and underarms. You should also pay special attention to your hands and feet now that they are more on show, especially if you wear sleeveless dresses and open sandals. A regular manicure and pedicure will keep them looking good. And moisturising is more important than ever before in order to keep your skin silky smooth and soft.

To stay slim and shapely, you should continue with your regular exercise routine, especially if you are planning a beach holiday and want to look good in a swimsuit. Opportunities for exercise are all around you and it is a splendid time for getting out into the fresh air and getting fit.

Look after your legs

Legs are more evident in the summer, especially if you wear shorter skirts, shorts, swimsuits or leave off stockings and bare them to the sun. Yet most of us forget about our legs for much of the year and overlook them completely. Now is the time to get them into shape and make the skin soft and beautiful. You should make leg grooming part of your regular beauty routine.

Before you go any further, inspect your legs and cast a critical eye over them. Are they hairy, or stubbly from a rushed shaving session? Are there dry, flaky patches of skin on your shins? Do your knees look rough and red? Are your thighs heavy and puckered with the tell-tale signs of cellulite? Now read on and discover how you can make your legs look good.

Keeping them smooth

Beautiful legs are silky so you should attack any unsightly rough skin, especially on your knees. Next time you take a bath or shower, massage your knees with a friction mit or massage glove. Work up a good soapy lather as you set about removing any dead, dry skin. Adding a few drops of scented bath oil to the water will help keep skin soft and supple as well as smelling deliciously fragrant. Rub dry and moisturise well.

Regular exfoliation throughout the summer will keep your bare legs looking great. You can also use a specially formulated skin sloughing product which contains tiny rough grains. Rub briskly, wash off and dry. Afterwards, apply a good body lotion or moisturiser.

Removing unwanted hair

Tanned, silky, hairless legs look best in summer, although in many European countries, some fine downy fair hair on the legs is considered very attractive. However, in the United Kingdom, Australia, the United States and other English-speaking countries we generally prefer to be hairless. There are several methods of hair removal that you can use — notably shaving, depilation, waxing and electrolysis. They all have their benefits and disadvantages and you will have to weigh up which suits you best.

Shaving

This is the quickest, easiest and most frequently used method of hair removal. Although it is fast and effective, it must be done regularly as a stubbly dark regrowth appears when the hairs start to grow back. Many women worry that the hair will then be thicker and more prolific than ever but this is not true. However, the hairs will be rough and coarse as shaving blunts them. The best model of razor to use is one of the specially designed ladies' shavers which are safer than the ordinary kind and reduce the risk of cutting yourself. Otherwise an ordinary man's safety razor or the disposable sort will suffice.

Before you start shaving, moisturise the skin well to counteract some of its drying effects. Then smear your legs thickly with a good lather of shaving foam or ordinary soap. Shave in the opposite direction to the growth and keep rinsing out the razor between strokes. Afterwards, wash away any traces of soap and look for the patches of hairs that you might have missed. Gently pat dry with a towel or tissues and moisturise thoroughly. The best time to shave your legs is immediately after a warm bath or shower when the skin pores are open and at their most receptive.

Remember that hair grows back more quickly after shaving than any other method of hair removal so you must keep checking for regrowth and repeat the process as soon as new hairs appear.

Depilation

With these creams, gels, lotions, foams and sprays, there is no stubble and your legs look smoother and feel softer to the touch. Their effects also last longer and therefore you can use them less often – about once a month if you want to keep your legs hairless. However, although they soften and dissolve the hair shafts they do not affect the roots and therefore the hair will grow back eventually.

Some products may irritate sensitive skin as they contain powerful chemicals, so if you are using one for the first time, you should do a small patch test on your leg or arm and then wait for 24 hours in case of allergic reactions – redness or a rash, for instance.

You usually have to set aside about 15 minutes for depilation. Apply the product according to the instructions on the depilatory tube or packet and leave for the specified time (not less.) Rinse off afterwards in the bath or shower and moisturise well.

Waxing

This is the most effective hair removal method of all, especially in early summer when hairs may be longer after a winter of neglect. Its advantages over other methods are that it leaves legs silky smooth and hairs take longer to grow back. In fact, if you wax your legs regularly it will have a cumulative effect and the regrowth will get gradually weaker and less obvious. Also, there is no risk of stubble or chemical irritation. The disadvantage of waxing is that some women find it quite painful when the strips of wax are pulled off, although it is more bearable when done by a professional in a salon rather than self-administered at home.

Before waxing, you should always make sure that your legs are clean and perfectly dry. Moisturise the skin lightly and then gently pat dry with tissues and dust with a little talcum powder. The wax is usually heated before applying (although there are cold wax treatments available). When it is ripped off, it removes the hairs from quite deep inside the follicles so that your skin feels really smooth. Afterwards, you should remoisturise, perhaps with one of the special soothing brands that have been formulated for this purpose.

Electrolysis

Diathermy and galvanism are the most common forms of electrolysis and as they are both quite painful, you have to be very dedicated indeed to the hairless image to try them. Although they are ideal for moving small areas of facial hair, they are not really suitable for dealing with legs as they are expensive and require a course of several treatments. Their advantage is that they destroy the hair root bulb to make hair removal permanent.

Bleaching your hair

If you feel that all this hair removal is somehow rather artificial and prefer to go about *au naturel*, then you might consider bleaching your hair if it is fine and downy. This process works very well on even the darkest hairs and will last from about four to six weeks before it needs repeating. Because it is a chemical process, you will need to do a small spot test for allergic reactions before bleaching the whole length of your legs.

Keeping legs shapely and slim

Regular exercise such as walking, running, swimming and cycling will help keep your legs slender but there are many special exercises you can practise to keep trouble-spots like ankles, calves and inner thighs looking good and firm.

Ankles: trim thick ankles with the following exercise. Sitting on the floor with your arms extended behind you, supporting yourself with your hands flat on the floor, bend your knees so that your feet are close to your hips. Now alternately flex your ankles up and down. Repeat 10 times with each foot.

Calves: you can tone up and slim down flabby calves with this easy daily exercise.

Stand facing a wall at arms' length with your palms resting lightly on the wall for support. Now raise yourself up onto your toes, hold the position and count for three, and lower your feet to the floor. Repeat about 30 times, building up the repetitions each day.

Thighs: these are the most serious problem for most women. Get them back into shape with the following exercise for reducing and toning inner thighs.
Lie on your right side with your arm extended on the floor and your left arm bent in front of you with the palm flat on the floor for support. Your legs should be outstretched and toes pointed. Now, without rolling back, raise your left leg as high as it will go and lower it to the floor. Repeat 10 times, then flex your foot and do another 10 repetitions. Now try it raising both legs – this is much harder and will take practice. Change sides and repeat the whole sequence lying on your left side. This is a wonderful exercise for slimming down inner thighs.

How to have beautiful hands and feet

At this time of year, hands and feet are on view and rarely covered up, so you should try to keep them looking their best. Regular care and maintenance takes only a few minutes a day while a weekly manicure and pedicure will pay dividends. Yet they are probably the two most neglected areas of your body. You ill-treat them by forcing your feet into tight shoes which cause painful corns, and allowing your hands to come into contact with all sorts of harmful chemicals, detergents and cold winds which dry and chap them.

Caring for your hands

Your hands and nails can tell you quite a lot about your general condition and health. Healthy nails are strong, pink and smooth. They should not be ridged, dotted with white spots, brittle and liable to break easily. They are a reflection of what you eat and your overall lifestyle. Made up of a tough form of protein called keratin, nails need a good supply of nutrients to stay healthy. For example, if your nails split easily and snap off, you may not be getting enough protein and vitamin A. Make sure that you include some carrot juice, cod liver oil, apricots and yellow fruit and vegetables in your diet, and watch the condition gradually improve.

If your nails are slow-growing it may be due to several reasons – taking drugs, over-rigorous slimming, poor diet, cold weather or illness. White spots and weak, brittle nails are usually a sign of zinc deficiency and a low intake of vitamin B6. This condition is particularly common among women who take the contraceptive pill. Taking daily supplements of these two nutrients will help improve your nails.

The greatest dangers to your nails and hands come from environmental influences – cold, wind, hot sun, detergents, disinfectants, chlorine, strong soaps and cheap bath salts. Remember to protect your hands at all times. Here is a list of protective measures you can make a part of your beauty awareness and routine:

1 Always wear rubber gloves when washing up dishes, cleaning, making fires, sterilising the baby's bottles and other jobs around the house.
2 Wear strong gloves for gardening to prevent dirt getting ingrained in your skin and under your nails.
3 Wear warm gloves in cold weather to stop any chapping, dryness and sore, red patches.
4 Apply a good sunscreen in the sun to prevent drying and unsightly liver spots.
5 Use only very mild soaps to wash your hands.
6 Massage your hands regularly with hand cream to keep the skin smooth and moist. Make it part of your bedtime routine. Also keep a pot of hand cream handy in the bathroom and beside the kitchen sink just in case you need to use it after washing.
7 Add a few dops of soothing bath oil to your bath.

Hand creams

These may be light and moisturising, soothing to sore, chapped hands, nourishing with a special deep action formula for night-wear, or water-resistant and forming a protective barrier in cold weather. Trial and error will help you find the best hand cream for you. Generally, barrier creams are best for daytime use and nourishing ones for night-time, so you may need to invest in two different products in order to keep your hands moist and smooth. It is best to buy a good hand cream and not to balk at the price. After all, your hands tend to show your age more than any other part of your body, even your face, and if they look rough, wrinkled or blotchy you will feel less confident and attractive. Hand creams which contain soothing aloe are particularly good for red, sore and cracked hands.

Manicuring your nails

A weekly manicure will keep your hands in tip-top condition and although you can have it done professionally at a beauty salon it is just as easy to do it yourself at home when you have some spare time or are spending an evening in relaxing and watching television. You might be a little clumsy at first but you will soon become more skilful. Manicuring not only makes your hands and nails look good – it protects and conditions them, too, so that they stay that way. The whole process from start to finish should take only about half an hour. Follow our easy step-by-step guide to see how it should be done.

Before you start, you should get together all the things you will need:

1 Some nail remover polish and cotton wool balls.
2 Emery boards – not the metal nail files which are damaging.
3 Some cuticle cream, remover and orange sticks.
4 A bowl of warm soapy water and a soft towel.
5 Moisturising hand lotion.
6 A nail buffer (optional).

7 Nail clippers or scissors.
8 Nail varnish – base and colour coats and a final sealing coat.

Treating common hand problems

Here are a few tips for dealing with some of the problems you may encounter with your hands. Good regular handcare and manicuring should prevent them occurring but you ought to know how to treat them if they arise.

1 Rough, stained hands: these usually happen when you garden without gloves or do any rough, heavy work. You can gently rub away any patches of hard skin with a pumice stone and soapy water. Remove any dirt from cracked skin with half a lemon and then moisturise with hand cream or rub in some olive oil. This treatment is also suitable for removing disfiguring nicotine stains although you will have to rub them very hard. Use an especially rich, emollient hand cream afterwards.

2 Red, sore hands: these may be caused by very cold winds and weather or immersing your hands in detergents. Massage them regularly with a good hand cream and wear gloves whenever necessary — doing household chores and gardening.

3 Brown liver spots: the sun is the culprit in this case and you should always protect your hands with a protective sunscreen. This is a case where prevention is better than cure as it is practically impossible to get rid of these ugly brown marks. A beautician can partially lighten them with a de-pigmentation cream or bleach but the traces will always be there and nothing is more ageing to your hands.

Caring for your feet

Feet are often even more overlooked than hands and in the summer you should make a special effort to repair the damage of months of neglect. Feet should not only look good – they should feel right, too. For aching, tired and sore feet can affect your posture, your mood, your movement and your energy. There is nothing like ill-fitting shoes or the start of a corn of blister to make you feel low and fatigued, especially if you have a long way to walk or are trailing around shops.

Feet need frequent exercise, beauty care and comfortable shoes to keep them in pristine condition. If you always drive everywhere or have a very sedentary job and rarely walk, you may develop poor circulation in your feet and slack muscles. This, in turn, can lead to fallen arches, corns, callouses and bunions – none of which are very attractive in open summer sandals.

Choosing the right shoes

Always wear comfortable shoes which fit properly with plenty of room for your toes and don't rub your heels. They should not be too high, too narrow, too small, too pointed or too tight. It is no good buying a pair of shoes with the intention of 'breaking them in'. Although leather will give and stretch a little, shoes should fit properly when you first try them on in the shop. If they feel uncomfortable in any way, try another pair on instead. Any pressure on your toes and feet may lead to corns and bunions. Although high heels are fine for the occasional evening out or special function, you should not wear them all the time as they contribute to the formation of varicose veins, cellulite build-up on thighs and throw your natural posture out of alignment. Flat shoes are fashionable and exercise your feet and legs naturally, but for many women the best heel height is about 3-5cm/1½-2 inches. Too high a heel can tile the pelvis to form a hollow in your back and cause excruciating backache.

When you buy a new pair of shoes, try to do it in the afternoon when your feet are probably more tired and swollen than first thing in the morning. If the shoes feel comfortable then, you will know that they are the right fit for you.

Daily foot care

Every day you should wash your feet in warm soapy water and rub away any patches of hard, dry skin with a pumice stone. Always dry them thoroughly afterwards, not forgetting to dry between the toes as this is a good breeding ground for fungus (athlete's foot). Massage well with a moisturising hand or body lotion. then dust lightly with talc to absorb any excess moisture.

If your feet are tired, give them a soothing soak in a warm footbath of Epsom salts or add a few drops of bath oil to the water. Then plunge into cold water, dry, moisturise and put them up for a little while. Every seven to ten days you should treat them to a pedicure. You will need the same cream, varnishes, emery boards and other equipment as listed under '*Manicuring your nails*' above. Proceed as follows:

1 Remove every speck of old nail polish with cotton wool and some remover. Then soak your feet in warm water for about 10 minutes. Dip quickly in and out of cold water and dry thoroughly. This will prevent the nails splitting.
2 Using nail scissors or clippers, neatly trim your nails back to the end of each toe. If the edges are rough, smooth them down with an emery board.
3 Wrap an orange stick in some cotton wool, dip into warm water and gently clean around the nails. Apply some cuticle remover and rinse off. Dry and massage a little cuticle cream into the surrounding area. Ease back the cuticles with an orange stick.
4 Rinse your feet once more in warm water and rub away any hard patches of skin with a pumice stone or friction pad. For very bad cases, you could use a liquid skin remover to help get it really smooth.

5 Dry your feet and rub in some hand or body moisturising lotion. Now gently buff your nails in the same direction to make them pink and boost circulation.
6 Separate your toes with cotton wool, tissue or sponge pads, apply a base primer coat of varnish and dry.
7 Now add a coat of colour – bright reds and pinks look good for evenings while pearly pinks and silvers may be better for day and beach wear in the summer. When it dries, carefully add another coat, taking care not to streak it. You can protect it with a clear top coat to prevent it chipping. Do not remove the separation pads until the varnish is thoroughly dry and hard.
8 Last of all, dab your feet generously with soothing eau-de-cologne or treat them to a special reviving spray.

Treating common foot problems

If you look after your feet you are unlikely to encounter any problems. Most disorders stem from neglect and you may have to seek professional advice and visit your local chiropodist. As soon as the first signs appear, act quickly to nip them in the bud.
1 Athlete's foot: if you tend to walk barefoot in gyms, health clubs, showers and public swimming pools, you may pick up this fungus infection. The skin between and behind the toes becomes flaky and dry and eventually cracks. Remove any dead skin with a pumice stone and then apply a medicated fungicidal powder, cream or lotion (available from most chemists). Expose your feet as much as possible in open sandals so that the air can circulate freely, and never wear the same tights or socks two days running. If your feet start to perspire, dry them and change footwear immediately.
2 Bunions: this is a painful swelling at the base and side of the big toe. Tight, pointed, badly fitting shoes are always the cause so throw out your old shoes which were the culprits. By getting professional treatment promptly as soon as the first signs appear, you could save yourself a lot of pain and some corrective surgery later on. There are no home remedies.
3 Callouses: this hard skin is really a protective reaction to prevent tight shoes causing more damage. Every day, you should attack the callouses with pumice stone or a special scraper. They will gradually disappear.
4 Corns: yet another result of ill-fitting shoes which pinch the toes. The point of the corn presses inwards unfortunately and may prove exceptionally troublesome if it presses on a nerve. You can treat small newly formed corns yourself with a pumice stone after immersing your feet for at least 10 minutes in warm water to soften the skin. A corn plaster will give some relief but really bad corns have to be cut out professionally.
5 Verrucas: like athlete's foot, these are picked up in places where people tend to go barefoot. These inward-growing warts are painful and have to be burned out by a chiropodist. Sometimes regular anointing with ink helps them to clear up and disappear although there is no scientific explanation for this.

Keeping fit in the sun

There are so many ways to be active and exercise when you can enjoy the fresh air and warm sunshine of long summer days. Swimming in the sea or an open-air pool, jogging in the park or cycling to work are all good ways of getting and staying fit. Remember to wear a good sunscreen to protect your skin and to limit your make-up to a minimum.

Summer is also a good time for playing tennis on a hard or grass court. If you do not play regularly or have let your game lapse in recent years, you might benefit from a course of brush-up lessons to relearn the basic strokes. It's a good way to get some exercise and you can burn up a lot of calories dashing around the court in a strenuous game on a hot day.

If you go away on holiday, you can use your time on the beach to get fit – don't just lie there; get moving. Jog along the water's edge or up the cliff path; explore your surroundings by going for a long walk or hiring a bike. Enjoy a beach game of handball or volleyball, or just chase a frisbee around the sand. You can even do a little weight-training, performing your usual work-out and stretching exercises and using cans of soft drinks as dumb-bells. There may also be opportunities for swimming and a whole range of watersports including sailing, water-skiing, para-gliding, windsurfing and conventional surfing.

A last word of warning: if the heat is intense and the sun very fierce, be sensible about when you choose to exercise. Avoid the hottest part of the day (around noon) or you may quickly become dehydrated and even get a nasty case of sunstroke. The best times to exercise are early in the morning or in the late afternoon and evening when the heat of the day is subsiding. If you tend to perspire a lot, drink plenty of fluids after exercise to replace any water loss.

Summer tip

If you overdo it and exercise too long and too hard, you may get heatstroke as mentioned above. If you start to feel dizzy, faint or nauseous, stop exercising immediately and rest. Taking adequate fluid on a hot day will help to minimise the risk. Your skin may get cold and clammy and your pulse rapid. If this happens, it is important to rehydrate your body and drink plenty of fluid. Better still, avoid heatstroke altogether by exercising in the coolest part of the day – early morning or evening when the sun is at its weakest.

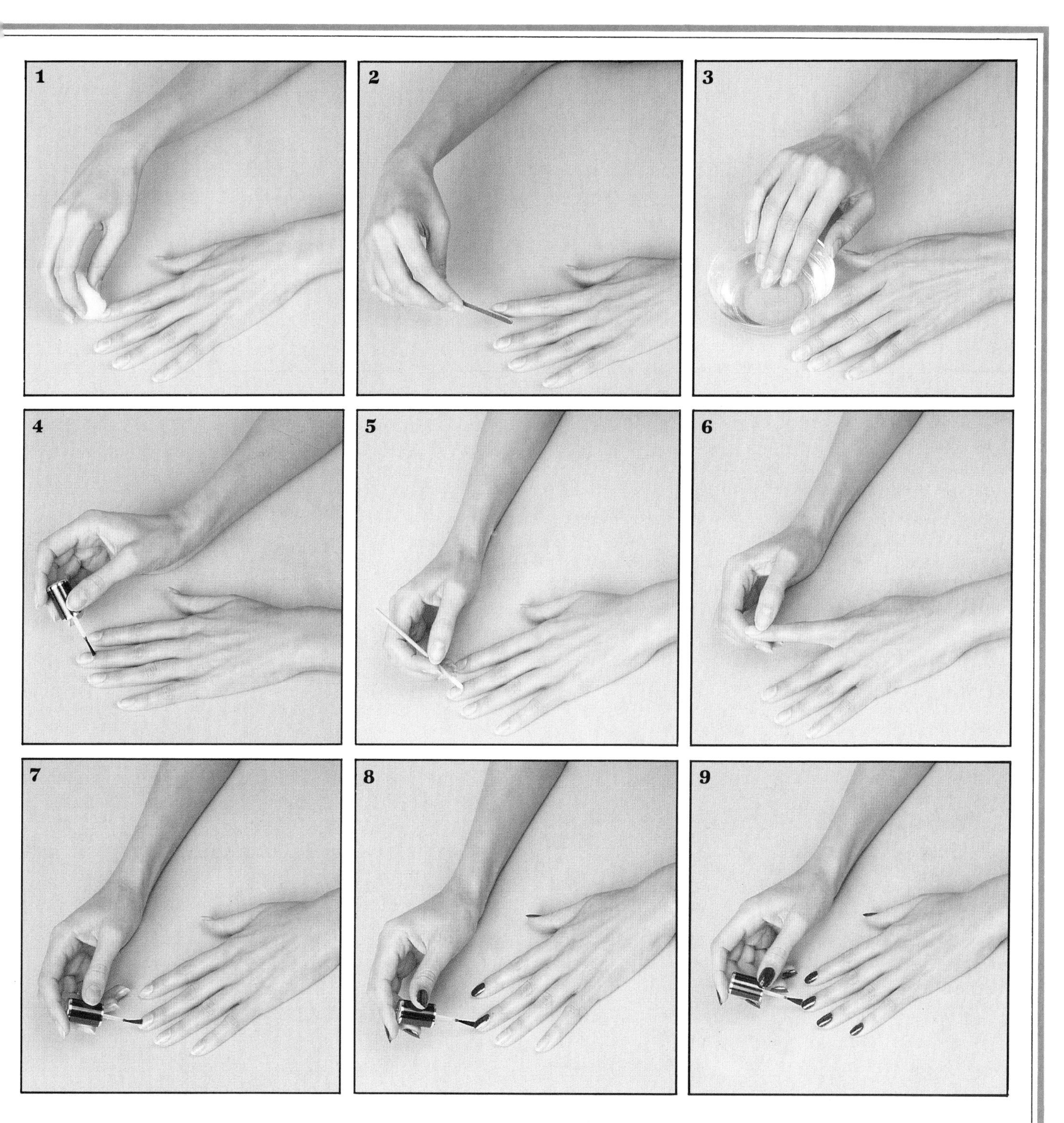

Manicure routine

1 *Wash your hands and remove any traces of old nail varnish with cotton wool soaked in varnish remover.* **2** *Use an emery board to file the nails to an oval. File from the sides towards the centre of each nail, holding the emery board at a slant.* **3** *Immerse your fingers in warm water for a few minutes.*

4 *Apply some cuticle remover to each nail and rinse off with warm soapy water.* **5** *Use an orange stick, moistened with cuticle cream, to clean around the nails and gently ease back the cuticles and remove dead skin.* **6** *Now massage in some more cuticle cream. Wash your hands and moisturise them with a good hand cream for soft skin.*

7 *Apply a base coat of clear varnish to each nail. Leave to dry hard.* **8** *Carefully apply a coat of coloured varnish on top of the base coat. Be careful not to streak it - it should be even. Dry and apply another coat on top. Allow to dry.* **9** *Apply a protective clear top coat of varnish to prevent chipping. Dry thoroughly before touching anything.*

SUPER SALADS FOR HEALTHY SUMMER LIVING

When the weather's hot and sunny and you're feeling slimmer and healthier, you won't want to eat large filling meals. Salads and juices are the ideal food for summer – cool, refreshing, delicious and nutritious. At this time of the year, you can be more adventurous and experiment with the wide range of fruit and vegetables you can buy or grow yourself. For the figure-conscious woman, salads are the perfect food. Yet too many women still think only of a limp lettuce leaf, sliced tomato and wilting cucumber when they make a salad. If you have been put off eating salads by such boring, tasteless food, then think again. Salads can be colourful and interesting if made with contrasting textures and flavours and tossed in an unusual dressing. If you want to be really healthy, you should try to eat a raw salad every day. It is a good way of providing most of the vitamins and minerals your body needs. Adding cooked beans, low-fat cheese, cold fish or poultry, wholewheat pasta or brown rice povides protein, too.

Your salads can be based on different foods. For instance, the principal ingredients may be:

1 Vegetable: crisp lettuce, cucumber, tomato, avocado, grated carrot, chopped onion, radish, beetroot, fresh herbs, watercress, spinach, shredded cabbage, celery, garden peas, cooked French beans, endive, courgettes/zucchini, mushrooms, peppers, cauliflower florets, raw broad beans, cooked potatoes, beansprouts, fennel, aubergine/eggplant, sweetcorn kernels.

2 Fruit: apples, apricots, strawberries, raspberries, redcurrants, banana, cherries, peaches, nectarines, oranges, grapefruit, pears, melon, pineapple, grapes.

3 Nuts and seeds: almonds, hazelnuts, walnuts, pecans, brazil nuts, pine nuts, sunflower, pumpkin and sesame seeds.

4 Cereals and grains: wholewheat pasta, brown rice, bulgur wheat, buckwheat, millet, sprouted grains.

5 Beans and lentils: cooked kidney, butter, soya, black-eye and borlotti beans, chick peas, lentils.

6 Cold fish, poultry or meat: salmon, tuna, sardines, smoked haddock and mackerel, white fish, mullet, squid, shellfish (prawns, shrimps, crab, lobster), chicken, turkey, duck, beef, lamb and pork.

7 Cheese and eggs: low-fat soft cheeses, (quark, cottage, ricotta), hard-boiled eggs.

When you make a salad, you can mix these ingredients from different groups for a really unusual and mouth-watering result. Think of salads as a main meal, not just something to nibble at on a side plate. And when choosing salad fruit and vegetables, opt for the freshest produce at its peak for eating – discard anything that looks wilted, limp, discoloured or past its best even if it is cheaper. Use only the crispest, freshest green stuff, discarding any damaged or browning outer leaves. Wash well in cold water to get rid of any chemical residues, insects or dirt, and then shake or spin dry. Use a good sharp knife when chopping and slicing.

The best-dressed salads are not coated in bottled mayonnaise or salad cream, even if they are the low-calorie sort. It is better to make your own – either oil-based dressings which can be stored in a large screwtop jar in the refrigerator and used as required, or a healthy yoghurt- or avocado-based one. Many commercially manufactured dressings contain additives and other potentially harmful ingredients. It is healthier and cheaper to make your own.

Use the best-quality oils for dressing salads – olive, sunflower, safflower, arachide (peanut) or walnut – and try experimenting with different flavoured herb vinegars – tarragon, sage, basil and garlic. If you dislike vinegar, you can always use lemon juice instead. If you like your salad to taste of garlic (which incidentally is very healthy and a natural cleansing agent), then try rubbing the bowl with a cut clove or place a peeled clove in the bottom of the dish before serving. Adding crushed raw garlic to the dressing itself can be overpowering and may produce unpleasant smelling breath.

Salads are best dressed immediately before serving and should not be left to stand for too long or they will wilt, go soggy and lose their freshness and crispness. Herbs are also best added at the last minute in order to preserve their bright colours and aromatic flavour. Remember that salad-making is an art – far from being the easiest thing in the world as many people seem to think. You must know how to mix and match the right ingredients which complement each other perfectly to get the correct balance and colours.

Salad recipes

All these recipes serve one person only. If you are sharing your meal, then you should double up accordingly. They are all quick and easy to make when you are in a hurry, and most can be packed into a Tupperware or airtight container and carried to the office for a working, healthy lunch.

Minty rice salad

75g/3oz cooked American long-grain rice
25g/1oz cooked peas
25g/1oz chopped celery
1 spring onion, chopped
5ml/1 teaspoon chopped fresh mint
22.5ml/1½ tablespoons natural yoghurt
black pepper

Mix together the rice and vegetables. Blend the mint, yoghurt and seasoning and toss with the rice salad.

Curried rice salad

75g/3oz cooked American long-grain rice
½ dessert apple, cored and chopped
10ml/2 teaspoons lemon juice
small piece green pepper, chopped
15ml/1 tablespoon peanuts
22.5ml/1½ tablespoons natural yoghurt
good pinch curry powder
15ml/1 tablespoon seedless raisins

Mix the cooked rice with apples in lemon juice. Add the pepper and peanuts. Blend the yoghurt, curry powder and raisins and toss the salad in this dressing.

Quick rice salad

75g/3oz cooked American long-grain rice
30ml/2 tablespoons sweetcorn kernels
small piece red pepper, chopped
15ml/1 tablespoon oil and vinegar dressing
1 small tomato, quartered
3 slices cucumber

Mix the rice, sweetcorn, peppers and the dressing. Garnish with tomato and cucumber.

Carrot and raisin salad

100g/4oz grated carrot
25g/1oz California raisins
15ml/1 tablespoon soured cream or natural yoghurt
10ml/2 teaspoons chopped hazelnuts
salt and pepper
chives or chopped parsley

Put the carrot and raisins in a bowl. Blend the soured cream with the hazelnuts and season. Mix into the salad and sprinkle with herbs.

Fruit cabbage salad

100g/4oz shredded white cabbage
25g/1oz chopped dried apricots
25g/1oz California raisins
1 spring onion, chopped
small piece green pepper, chopped
1 radish, sliced
Dressing:
30ml/2 tablespoons natural yoghurt
2.5ml/½ teaspoon French mustard
½ small clove garlic, crushed
salt and pepper

Mix all the salad ingredients together in a bowl.Blend the dressing and toss with the salad.

California salad

few crisp lettuce leaves
25g/1oz grated carrot
small piece each red and green pepper, chopped
1 stick celery, chopped
½ courgette/zucchini, sliced
1 small tomato, quartered
salt and pepper
½ avocado, stoned and peeled
30ml/2 tablespoons French dressing
1 clove garlic, crushed

Put the salad vegetables in a bowl with the seasoning. Mash the avocado flesh to a purée. Blend with the French dressing and garlic and toss the salad.

Watercress and orange salad

1 small bunch watercress
1 orange, peeled and sliced
1 spring onion, chopped
3 black olives
15ml/1 tablespoon toasted flaked almonds
30ml/2 tablespoons sunflower oil
juice of ½ orange

Pick over the watercress and wash well. Place in a salad bowl with the orange, onion, olives and almonds. Blend the oil and orange juice and toss the salad gently.

Spinach salad

few young spinach leaves
50g/2oz button mushrooms, thinly sliced
25g/1oz blue cheese
1 rasher grilled bacon
30ml/2 tablespoons olive oil
juice of ½ lemon
dash tarragon vinegar
pinch of sugar
salt and pepper

Remove any tough stalks from the spinach. Wash and

dry. Place in a bowl with the mushrooms and cheese and crumble in the bacon. Blend the remaining ingredients to make a dressing and gently toss the salad.

New potato salad
3-4 small new potatoes, cooked in their skins
1 rasher grilled bacon
1 spring onion, chopped
30ml/2 tablespoons natural yoghurt
good squeeze of lemon juice
15ml/1 tablespoon chopped dill or parsley
salt and pepper
chopped chives

Cut the potatoes into small chunks and place in a bowl with the crumbled bacon and onion. Mix the yoghurt, lemon juice, herbs and seasoning, and toss the salad gently. Sprinkle with chives.

Mexican bean salad
100g/4oz cooked kidney beans
½ small red pepper, cut in rings
½ small green pepper, cut in rings
1 spring onion, chopped
chopped chives and parsley
22.5ml/1½ tablespoons olive oil
juice of ½ small lemon
dash of wine or herb vinegar
salt and pepper

Put the beans, pepper rings, onion and herbs in a bowl. Mix the remaining dressing ingredients together and toss the salad gently.

Curried pasta salad
50g/2oz cooked pasta shells
50g/2oz canned tuna chunks
1 spring onion, chopped
30ml/2 tablespoons natural yoghurt
2.5ml/½ teaspoon mild curry powder
good squeeze of lemon juice

Curried rice salad; Quick rice salad; and Minty rice salad (all recipes on the opposite page).

5ml/1 teaspoon mayonnaise
chopped parsley

Put the pasta, tuna and onion in a bowl. Mix the remaining dressing ingredients and toss well so that the pasta is well-coated.

Italian seafood salad
50g/2oz shrimps or prawns
few slices cooked squid
5-6 cooked mussels (or canned)
3-4 cooked clams (or canned)
2 black olives, stoned and quartered
piece red pepper
30ml/2 tablespoons olive oil
15ml/1 tablespoon lemon juice
1 clove garlic, crushed
salt and pepper
chopped fresh oregano or marjoram

Put the seafood and olives in a bowl. Grill the pepper until charred and skin it. Cut into strips and add to the other salad ingredients. Mix the oil, lemon juice, garlic, seasoning and herbs to make the dressing and toss well. Chill before eating.

Tomato and avocado salad
1 large tomato, skinned and sliced
4 slices Italian mozzarella cheese
1 spring onion, chopped
chopped fresh basil (or dried) and oregano
salt and pepper
½ small avocado, sliced
30ml/2 tablespoons olive oil
juice of ½ lemon
dash herb vinegar
salt and pepper

Place the tomato slices on a plate. Arrange the mozzarella on top and sprinkle with the onion, herbs and seasoning. Overlap the avocado slices along the top. Mix the dressing and pour over the salad.

Sicilian mixed salad
1 large tomato, skinned and quartered
50g/2oz cooked green string beans
1 boiled new potato, sliced
few slices cucumber
3 black olives, stoned and quartered
salt and pepper
50g/2oz tuna (optional)
22.5ml/1½ tablespoons olive oil
dash wine vinegar

Mix the tomato, beans, potato, cucumber, olives and seeasoning (with the tuna if used). Mix the dressing and toss gently. Serve if wished with hard-boiled egg.

Greek tomato salad
1 large tomato, quartered and sliced
few cos lettuce leaves
1 small onion, thinly sliced
½ small green pepper, sliced
few slices cucumber
30ml/2 tablespoons olive oil
salt and pepper
chopped oregano
few thin slices feta cheese
3 black olives, stoned

Mix the salad vegetables together in a bowl. Toss gently in the oil and season. Top with the herbs, feta cheese and olives.

Beansprout fruit salad
50g/2oz fresh beansprouts
small piece red pepper, sliced
1 spring onion, chopped
25g/1oz cashew nuts
50g/2oz chopped fresh pineapple
50g/2oz diced melon
½ small avocado, stoned, peeled and sliced
15ml/1 tablespoon chopped parsley
45ml/3 tablespoons natural yoghurt
juice of ½ orange
dash of lemon juice
salt and pepper

Mix the salad vegetables, nuts and fruit together in a bowl with the parsley. Blend the yoghurt with the citrus juice and seasoning and toss the salad.

Pasta fruit salad
50g/2oz cooked pasta shells or rings
½ small red apple, cored and diced
15ml/1 tablespoon walnuts, chopped
1 stick celery, chopped
1 small orange, peeled and segmented
few sprigs watercress
30ml/2 tablespoons natural yoghurt
juice of ½ orange
chopped parsley

Mix the pasta, fruit, nuts, celery and watercress together. Blend the yoghurt and orange juice and toss the salad. Top with fresh parsley.

Cacik and lettuce salad
½ small cucumber, grated coarsely
sea salt
75ml/3floz natural yoghurt
1 clove garlic crushed
5ml/1 teaspoon chopped parsley
5ml/1 teaspoon chopped chives
10ml/2 teaspoons chopped mint

Fruit cabbage salad (top); and Carrot and raisin salad (below). The recipes are on page 80

freshly ground black pepper
1 crisp lettuce heart

Put the cucumber in a colander, sprinkle with salt and leave for 30 minutes to draw out moisture. Press gently to extract more liquid and place in a bowl with the yoghurt, garlic, herbs and a good sprinkle of black pepper. Mix well. Chill for at least half an hour and serve spooned over a crisp lettuce heart. Garnish if wished with black olives and tomato quarters.

Avocado and raisin salad
½ avocado, peeled, stoned and thinly sliced
freshly squeezed lemon juice
25g/1oz raisins
1 carrot, coarsely grated
1 spring onion, chopped
10ml/2 teaspoons olive oil
juice of ½ orange
salt and pepper
few chopped chives

Sprinkle the avocado with lemon juice to prevent discolouration. Mix with the raisins, carrot and onion. Blend the oil and orange juice, season and gently toss the salad. Sprinkle with a mist of chives.

Crunchy cauliflower salad
½ small cauliflower, divided into florets
1 stick celery, chopped
1 small red-skinned apple, cored and diced
25g/1oz peanuts
50ml/2floz natural yoghurt
juice of ½ orange
sprig parsley, chopped

Mix the cauliflower, celery, apple and peanuts together in a bowl. Blend the yoghurt and orange juice and season. Toss the salad gently and sprinkle with parsley.

Three bean salad
75g/3oz cooked red kidney beans
75g/3oz cooked chick peas
75g/3oz cooked haricot or flageolet beans
1 spring onion, chopped
1 clove garlic, crushed
15ml/1 tablespoon chopped parsley
15ml/1 tablespoon olive oil
good squeeze of lemon juice
dash wine vinegar
salt and pepper

Mix the beans, spring onion, garlic and parsley in a bowl. Blend the remaining ingredients and gently toss the salad. Chill before serving.

Mediterranean tomato and tuna salad
1 large tomato, sliced thinly
1 hard-boiled egg, sliced
100g/4oz tuna cut in chunks
15ml/1 tablespoon olive oil
5ml/1 teaspoon herb vinegar
salt and pepper
chopped chives and parsley

Arrange the tomato and egg slices in an overlapping circle. Fill the hole in the centre with tuna and make a vinaigrette with the oil, vinegar and seasoning. Scatter with plenty of chopped fresh herbs.

North African salad
1 tomato, skinned and chopped
½ small green pepper, chopped
½ small chilli pepper, seeded and chopped
1 spring onion, chopped
1 small clove garlic, crushed
½ small red pepper, chopped
5ml/1 teaspoon chopped mint
5ml/1 teaspoon chopped parsley
15ml/1 tablespoon olive oil

juice of ½ lemon
salt and pepper
small chunk cucumber, chopped

Mix the tomato, peppers, chilli, onion, garlic and herbs in a bowl. Blend the oil and lemon. Pour over the salad and chill. Stir in the cucumber and serve.

Chinese leaf salad
few sliced Chinese leaves
½ onion, chopped
½ small red pepper, sliced
2 slices pineapple, chopped
25g/1oz chopped walnuts
few sprigs watercress
45ml/3 tablespoons yoghurt
good pinch curry powder
juice of ½ lemon

Put the Chinese leaves, onion, pepper, pineapple, walnuts and watercress in a bowl. Blend the yoghurt, curry powder and lemon juice and gently toss the salad.

Caribbean curried chicken salad
100g/4oz shredded cooked chicken
2 slices pineapple, chopped
few crisp lettuce leaves
15ml/1 tablespoon raisins
15ml/1 tablespoon shredded coconut
5ml/1 teaspoon mango chutney
few peanuts
30ml/2 tablespoons natural yoghurt
15ml/1 tablespoon mayonnaise
good pinch curry powder
chopped parsley

Mix the chicken and pineapple and arrange on top of the lettuce. Pile the raisins, coconut, chutney and peanuts on top. Blend the yoghurt, mayonnaise and curry powder and spoon over the salad. Sprinkle with chopped parsley.

Pasta, shrimp and avocado salad
½ avocado, peeled, stoned and cubed
100g/4oz shrimps or prawns
lemon juice
100g/4oz cooked pasta shells or macaroni
15ml/1 tablespoon chopped parsley
15ml/1 tablespoon olive oil
dash wine vinegar
small clove garlic, crushed
salt and pepper

Marinate the avocado and shrimps in lemon juice and mix with the pasta and parsley. Mix the oil and vinegar and add the garlic and seasoning. Gently toss the salad.

Radish, orange and watercress salad
1 large orange
small bunch watercress
4-5 radishes, sliced
45ml/3 tablespoons natural yoghurt
good pinch ground cinnamon
15ml/1 tablespoon chopped chives

Peel the orange, removing the white pith and slice thinly crossways. Blend in a bowl with the watercress and radishes. Blend the yoghurt, cinnamon and any leftover orange juice and spoon over the salad. Sprinkle with chives and serve.

Italian fennel salad
1 small fennel bulb
1 spring onion, chopped
3 anchovy fillets
1 tomato, quartered
small piece cucumber, sliced
50g/2oz ricotta cheese
15ml/1 tablespoon olive oil
dash herb vinegar
juice of ½ lemon
pinch sugar
salt and pepper
few slivers lemon peel
chopped parsley

Slice the fennel thinly, and mix with the onion, anchovies, tomato, cucumber and ricotta. Blend the oil, vinegar and lemon juice with the sugar and seasoning and gently toss the salad. Top with thin slivers of lemon peel and parsley.

Orange and pepper salad
1 small green pepper, thinly sliced in rings
1 spring onion, chopped
1 large orange, peeled and sliced
few leaves curly endive
15ml/1 tablespoon olive oil
juice of ½ orange or lemon
1 clove garlic, crushed
salt and pepper
chopped chives

Mix the pepper, onion, orange and endive. Blend the oil, juice and garlic and seasoning to make a tangy dressing. Toss the salad and sprinkle with chives.

French red cabbage salad
½ red cabbage, shredded
few leaves curly endive or chicory
2 rashers crisply sautéed bacon, chopped
50g/2oz blue cheese, crumbled (Roquefort ideally)
crisp-fried bread croûtons

30ml/2 tablespoons olive oil
10ml/2 teaspoons herb vinegar
5ml/1 teaspoon Dijon mustard
pinch sugar
salt and pepper

Put the red cabbage, endive, bacon, cheese and croûtons in a salad bowl. Mix the remaining dressing ingredients until well-blended. Gently toss the salad.

Oriental salad
75g/3oz beansprouts and alfalfa
1 spring onion, chopped
1 carrot, grated
few sprigs watercress
15ml/1 tablespoon olive oil
10ml/2 teaspoons tamari sauce
juice of ½ lemon
5ml/1 teaspoon honey
a little grated fresh ginger or pinch ground

Mix the beansprouts, onion, carrot and watercress. Blend the dressing ingredients and gently toss the salad. Serve to accompany stir-fried Chinese dishes.

Salad brochettes
1 small cherry tomato
2 chunks green pepper
2 chunks red pepper
2 chunks cucumber
3 chunks pineapple
½ small avocado, peeled and cubed
2 stoned black olives
½ small peach, stoned and cubed
75g/3oz cooked chicken, cut in chunks
75ml/3floz natural yoghurt
15ml/1 tablespoon mayonnaise
squeeze lemon juice
pinch curry powder
chopped parsley

Thread all the salad and fruit ingredients and chicken onto 2 kebab skewers. Mix the remaining ingredients to make a spicy mayonnaise and serve the brochettes sprinkled with parsley.

Caesar salad
few crisp cos lettuce leaves
30ml/2 tablespoons olive oil
few drops wine vinegar
1 clove garlic, crushed
30ml/2 tablespoons grated Parmesan
salt and pepper
squeeze lemon juice
few fried bread croûtons
50g/2oz diced ham or cooked bacon
1 raw egg yolk
2 anchovy fillets

Wash and spin the lettuce and place in a salad bowl. Blend the oil, vinegar, garlic, Parmesan, seasoning and lemon juice. Pour over the lettuce and toss with the croûtons and ham. Add the egg yolks and toss again until all the ingredients glisten. Garnish with the anchovy fillets.

Waldorf salad
1 large red-skinned dessert apple
juice of 1 small lemon
1 stick celery
15ml/1 tablespoon chopped walnuts
45ml/3 tablespoons mayonnaise mixed with yoghurt
salt and pepper
few lettuce leaves

Cut the apple into quarters and remove the core, leaving the peel intact. Dice and sprinkle with lemon juice to prevent discolouration. Chop the celery and toss with the walnuts in the yoghurt and mayonnaise dressing. Season and arrange on a bed of lettuce leaves.

Avocado and nut salad
½ avocado pear, peeled and sliced
1 small red-skinned apple
juice of 1 small lemon
30ml/2 tablespoons cashew nuts
45ml/3 tablespoons natural yoghurt
pinch curry powder
chopped fresh herbs
small bunch watercress

Place the avocado in a bowl. Core and dice the apple and add to the bowl. Sprinkle with lemon juice. Add the nuts, yoghurt, curry powder and herbs and toss gently. Arrange on the watercress.

Cheese, ham and pineapple salad
50g/2oz diced cooked ham
1 small cooked potato, diced
25g/1oz diced Swiss cheese
few seedless grapes
1 sliced fresh pineapple, cut in chunks
30ml/2 tablespoons mayonnaise
15ml/1 tablespoon pineapple juice
salt and pepper
chopped parsley

Place the ham, potato, cheese and fruit in a bowl. Blend the mayonnaise, pineapple juice and seasoning and toss the salad. Sprinkle with chopped parsley.

A NEW BEAUTY PLAN FOR AUTUMN'S CHANGING SCENE

In autumn, the time is ripe for change – a new hairstyle or hair colour; a different beauty and skincare system; and new make-up colours to match the latest fashions. You need to adapt your 'look' to cooler shorter days and the demands of work. It may come as a shock to the system after the long lazy days of summer, but going back to work and experimenting with a whole new range of seasonal colours can be interesting and fun. Explore the shops and glance through the fashion-filled pages of the glossy magazines to discover what is new and appealing to you on the autumn beauty scene this year.

Now is the time to repair any sun damage to your skin and build up cold weather protection with nourishing, moisturising treatment creams. You may have to deal with a fading tan problem – either by topping it up and prolonging it with a course of sun-bed treatments, or by giving in to your skin's natural tendency to shed the top layers of dead skin cells and opting to go paler. It sometimes makes a pleasant change to tone down your summer colour and try out a new make-up for autumn.

Autumn calls for a new colour strategy, especially for work, and interviews, too, if you are busy job-hunting. There are beauty tips and advice for busy working women to help them look the part for their job. You need to assess your lifestyle and ascertain which make-up is best for you. Speed is important when you are rushing to get ready in the morning, and the special fast basic make-up routine will enable you to look good with the minimum of time and effort.

Your hair will need reconditioning after the wear and tear of summer and perhaps you might like to treat it to a new autumn colour which looks natural but sensational. Autumnal shades of copper, rust, titian, burgundy and gold all look great and very seasonal.

Just because the weather is getting colder does not mean that you should stop exercising. On the contrary, you should make a bigger effort to keep in shape when there is a greater temptation to skip your regular session and eat larger, calorie-laden meals. You can even perform mini-exercises at your desk to keep your legs and ankles trim. Or why not try a new form of exercise and work-out with weights?

Busy women may have little time to cook when they arrive home in the evenings and they can benefit from the ideas for healthy fast food – a complete meal in 30 minutes or less! They can also learn how to dine out in restaurants the slimming, healthy way and prepare delicious packed lunches which are highly nutritious and low in calories to eat at their desks when they are in a hurry.

Last but not least, don't let the stress and strain of a busy lifestyle take its toll on your body, physical and mental health, especially if you are combining the roles of running a job, home and family. You need to learn the secrets of conscious relaxation and the benefits of yoga. Make some time every day for deep breathing exercises and meditation. This is a more beneficial form of relaxation than just flaking out in front of the television. Use your leisure time positively to improve your beauty potential.

PAMPER YOUR SKIN AND SOLVE ANY PROBLEMS

At the beginning of autumn many women's skin is left with less than happy memories of summer holidays. Not only does it appear dull, lifeless and perhaps lined, it also has a jaundiced look which is the result of a fading tan. Your skin is probably less healthy at this time of the year than at any other season. The damaging effects of sun and sea water, not so noticeable then, are all too apparent now. Your skin has literally 'aged' over the summer months. This can be very dispiriting unless you adopt an optimistic attitude and take positive action to repair summer damage. Fortunately, skin is a fairly resilient organ and it will respond to care and nourishment if it has not been neglected for too long.

Preserving your tan

If you have spent time, trouble and money acquiring a summer tan which suits you, you naturally want to keep it for as long as possible. Back in your everyday routine there are a number of things you can do to preserve it. The main destroyers of a tan are bathing, the action of soap and the friction of bath towels. Add oil to your bath water, or oil your skin before bathing. Do not use bubble bath, bath salts or any other bath additive which contains drying agents or detergents. Try to pat the skin dry and above all avoid vigorous rubbing with a towel. After bathing moisturise the body with a rich skin lotion. If the weather is warm and sunny, as it often is in early autumn, make sure that your face and limbs (if they are exposed) are well-lubricated to prevent further drying out. If you are really keen on keeping your tan, then you should invest in a course of sun lamp treatments to boost your colour as it begins to fade.

Have a professional facial

One of the best ways of revitalising and nourishing your skin after summer damage is to have a professional treatment at a beauty salon or clinic. It is money well-spent, since it is a great morale booster and the treatment will be adapted to suit your individual skin type, whether oily, dry or normal, and condition. It can also be a most relaxing and therapeutic experience – a welcome 'pause' in the life of many busy women.

You can, of course, give yourself a facial at home, and if you really cannot get to a salon, do give yourself a skin revitalising treatment at this time of the year. However, a home treatment is rarely as pleasurable or as thorough as one you would get professionally in a proper salon.

A salon facial usually starts with thorough cleansing of the face and neck with cream or lotion. The skin is then examined for blocked pores, blackheads and other blemishes. The face is then steamed, often with ozone, for about 15 to 20 minutes to encourage the pores to push out dirt and impurities. Blackheads are then removed from the centre of the face where the skin is oily. The face and neck are then massaged in gentle circular movements to stimulate circulation and reduce puffiness caused by fluid retention. Finally the forehead is massaged to reduce stress and tension lines.

A few salons now use an electric current to deep cleanse the skin and extract impurities. This is particularly effective for sun-damaged skins. This is because the sun thickens the outer layers of the skin and so makes it less able to absorb nourishing creams. A very mild electric current allows nourishing liquids to penetrate deep into the lower layers of the skin, whereas a simple facial massage cannot do this. Another electrical treatment for greasy skins passes serums deep into the skin which helps to dry out excess oil. These deep-penetration treatments are usually followed by a second form of electrical stimulation which closes the pores and tones and smoothes the skin. There is a definite improvement in appearance and the skin looks clearer and healthier after treatment.

Beauty salons and clinics are also well-equipped to deal with skin problems such as acne and whiteheads although there are some effective remedies you can carry out yourself for skin blemishes. Once you know what causes your particular skin problem, you may be able to cure it quite easily.

Dealing with skin problems

Most women suffer from skin problems from time to time, ranging from the odd pimple to acne, allergies, broken veins and skin rashes. Some are temporary and easily cleared up, others more persistent.

Acne: this is a distressing problem, especially for young people whom it most afflicts. Basically it occurs when the male and female hormones are imbalanced and do not regulate the output of oil from the sebaceous glands. Overactivity results in excess oil secretion and thickening of the pore openings. The pores becomes blocked and after a while they form a pimple, a whitehead or a blackhead. If these become infected, producing red, swollen acne spots, the skin's inner layers can be damaged, resulting in permanent scars.

Good skin hygiene and really deep cleansing are important. Do clean the skin at least twice daily with a mild soap or cleanser and do not use astringent or alkaline products which could aggravate the problem. Gentle medicated products can be helpful but use them in moderation. Diet is also important and an excess of fatty foods and sweet things will not help the condition. You can try taking additional supplements of vitamins A, B3, B6 and C as these are thought to be beneficial in treating acne.

Although healthy diet, good skin hygiene and some medicated products are useful, acne is not something that can be easily cured with do-it-yourself treatments. Seek medical advice. Antibiotics and X-rays have been successful with some sufferers and natural sunlight and ultra-violet treatments have also been used. However, rely on your doctor or dermatologist to advise the best treatment for you.

Blackheads: these are simply pores blocked with oil which blacken on exposure to the air. They are not formed by dirt trapped underneath the skin, as many people mistakenly believe. They are probably the most common form of skin blemish and most women have had them on the forehead, nose or chin where they tend to form. Scrupulous cleansing, regular exfoliation and a weekly face mask will help prevent them as will the use of a facial washing brush or rough face cloth. It is not advisable to squeeze out offending blackheads yourself – you run the risk of infection and possible scarring. Go to a professional salon where removal is carried out expertly however tempting and easy it may be to have a go yourself.

Spots and pimples: there are few women who have not had the occasional spot or pimple – usually just before a period or when they are unhealthy or under stress. Thorough cleansing and regular exfoliation can help prevent spots – give yourself a deep-cleansing and exfoliation treatment before your period as a preventative measure. When pimples do appear, keep the spot area scrupulously clean and use a medicated lotion or cream on the spot until it clears up. Do not squeeze spots, however pus-filled and unsightly they are. The infection could spread and lead to permanent scarring. Use a concealing stick to hide blemishes of this kind.

Whiteheads: these are tiny beads of trapped oil just below the surface of the skin and show up as tiny hard bumps the size of a pinhead. They usually form on bony areas of the face such as the cheekbones or around the eye socket. Massage often helps to get rid of newly-formed whiteheads and they may disappear in a few weeks with the use of a mild medicated lotion. If they persist, it is not wise to try and remove them yourself. Go to a trained beautician who will do it correctly, without risk of infection.

Brown patches: these can occur on the skin at any age but appear frequently in women who are taking a contraceptive pill or pregnant. They seem to be triggered off by hormonal changes and exposure to the sun. Unfortunately, they are not easily removed except with bleaching creams, which are very harsh on the skin, or by skin peeling. Both methods are fairly drastic and should not be undertaken without expert advice. On the whole it is better to disguise brown patches with clever make-up – and stay out ot the sun, otherwise the patches will become even more prominent.

Red or broken veins: these occur mostly in women with fine-textured, dry skin in the form of a fine red tracery of veins on the cheeks. They can be caused by exposure to extremes of temperature, by over-use of harsh alcohol toners or simply by age. Severe broken veins will need professional treatment, usually sclerotherapy which involves injecting a chemical fluid which dries out traces of blood and seals off broken capillary walls. Milder cases can be treated with electrolysis which cauterises each capillary. Clever make-up can also help to conceal broken veins.

Sensitive and allergic skin: there is little doubt that over the last two decades, the incidence of allergic reaction has increased considerably. It is certain that pollution of the atmosphere has something to do with it and that the regular and widespread use of perfumed soaps and cosmetics, deodorants, household cleaners and washing powders, particularly of the biological sort, is a major factor. There is also a vast range of foods, chemical additives and products to which people develop allergic reactions – and to complicate matters, some suddenly develop allergies to substances and products they have used for some time for no apparent reason and they may not even be aware of this or what substance is causing the trouble.

On a purely practical level, if your skin develops an irritating rash, try to find out what is causing it. This means keeping a record of what you eat and the cleaners and cosmetics you use. Gradually eliminate the suspect products until you find the offending substance. This may take time, particularly if your allergic reaction is to some common foodstuff, but is well worth the effort in the long run. Perfumes, certain metals, detergents and some cosmetics are known irritants for many people so start with them first. Most women find the culprit relatively easily.

If you suspect you are allergic to ingredients in some cosmetics, then try a patch test by putting a trace of the product in the crook of your arm and leave for 24 hours. If there is any redness on the spot or you feel any irritation do not buy the product. One answer for many women who suspect a cosmetic allergy is to use hypo-allergenic cleansers and make-up. Known irritants, such as perfumes, have been kept out of the formulation of these products and they have been exhaustively tested. However, a few women may still react adversely to one or other constituent in such products. If, after some effort, you cannot isolate the allergenic substance, you should consult your doctor or a dermatologist who will carry out more exhaustive tests with a wide range of known allergens.

Moles: these can be most attractive as the past use of beauty spots as a cosmetic aid proves, but they can be unsightly when sprouting isolated hairs. Do not attempt to remove hairs yourself. Consult a dermatologist (not a beautician) who will recommend the safest treatment.

Sallow skin: this often goes with dark hair and eyes and an olive or greasy complexion that tans easily. Basically, this skin tone is inherited and there is little you can do to change it except liven up the skin's appearance. Stimulate circulation by taking more exercise, preferably out of doors, and help the skin to shed dead cells more quickly by regular massage and toning treatments. Use a complexion brush to clean the skin and treat yourself to a face mask once a week, and to exfoliation frequently. One advantage of sallow skin types is that it does not dry out or wrinkle as quickly as other skins; it therefore looks more youthful for longer. Skilful make-up, including a well-chosen blusher, can lift a sallow skin.

Puffy eyes: lack of sleep will obviously produce puffy eyes, but quite often they are caused by using too much or too heavy an eye cream at night. Splash the eyes with cold water in the morning to reduce puffiness and change to a lighter cream or give it up altogether. Puffy eyes may also be hereditary. You can also soak two cotton wool pads in toner and place one over each eye. On relatively youthful faces these can be disguised by make-up, but as you grow older puffy eyes may turn into drooping lids. At this stage there is very little you can do about them except have them removed by cosmetic surgery.

Open pores: these inevitably go with coarse, greasy skins. There is very little you can really do to close the pores, except temporarily. Be careful about what products you use. Some contain irritants which cause localised swelling and shrinking of the pores but these can also stimulate the glands into further oil production, so adding to the problem. Thorough cleansing, regular exfoliation, using a complexion brush, and a stimulating mud mask will all help. Use oil-free foundation to minimise their appearance and prevent the formation of blackheads and spots.

Facial rejuvenation

After the damage the sun has done to your skin, it is a good idea to take stock in autumn and try a short rejuvenation programme to get it back in condition – moist and smooth. Remember that healthy skin depends on blood flow, good diet, relaxation (because stress can tense your facial muscles and lead to frown lines) and a skincare system that is practised twice-daily and suits your skin. Don't just assume that your skin is its normal, oily or dry self. Re-examine it in the light of autumn and reassess its condition. As stated before, skin changes all the time due to environmental conditions beyond your control, hormonal changes in your body and the harmful agents with which you come into contact. If you spent some time in the summer outside in the hot sun, then your skin may be drier than you think.

Make some resolutions for autumn that will help rejuvenate your skin and give yourself a beauty boost.

1 Give up smoking

The nicotine in cigarettes interferes with blood supply and waste removal from your skin by constricting its tiny blood vessels. Smoking can even lead eventually to wrinkles and ageing of the skin, so if you are a regular smoker, try to cut down or give up completely. There are so many health benefits as well as beauty pluses to be gained.

2 Drink less alcohol

Too much alcohol can affect your skin, too, by dilating the blood vessels. You may have noticed how people who drink very heavily sometimes have puffy-looking skin and bags under their eyes. Try to limit your alcohol consumption to, say, one glass of wine a day.

3 Check out your environment

Hot central heating, low humidity, drying air-conditioning systems and cold weather all dehydrate your skin and it can ill afford to lose moisture at this time of year. If you live or work in a very hot atmosphere, then a humidifier or some potted plants will help to restore some moisture to the air. If you can control the temperature, don't have the heating blazing away all the time full blast – it is not good for you. Also, if you live or work in a big city, you may have noticed how dirty and grimy your skin is at the end of the day. Always cleanse extra-thoroughly in this sort of environment to get rid of any pollutants and dirt. Then tone and moisturise as usual.

4 Give your skin an autumn boost

Invest in a new moisturising cream to rejuvenate your skin this autumn. There are many good moisturisers that protect you against dehydration yet leave no greasy residue. Some can even be used during the day under your usual make-up. Older women might even like to try an ampoule system which stimulates cell metabolism and restores cell vitality to lacklustre skin.

A NEW COLOUR STRATEGY FOR YOUR MAKE~UP

Autumn make-up

Now that the autumn's come and you are back into your work routine you need to develop a fast make-up system which is easy to apply and looks good. Our step-by-step system is easy to administer and takes only about 10 minutes – perfect if you are busy and rushed, getting up in the morning or late for work. No matter how sleepy you are feeling, you can tackle it and be confident that you are looking good. You could try a new look for autumn and subtly change the colours fom brighter summer shades to more autumnal golds, bronzes, browns and russets. Unless you are striving to keep your tan through the coming months, it may be better to tone down your foundation, too, and opt for a paler more seasonal colour.

If you are thinking of changing your job and making new applications for work, you might consider what kind of make-up looks best for an important interview. There is practical advice on this and how it may help you to clinch the job you want.

Adapt your make-up to the changing light

After the harsh bright sunlight of summer which showed up every imperfection in your skin, the light at this time of year is softer and more flattering. Unless you are trying to keep your suntan going throughout the coming months with top-up tanning treatments and artificial creams or dark foundations, it is best to opt for a paler shade which is the perfect match for your skin tone. If you go to buy a new foundation, remember that the colour it appears to be in the jar is rarely the same as it will look on your skin so do try some out on the inside of your wrist before investing in an expensive pot. A warm beige or slightly pinky foundation with a hint of peach or rose will look warm and natural on most skins. The secret is to warm up your autumn complexion without making it look too vibrant, tanned, dramatic or winter-pale. Study the new shades and cosmetic ranges in glossy magazines or on the beauty counters of a big department store, and see what seems best for your skin type and tone.

For work, especially in a big city, you need a foundation that will stay looking good all day without constant retouching – a perfect base which stays matt and even without going blotchy or oily as the day wears on. Then, if you are going out in the evening, you need only touch it up faintly or redust with a little powder. You can make your skin look more autumnal by choosing a more earthy shade of blusher in a rich brownish tone – natural and understated, and only lightly blushed or applied along the cheekbones. The total effect will be chic and businesslike – just perfect for a careerwoman with a demanding job.

Interplay light and shade

The subtle use of highlights and shaders will help you contour your face, giving it shape and depth. Apply on top of your flawlessly matt foundation in soft, shimmering tones – but not in too dramatic or heavy-handed a manner. You really must take care when doing this and apply only very light touches or the result will look unnatural, streaky or blotchy. Dab a touch of highlighter on your upper cheekbone, and on browbones above your eye shadow. Smooth darker shaders well into your foundation so that there are no visible 'joins'. Try out one of the new range of colours, perhaps in a cinnamon or an earthy terracotta to add some warmth to your natural skin tone.

Spotlight on your eyes

Your eyes are probably one of your best features and the focal point of your face, so they deserve special attention. There are so many lovely colours to choose from, and for a smart businesslike effect which reflects the new season, too, you could try out a palette of golds, bronzes, russets, coppers and browns. The main thing is to choose shades that will blend in well with your eye colour and hair colour and match the clothes you wear. Try to match up all these different factors to get the right shade. Having said that, browns and golds suit most women, whatever their colouring. After the natural look you adopted for summer, now you can really go to town on your eyes and outline them with a soft dark kohl pencil or liner to make them more stunning and noticeable. Apply a couple of coats of mascara to give your lashes extra length and thickness. However, bear in mind while doing this that the effect should still be suitable for work and the office. What looks terribly glamorous for evening might be too harsh or overdressy for the daytime.

Lips should look rich

Dark lips in uncompromising shades of red, brown, brick and orange can all be very effective in autumn, adding depth and richness to your face. Warm colours will make lips look fashionably strong-looking and you should outline them carefully to prevent a smudged effect. Choose a lipstick that has built-in moisturisers to protect lips from dehydrating colder weather, central heating and air-conditioning. A lipstick that has staying power, even through cups of coffee and snacks, will help keep lips moist and prevent cracking. It is annoying to have to keep reapplying lipstick so opt for one of the expensive ones that lasts well.

Create the right interview face

If you are being interviewed for a new job it is always best not to wear too-dramatic and over-colourful make-up. The total effect you create should be efficient, tidy and competent, and your make-up can reflect this in the same way as your attitude and your clothes. A pale foundation, some understated blusher and a natural-looking eye make-up usually look businesslike. You need to use your make-up to create a cool and sophisticated image which looks attractive and gives you confidence in an interview situation. Above all, never do the following things with your make-up:

1 Use sparkly, metallic eye glosses and shadows. These are better suited to evenings out than interviews.
2 Overdo your face shaping and contouring. If it does not look understated and subtle, then leave it out altogether. Just use a concealer to hide any blemishes and blend into your normal make-up.
3 Wear a bright shade of blusher which stands out in spots of colour on your cheeks.
4 Apply several coats of mascara – keep them looking as natural as possible.
5 Wear very trendy colours, unless it is a job in a young bright company which wants someone with a youthful, fashionable image. If possible, stick to soft earthy tones which look natural and sophisticated. There is no point dressing soberly in a slick city suit if you top it with wild and colourful make-up. Be sensible in your approach. Before you arrive, pop into a powder room to check your make-up, touch up skin, eyes or lipstick if necessary and brush your hair. If you are happy about your appearance, it will give your confidence a much-needed boost and you may perform better in the interview situation itself. Try to combine acting naturally with being assertive and individual.

Using the right tools

When you have a busy job and little time to make-up in the morning, good tools can help you be quicker and more efficient – good-quality brushes for applying powder and brushing eyebrows; a make-up sponge for an even foundation; a face-sized mirror on its own stand; a headband to keep back strands of loose hair; and boxes of tissues and cotton wool balls will all help. Always make-up in daylight if you can and do this near a window so that the light cannot play tricks on you. Making-up quickly in artificial light can create too harsh an effect which will look odd when you get to the office and the sun is up. Check that there are no shadows falling on your face and that it is in the full light for the best results.

The no-fuss guide to a quick face

Even if you are in a hurry, you can still achieve a perfect make-up in about 10 minutes. The more you practise, the quicker and easier it will be as a natural look to suit you evolves. Even if you are still half-asleep you will be able to go through the motions of making-up and the results will look flattering. To achieve this you have to opt for an uncomplicated colour-coordinated approach which looks light and natural – nothing too fussy or dramatic. You will need a few basic cosmetics and tools: foundation in a soft shade, concealer, blusher and powder for your skin. Liner or eye pencil, shadow and mascara for eyes. And a lip brush and lipstick for your mouth. For speed, cosmetic pencils are best – a colourful lip pencil, kohl liner pencil and eye pencils in different shadow colours. They are so easy to use and need not be applied as carefully as liner, lipstick and shadows, but you must choose what suits you best. Follow the step-by-step guide to achieving a perfect look with the minimum of effort.

You will see from studying the pictures overleaf that you do not require any special skills to apply your make-up really quickly and get your routine down to a fine art. However, you should not attempt to rush this basic system and take short-cuts unless you know they work, or you may bungle the job and spoil the overall effect. Nothing looks worse than streaky foundation showing the 'join' where chin meets neck; or inexpertly applied and smudged liner and mascara which makes eyes look bruised instead of glowing.

When the evening comes and you want to go out to a party, the theatre or dinner, you need not remove all your make-up and start again. Just retouch your foundation, blusher and concealer, and apply more eye make-up and lipstick on top of the old, either in the same colours or using totally different ones. Nothing could be simpler and less trouble. This transformation can take place in minutes seated at your desk in the office or in front of the powder room mirror if necessary. For more advice on changing daytime into evening make-up with easy-to-follow step-by-step pictures, turn to the section on Winter make-up on page 126.

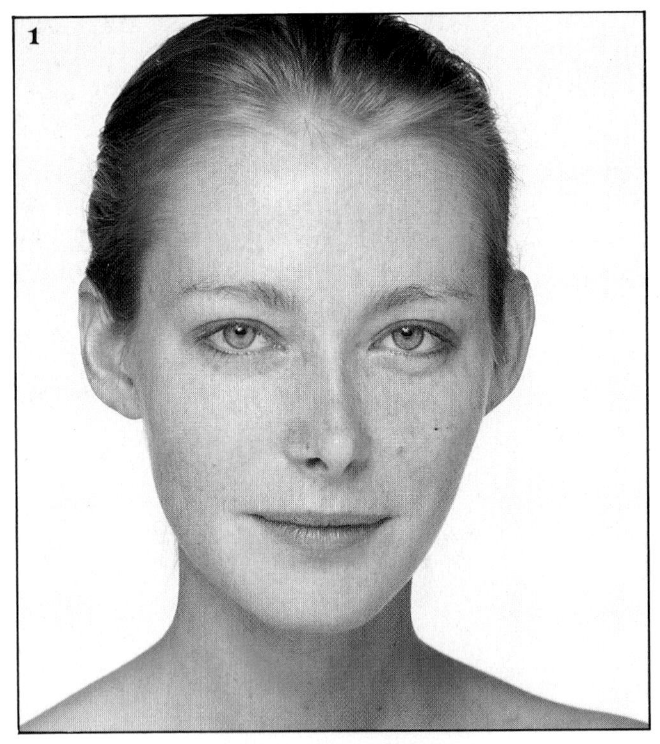

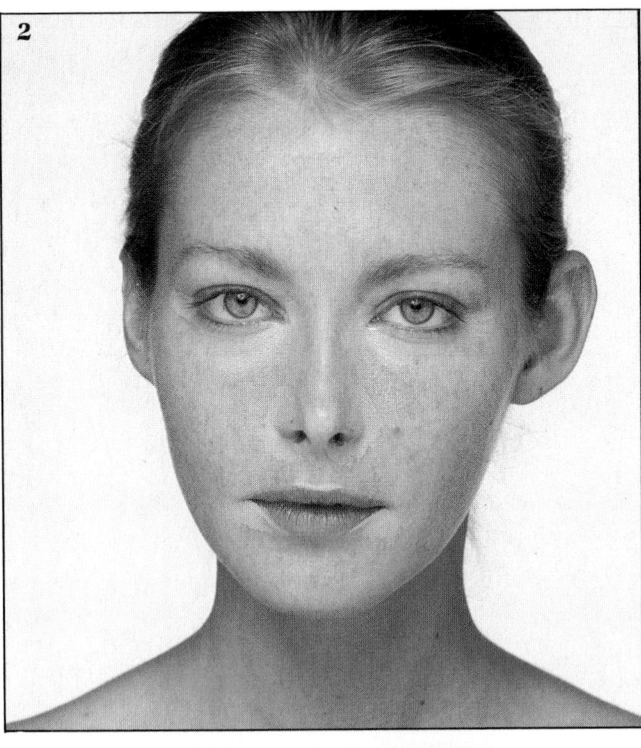

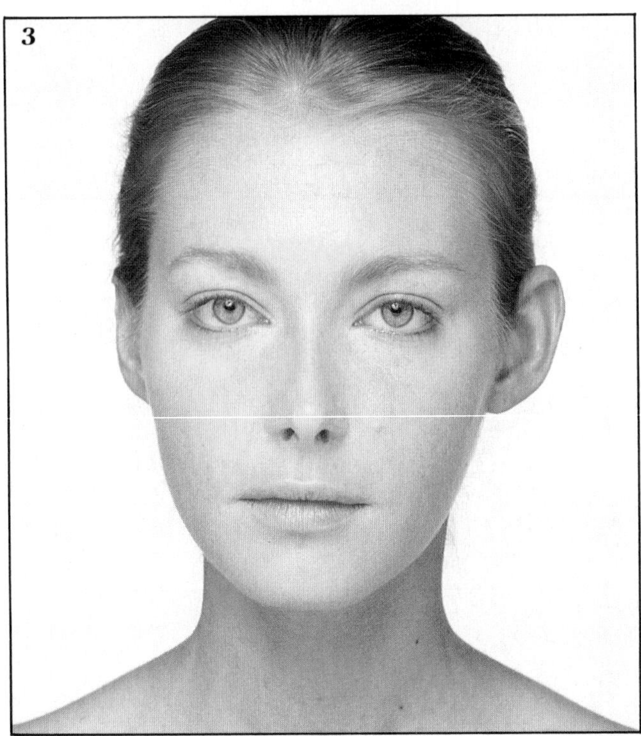

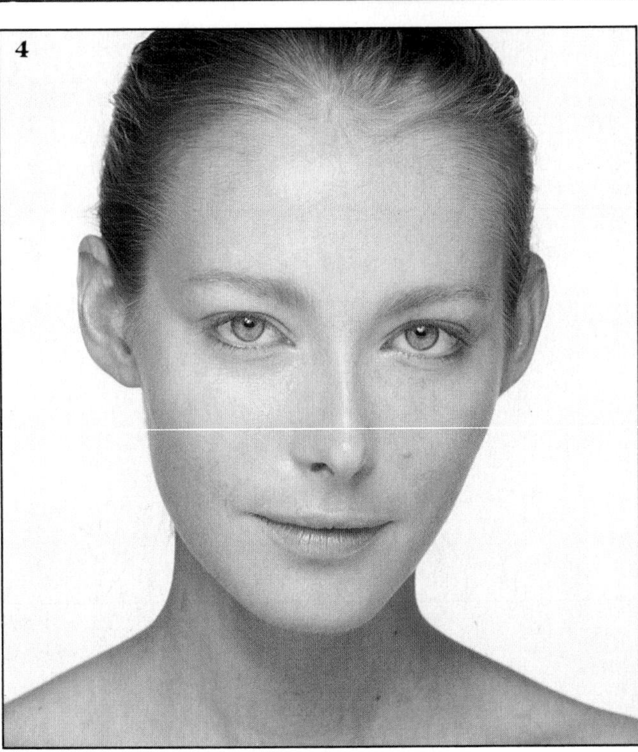

10-minute make-up

1 *Cleanse your face thoroughly and tone and moisturise before applying make-up. Do this every morning.*

2 *Gently smooth concealer into skin around the mouth, the nose and under the eyes. You can also use it to cover up any spots or skin blemishes.*

3 *Now dab some foundation onto cheeks, chin and forehead and smooth into your skin to give an even finish. Do this gently and don't drag the skin, especially delicate tissue under eyes. Smooth foundation just under the chin so there is no 'join' mark under the chin and it is evenly blended.*

4 *Shape your face by applying softly a little blusher in a subtle pink or shade that suits your skin colour, along the cheekbones and the sides of the forehead along the hairline. If it is powder-based, fluff on gently, or blend lightly if it is creamy. Dust face with translucent powder.*

5

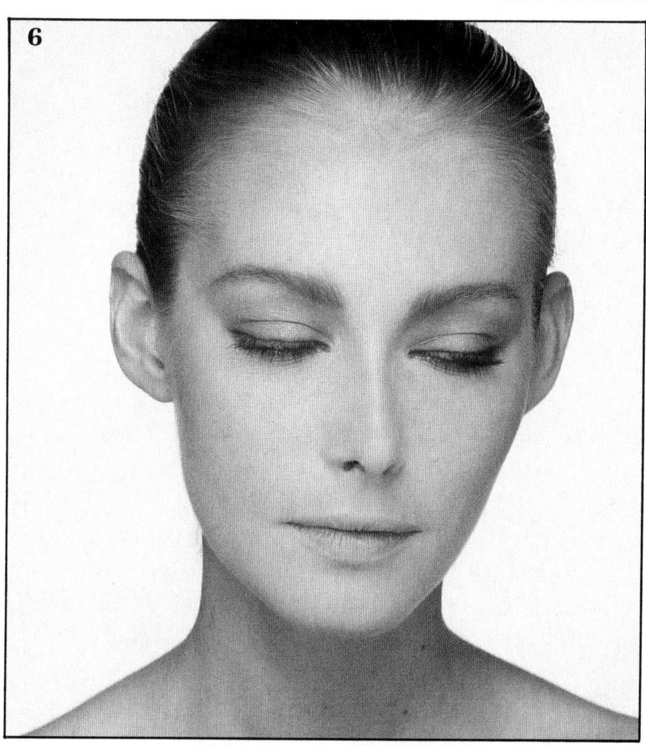
6

7

8

5 Outline your eyes subtly with soft pencil in black or brown along the edge of the top lid just above the eye lashes and below the lower lid. Don't fill in the corners of the eyes. Smudge the lines gently for a more natural effect, especially the corners.
6 Apply some eye shadow, darker shade in the socket, blending it upwards towards brow line. Use paler shade on the lids, getting darker at the outer edges. Smooth on gently and subtly.
7 This step shows the effect of the eye make-up with eyes wide open. Add a little dark shadow under the eyes at the outer corners if wished.
8 Finally, apply one or two coats of mascara to the eye lashes to make them look thicker, longer and more lustrous. This will add the finishing touch to your eyes. Lastly, outline your lips with a lip brush and fill them in with lipstick. Blot or powder and apply another top coat.

AUTUMN COLOURS FOR GLOSSY, SHINING HAIR

Even if you have looked after your hair in the sun, it will have suffered some inevitable wear and tear. Fairish hair, attractively lightened by the sun's rays, looks fine in warm weather and bright light, but as the days close in in autumn the sun's damage can become apparent in the form of dull, lifeless hair. Now is the time to repair this damage and to think about your general 'back to work' looks. Adapt new seasonal fashions to styles which take you through into winter. This applies to your hair, as well as your make-up and clothes.

Recondition your hair

First of all, recondition your hair. There are few women who will not need to do this after summer. Remember that instant conditioners merely 'paint over' damaged hair; they mask but do not repair torn or broken hair. For this you will need a treatment that penetrates to the cortex, supplying protein that bonds and strengthens the hair. A deep conditioning treatment really is important to get your hair back into peak condition, particularly if you intend to colour or curl it as part of your autumn look. Try one of the many protein treatments on the market which will restore suppleness to hair of all types, lengths and colours.

If your hair is very dry and lifeless, you may need an oil or wax treatment. These have to be steamed or heated into the hair to provide nourishment and are rather time-consuming and messy – but they are invaluable for hair that has been 'processed' by tinting or perming. Try a non-colouring henna conditioning wax, available from many cosmetic manufacturers and suitable for fair as well as dark hair. Henna, as well as being a colouring agent, is also a natural conditioner. Non-colouring henna wax is made from leaves of older plants that have lost their dyeing properties but still retain their natural organic conditioning properties. If this does not agree with your hair, do not worry because there are many other hot oil treatments that you can try.

Autumnal hair tones

One way of acquiring a new seasonal look is to colour your hair. Fortunately, modern hair tints are relatively safe and well-formulated – most change the tone rather than the shade of hair and the aim of a good colourist is to create an effect that is so subtle and natural it is almost impossible to tell if hair colour has been used. Your goal should be to enhance and highlight your hair's natural tones so that it provides an attractive frame for your face and make-up. Autumn is a particularly suitable time to shade your hair since the hair generally suffers less damage in cooler months, and you will also be able to set aside time for retouching more easily than in summer.

What colour?

Whatever your hair colouring, you should only go two or three shades lighter than your natural colour and you should never attempt to go darker. Never try to completely alter your hair colour. Blonde hair on women with naturally dark hair and skin colouring looks distinctly odd (and vice versa).

The most popular colours nowadays are honey, hazel, chestnut, russet and, for brunettes, burgundy browns. For blonde and light brown hair which is going grey, use a soft tone, the same as your natural colouring. Grey-haired women should never be tempted by blue or mauve rinses which are terribly ageing. In autumn, you may wish to opt for a seasonal shade such as copper, auburn, burgundy or gold. This will depend on your natural hair colouring and skin tone, of course.

Types of hair colouring

Temporary rinses last from one shampoo to the next. They work by adding colour to the outer cuticle of the hair and do not penetrate the hair shaft itself. Many contain softening conditioners and they do not damage the hair. Rinses can add highlights to your own natural colour or tone down shades, and they can help to disguise grey hair. Their effects are very subtle. You can also use them for a trial run before you decide to have your hair permanently coloured.

Semi-permanent tints coat the hair shafts and also slightly penetrate them. Their effects only last through four or five shampoos with the colour fading gradually. They have an enriching effect on hair tones but because they contain no peroxide, they cannot lighten the hair. They can add golden tints to blonde hair and liven up dull, mousy hair. Like temporary rinses, semi-permanent tints can be applied at home and again they are useful for trying out a hair colour to see if it suits you.

Permanent colourings: contain both bleaching and penetration agents which can strip away natural colour and alter the hair's structure. These are the most versatile of all tints since any colour change is possible – lighter, darker and colouring grey hair. Although over the counter products are available for home use, you are best advised to go to a professional for permanent colouring, where patch tests (to test your skin for allergic reactions to the dye chemicals) and strand tests (to test the colour reaction of your hair) are automatically carried out. If you must colour your hair at home, these two tests are essential. Rubber gloves should be worn to protect your hands and a barrier cream smoothed around the hairline to prevent the forehead from being dyed. It is important to read the manufacturer's instructions very carefully. Be strict about timing. Too many minutes can not only greatly affect colour depth but also badly damage the hair. Permanent hair colouring needs retouching every three or four weeks at the roots, especially if you opt for a lighter shade.

Vegetable/herbal colourants

Nowadays many women prefer to use natural substances which are non-toxic and do not alter the hair's structure. Henna has been used for thousands of years by brunette and black-haired women to add chestnut, rich auburn, mahogany or red tones to their hair. It is also one of the finest conditioners for the hair.

Henna is difficult to use because it varies in colour, and results depend on the henna, your hair and the desired result. It is best applied by professionals; amateurs at home, unused to controlling the colour, can end up with, at worst, garish orange hair or, more often, a colour quite different from what they expected. Henna must never be used as a colourant on blonde, fair or grey hair – it will turn it bright yellow or orange. It gives marvellous shine and richness to brunettes and those with very dark or black hair. When mixed with other vegetable dyes such as camomile, it can add brown to reddish tones to dull, mousy-brown hair. Unlike other permanent colourings, henna will not need retouching for several months.

Camomile is another natural herb and it is used to lighten fair and blonde hair. It highlights fair hair in a most subtle and attractive way but several applications are necessary to get the right blend of tones. Many hairdressers offer camomile treatments or you can make your own camomile rinse. Dried camomile flowers can be bought at most herbal beauty shops. Make an infusion by adding 30ml/2 tablespoons of dried flowers to 550ml/1 pint of boiling water and simmer for about 15 minutes. Strain, cool and use to rinse the hair after shampooing.

Sage can darken and improve the colour of the hair. It can add depth to brown tones and help disguise 'salt and pepper' hair. Make a strong infusion using 45ml 3 tablespoons of fresh sage (or 15ml 1 tablespoon of the dried herb) and 15ml 1 tablespoon of tea leaves. Pour over 550ml/1 pint of boiling water and simmer for 30 minutes. Leave for several hours before straining into a clean container. Dab into the hair every day until it reaches the desired shade.

Highlighting, streaking or tortoiseshelling the hair

One way you can give yourself a fantastic new look for the autumn is to highlight or streak your hair. When well done, this is one of the most attractive ways of transforming your hair. It is also the most expensive colouring process at your hairdresser because it is the most time-consuming. Highlighting, streaking or tortoiseshelling can only be done by a professional colourist – attempting it yourself could be a disaster.

There are two main methods of highlighting. The most successful way is to section off strands of hair and bleach them separately in strips of aluminium foil. Another quicker method is to place a plastic cap or layers of clingfilm punctured by tiny holes on the head. The hair is lifted through in fine strands with a crochet hook and bleach is applied to the strands outside the cap. The disadvantage of this method is that it is difficult to get to the roots of the hair and to get an even, all-over result.

Streaking involves lightening the edges of the hair in slender streaks, following the line of the hair cut. Tortoiseshelling or 'lowlighting' adds darker streaks, by tinting, to light hair to achieve a natural brighter effect. Another partial colouring method is the 'collage' when three shades are blended together in the hair. Fine sections of hair are bleached and then some of your natural hair is added and is tinted along with the bleached hair. The result is three shades of, say, brown – chestnut, blonde and caramel. It is very effective.

If you are thinking of colouring your own hair at home instead of visiting a qualified hairdresser, you should take great care and follow these general guidelines.

Rules for home-permanent colouring

1 Carry out a skin test. All permanent colourants have a toxic base and although few women react unfavourably to this, you could be one of them. Cleanse a small area of skin behind the ear with alcohol or surgical spirit. Prepare a small amount of colouring and apply to the skin. Leave for 24 hours and if there is no sign of irritation, the product is safe to use.

2 Carry out a strand test. This is to test the effect of colouring on your hair. Cut off several strands of hair near the scalp, and mix a little of your dye solution and apply to the hair following the timing instructions for colour development exactly. Look at the results in a strong light to check that they are favourable.

3 Do not colour the hair if bleaches, henna or treatments for restoring grey hair have been used recently.
4 Do not colour the hair if it has been permed or straightened within the last two weeks.
5 Allow plenty of time for a home-colouring treatment and read the instructions very carefully before beginning.
6 The equipment you will need is: a non-metallic bowl; the contents of the colouring pack; rubber gloves; cotton wool; a clock with a timer; an old towel or shirt; barrier cream to be applied around the hairline to prevent any staining of the skin.
7 Throw away any unused mixture after colouring hair. It could be harmful to children. Wash the bowl thoroughly immediately after use.
8 After colouring your hair, use only mild shampoos. Medicated shampoos could intensify the colour of your hair. Keep your hair well conditioned after colouring as it may have a slightly drying effect.

Your autumn hairstyle

Autumn means back to work for many women. While in summer you may have worn your hair in a simple drip-dry style suitable for sunbathing and swimming, your work-day hair may need to be a little less casual. It depends, of course, on where you work (if you work) and what you do. Jeans and long flowing hair look great in may work situations but a lot of women work in offices, shops and showrooms where such a style would be inappropriate. In general, your work style needs to be smart and practical, understated rather than too glamorous, outrageous or casual. This applies to your clothes, your make-up and your hairstyle. Consider your working lifestyle and think how best to dress and look the part for your job with as little effort as possible if you are very busy.

When it comes to your hair, short or long styles which do not need shaping every day are best. Remember the use of setting lotions, tongs and sprays is time-consuming, especially first thing in the morning. Choose a style that is chic and easy to manage. For short straight hair, a cap cut brushed forward over the forehead or a teddy boy style can look tailored without being severe. Curly or wavy hair can be cut into simple natural styles that neatly frame the face. With medium-length hair, try easing it away gently from the face with combs or pins for a more business-like look. Long hair can look elegant and attractive put up in a classic French twist or knot, or swathe it back into a loose bunch at the nape of the neck to keep it tidy, businesslike and off the face.

Dealing with problem hair

If you are in a tangle with your hair, you must find a solution to the problem now before it gets worse. There are so many sophisticated treatments for problem hair nowadays that there is bound to be a product to suit your needs. In the autumn, you are probably thinking of adopting a new hairstyle or colour to re-charge your batteries and get you in the right mood for the colder weather and latest fashions, so don't neglect any problems and hope that they will go away. Act now to put them right and have beautiful soft, shiny hair as a result.

Dry and damaged hair: this may have been caused by too much sun or even chemical damage from over-perming and colouring. It is worth splashing out on a really effective formula to restore it to its former glory. Choose a gentle shampoo with a built-in humectant to attract and bind moisture within the hair. This will also prevent water loss. Some products even contain chains of amino acids (proteins) that cling to the hair and strengthen it. Attached to the hair fibres, they perform a protective function and can even make fly-away hair more manageable if they have the ability to neutralise its electrostatic charges. Hair technology has come a long way and it is possible now for a product to restore the hair's cuticle and give a smooth, glossy finish. There are even special conditioning treatments for sun-damaged hair.

Oily hair and dandruff: you should not use too powerful a shampoo if you have an oil problem as it is important not to strip the hair completely of its natural oils. If you do so, far from making the hair dry, it is more likely to encourage the sebaceous glands to produce even more oil than before, and thus a vicious circle is formed from which there is no escape. Oily hair requires a gentle cleansing shampoo so that it can be washed frequently to keep it looking fresh and glossy. Dandruff often goes hand in hand with oily hair and this will benefit too from a mild cleanser rather than a harsh medicated one. This way, you can wash your hair as often as you like instead of feeling that you should wait several days between shampooing and suffer the oiliness and unpleasant appearance. There are even special finishing conditioning rinses formulated for oily hair which are free of fatty alcohols and oils but still add body and shine.

No time to wash your hair?

Now that you are back at work and very busy indeed you might find it hard sometimes to put adequate time aside for washing your hair. If this is the case, then you should choose a short cut that will pretty well take care of itself and need the minimum of blow-drying and setting (certainly, no rollers). But however rushed you are you should always shampoo thoroughly with the correct hair cleanser and condition if necessary. It does not take long to wash your hair in the shower before leaving home in the mornings or before you go to bed.

EXERCISE AND POSTURE FOR YOUR WORKING LIFESTYLE

This autumn, take a good look at your posture and avoid the debilitating back ache that often goes hand in hand with a sedentary office job and commuting to work. Do not stop exercising just because the nights are drawing in and the warmer days of summer have gone – you can still enyoy your favourite sports and work-out inside in a gym. You can even do mini-exercises at your desk to keep you fit and trim. Lastly, don't neglect your teeth – they often come a poor second best to the rest of your body but good dental hygiene should be an important part of your daily beauty routine. If you are starting a new job, a dazzling confident smile showing even white teeth will make a good impression.

The perfect spine — the secrets of good posture

If you have an office job, you may spend several hours every day sitting on an uncomfortable chair bent awkwardly over your work, strap-hanging on tubes, trains or buses, or hunched up over the steering wheel of your car. This can lead not only to bad posture but also to back problems, particularly tension and pain between the shoulder blades and in the lower back area. The way you hold yourself and move – in other words, your posture – is an intricate part of your beauty. You cannot be really beautiful if you collapse haphazardly into chairs and walk with a stoop, for instance. Naturally good posture helps you to move erect and gracefully without putting strain on the body, and as a result you will feel less tired.

Your spine is made up of a chain of vertebrae which are interlinked with discs of cartilage. Powerful muscles hold everything in place and support the structure. When your spine has a natural, easy alignment, it works as nature intended – nerves do not become trapped, vertebrae are not compressed and there is no danger of friction or bone and joint displacement.

You may have noticed that when you are feeling tired or depressed your posture reflects your mood – your shoulders stoop, your spine bends, you walk with a slouch, the muscles in your lower back ache and even your breathing may quicken and become more shallow. This does nothing at all for your health or looks. You will look taller and slimmer if you stand, sit and walk more erect with your stomach and buttocks tucked well in. You need not stand stiffly to attention like a soldier on parade with your shoulders thrown back unnaturally. Your spine is not meant to be pencil straight. It is naturally curved into a gentle 'S' shape, but the curves should be gradual, not exaggerated.

Strengthening your abdominal muscles

One way to improve your posture is to strengthen your stomach muscles. If these are weak, you will be more inclined to slouch and suffer from back ache. This is because you compensate automatically for the weakness in this area by shifting your weight backwards and letting the back muscles take the strain instead. This is a common fault in pregnant women. As the weight of the baby increases at the front, they shift their centre of gravity and let themselves in for a lot of unnecessary pain in the lower back region. One of the best ways to make your stomach muscles stronger and firmer is to do some sit-ups every day – when you get up in the morning or before you go to bed at night. They will help tone up these muscles and flatten them, too, so that you will end up not only with better posture but with a flatter tummy also. However you cannot rush into them – they have to be done carefully and gradually and the repetitions should be built up slowly, a few at a time, as you get stronger. Otherwise, you will feel very stiff and may even injure yourself.

Sit-ups: lie on the floor on a mat or towel with your arms at your sides and your knees bent, feet shoulder distance apart and flat on the ground. Slowly raise your head and upper body off the floor and roll up into a sitting position with your arms extended in front of you. Exhale as you do so and then roll gently down again without letting your head and shoulders touch the floor. Inhale and come up again. Repeat 10 times. Remember that it is most important that your feet should stay flat on the floor throughout. If you find this difficult, you can leave your legs flat on the floor and place your feet under a bar to hold them, or get somebody to sit on your legs and hold them down. When you can accomplish 10 sit-ups with relative ease, try adding on another five and so on until you can do 40 to 50 non-stop and without any discomfort.

Strengthening your back muscles

Swimming, yoga and general stretching exercises are all good ways to strengthen your back muscles and keep them well-toned. Here is a special exercise to help

strengthen your lower back and remove any lingering tension in this area. It is especially therapeutic if you have back pain. Perform it after your sit-ups to release the abdominal muscles.

Knee-ins: lie on your back flat on the floor on a mat or towel with your knees bent and feet together flat on the floor. Now bend your right knee in towards your chest and clasp it tightly to you in both hands. Really hug it hard and hold for a count of five. Lower it to the floor and repeat the exercise with the left knee. Now pull both knees tightly into your chest and hug them to you. Repeat the whole exercise five times and then relax.

The golden rules for avoiding back ache

Here are some hints on how to avoid back pain. Try to be aware of your posture and the way you sit, walk and stand at all times.

1 Never bend over from the waist to pick things up. Always bend at the knees with your back straight and then squat down to lift up an object. As you straighten your legs, slowly raise it up – this puts less strain on your back as your legs take the effort instead.

2 If you are carrying heavy bags, divide the weight between both hands so that it is evenly distributed and well-balanced. Try to carry them without any tensing of your shoulders.

3 When you walk, try to imagine an invisible thread running along your spine from the top of your head to your bottom and keep it straight. Hold in your stomach, tuck in your buttocks and let your arms swing naturally.

4 Do not wear high heels except for special occasions, parties and going out. They are not suitable for everyday wear and walking long distances. They contribute to bad posture by throwing your weight artificially forwards in such a way that your centre of gravity shifts and your spine is thrown into an exaggerated curve. As a result, your weight is not distributed evenly across the base of your feet and they will ache and may even develop callouses or curled-up toes.

5 Do not sleep on too soft a mattress. Feather beds are very nice and comfortable but your spine *needs* support and a firm mattress is best for this. Many back troubles and pulled muscles happen, amazingly enough, during the course of a normal night's sleep, caused by sleeping awkwardly on a soft mattress. If so, you will probably be told by your doctor to put a board underneath it to harden the surface. Avoid back pain and expensive visits to the osteopath for manipulation by investing in a good, hard mattress – it can still be very comfortable.

6 When you sit down, make sure that you support your back adequately, whether it's in your car, an armchair or at an awkward angle. Unfortunately, most chairs are not made with lumbar supports as an integral design feature. So although they may be aesthetically very attractive, you may have to place a cushion strategically behind you to fill any gaps and support your spine. When sitting down, you should also endeavour to put your feet flat on the ground at all times, so adjust the chair height if necessary.

Lastly, if you do get back ache and it won't go away, do not leave it unattended – seek medical advice without delay (unless, of course, if it is associated with your normal period pains). You may have to see a professional physiotherapist, chiropractor or osteopath for more instant relief. They often seem to get better results than just courses of tablets and painkillers or lying flat on one's back.

Keep that body moving

Regular exercise will keep you fit and slim and you should continue to run, cycle, swim in an indoor pool or work-out at least three times a week. In fact, by now exercise should be so instinctive to you and so integral a part of your routine that you will feel unhappy with yourself and even guilty if you skip it for whatever reason. If you still haven't discovered what you really enjoy most and seems right for you, then why not look further afield at some new areas of sport – perhaps, more exciting activities like wind-surfing on a local lake or reservoir, climbing or caving. Or you could visit the local riding stables or take up golf, badminton, squash or roller-skating. There are so many interesting activities for you to choose from and they will all help you get and stay trim and fit. This is very important as the weather gets colder and coughs, colds and other infections become commonplace. You need to be as fit and healthy as possible, in peak physical condition, if you are to stay beautiful and free from illness in the coming winter months.

It is a good investment to join a gym, health studio or exercise class – whichever is handy and affordable for you. Go along and attend the classes in your lunch hour or after work in the evenings. It is fun to exercise with other people and meet new friends. It may also give you the stimulus and moral support you need to stick at it, especially if you find it hard to discipline yourself to a regular committment. Go regularly, two or three times a week if you can.

Many healthclubs have now got their own facilities for women's weight-training. There may be a Nautilus machine or simple dumb-bells and Heavyhands-type equipment. If you want to lose some weight or stay trim, working-out with weights is a marvellous way to get into shape and make you leaner and firmer all over. Do not worry about building up unattractive muscle bulk – this is impossible if you work-out only with light weights and perform properly devised routines with lots of repetitions. Also, women do not have the male hormone testosterone which builds muscle. If you are interested in weight-training, find out the nearest gym to you and ask about joining. Make sure that there is a qualified instructor to advise you on the safety aspects of weights and how to use them properly. He may even devise a special programme to suit your individual needs.

If you want to try some weight training at home, you should start off with only light weights of, say, 1.25kg/ 2½lb. You can progress to heavier weights as you get fitter and stronger, but there is never any need to labour under really heavy ones. You should use weight training for getting fitter – not developing power and bulk. You can purchase the weights in most good sports shops or the sports departments of big stores. Small dumb-bells are quite suitable as is the Heavyhands euipment which is easier to hold and actually moulds to the shape of your hands.

Always warm-up before you work-out with weights with a few simple stretching exercises to ease out muscles, and even a short jog or some room-running. This will raise your pulse rate and warm-up your body, and there is less risk of injuring yourself with the weights. Here are a few simple exercises for you to try:

1 Warm-up swings

This exercise can be performed first as it will help warm-up muscles. You need a single dumb-bell. Stand up straight with your feet shoulder distance apart. Hold the weight in both hands and raise your arms above your head, extending them straight up above you. Now bend your knees and as you do so, swing your arms down in front of you and between your legs, still gripping the weight with both hands. Slowly raise them again and repeat the exercise 10 times.

2 Side lifts

Stand with your feet shoulder distance apart, arms outstretched to either side, holding a weight in each hand. Now slowly lower your arms until they hang at your sides and then slowly raise them again. Repeat the exercise 10 times for strengthening the upper arms.

3 Triceps extension

This exercise is particularly good for toning up and firming flabby upper arms, a common problem among many women. Stand with your feet shoulder distance apart, a weight in each hand. Now lean slightly forwards over your feet, keeping your back straight and with your arms bent close to your sides and elbows level with your back. At the same angle, keeping your back perfectly straight, extend your arms backwards from the elbows parallel to the sides of your body. Then slowly raise the lower arms to the original position. Repeat 10 times.

4 Open and close butterflies

Lie flat on your back on a bench or unpraised surface with your knees bent and feet flat on the bench. Now, holding a weight in each hand, raise your arms above your chest with elbows bent and hands touching in the centre above you. Slowly open your arms to the sides still keeping the elbows slightly bent and hold for a count of three. Slowly bring them back into the centre. Repeat the exercise 10 times. It is an excellent way of firming the bust and shoulders.

Do take care when working-out with weights and performing the above exercises as rushing them or performing them badly could lead to injuries – pulled or torn muscles.Use only very light weights and stop immediately if an exercise starts to hurt. Use smooth, slow movements – never jerky, fast ones.

Mini-exercises at work

Even at work, sitting in your desk, you can practise some mini-exercises to help keep you fit. Remember that the way you sit is important not only for avoiding back ache but also to prevent varicose veins forming. This is particularly important if you are pregnant. Never sit with your legs crossed – this constricts blood flow and contributes to bad circulation in your feet and lower legs. Neither should you sit on a hard chair that presses into the backs of your thighs. Over a long period of time, this may have similar effects. Now that you are sitting correctly and comfortably, here are some simple exercises for you to try:

Foot and ankle rotations: perform this exercise if you have been sitting down for a long time to tone up and improve circulation in the lower legs and feet. Keeping your legs still, rotate your feet in large circles exaggerating the movement through all the points of the compass. Rotate at least 10 times to the right and then reverse for 10 rotations to the left.

Stomach and buttock firmers: as you sit at your desk, practise pulling in your stomach muscles and holding them tight for a count of five. Relax and repeat several times. Now squeeze your buttocks tightly and hold for a count of five. Relax and repeat several times. Both these exercises will help strengthen and tone up flabby areas.

Ceiling kiss: you can even work on a double chin. Just stretch your head and neck backwards as far as they will go and hold for a count of eight. As you do so, purse your lips together and really reach up as if to kiss the ceiling. You will feel all the muscles in your neck and jaw tightening as you do so. Now lower, relax and repeat five times.

Teething problems – don't neglect dental care

Good dental hygiene and strong white teeth are among your greatest beauty assets. The state of your teeth and gums are exposed to all the world every time you laugh or smile so make sure that they can stand up to this attention. Every time you eat a sugary biscuit or cake, suck a sweet or forget to brush your teeth, you are putting your teeth and gums in danger. Gum disease and tooth decay are now commonplace in Western society, mostly as a result of our over-refined, too-sweet diet which is high in sugar. Many women have lost most of their teeth by the time they reach their forties, some even years before this. If you want to keep your own teeth and not end up with a mouthful of crowns or dentures, you should get into the habit of good dental hygiene. Most dental problems are caused by unhealthy gums and so you should be aware of the early-warning signals (swelling, soreness and bleeding when brushing) and act accordingly. Careful brushing, daily flossing, regular check-ups with the dentist, and cutting down on your sugar consumption will all help extend the life of your teeth and keep them looking clean and smelling sweetly. You can smile with confidence if you know that your teeth are pearly-white and looking good. Nobody wants to show blackened teeth or even stumps! So that they stay looking their best follow our dental care programme below:

1 Eat a healthy diet and cut out sugar:

Sugar attracts harmful bacteria which combine with your saliva to adhere to the surfaces of the teeth and in the cracks between the teeth and gums. They form acids which gradually erode the teeth and cause decay. This phenomenon is known as plaque. If you eat less sugar you will be less susceptible to plaque. Stop eating sweets, chocolate, cakes, pastries and sweetened desserts. Use other natural sweeteners instead such as dried fruits, fresh fruit, and honey (in moderation). They are healthier and better for your teeth.

2 Brush your teeth regularly

Regular brushing is one way of waging war on plaque. You should brush at least twice a day, certainly first thing in the morning when you get up and before you go to bed at night. It is also a good idea to carry a little toothbrush around with you in your bag and brush after meals. Choose a medium-hard brush which is multi-tufted with a good, straight handle. Squeeze the toothpaste straight onto the brush without wetting it first – water changes the bristle action and makes it less effective. Brush your upper teeth first in small circular movements working from the top of each tooth down, back and front. Then brush the lower teeth, working up from the base of each tooth. Do not rush this brushing – it doesn't matter if you spend five minutes on it. Just make sure that your teeth are really clean and rinse away any toothpaste thoroughly. Many experts believe that those pastes which contain fluoride are best but this has become a controversial issue, and it is best to find the product you like most – which tastes and smells pleasant and leaves your teeth really white and feeling fresh and clean. After brushing, you can check how effective it has all been with the help of a disclosing tablet (available from most chemists). This will show up any areas of plaque still remaining by turning them red, blueish or purple. It is a good test and the results will probably surprise you.

3 Floss to destroy plaque

To get rid of any plaque left after brushing, you should next floss your teeth and gums. This is a very simple procedure and a good habit to adopt. Most cavities start between the teeth themselves, and flossing is the only sure way to remove any plaque hiding in these cracks. Take a length of unwaxed dental floss, about 40cm/16in long, and wrap the ends round the middle fingers of both hands. Now coax the middle section which is free between two teeth and pull it backwards and forwards in a sawing motion getting deeper into the crevice. This will remove any food residues and plaque. Gradually work round your mouth, top and bottom. Your gums may bleed a little at first so be gentle on them, but they will get stronger and more resistant as they get used to regular flossing. Do not worry if they bleed initially however.

HEALTHY WORKING LUNCHES AND DELICIOUS FAST FOOD

Many working women complain that it is difficult to eat a really healthy diet when they have little time for cooking and shopping. They tend to eat snack foods and quickly heated convenience meals which lack important nutrients, especially the vitamins, minerals and protein which are essential for health and maintaining good skin. If you want to look your best at work, you should not skimp on meals nor eat too many 'junk' processed foods. When you are working hard in a demanding job or experiencing a particularly stressful period at work, you need to eat well and protect your body and beauty. To stay fit and healthy, you should have three nutritious meals a day. Snacking on unhealthy, high-calorie foods like chocolate bars and crisps or grabbing a cup of coffee between tasks will inevitably lead to weight gain, poor skin and a greater susceptibility to stress and tension.

The combination of stress and bad diet can produce a whole range of problems, ranging from digestive disorders, migraine, insomnia and nervous tension to high blood pressure and even gastric ulcers. Some women seem to thrive on a certain degree of stress. They need the challenges and excitement it brings to function at their full capacity and to be truly productive and creative. But however dynamic or aggressive you are in your work, you will feel even healthier and more energetic if you improve your diet.

It is easy to feel tense or depressed in the autumn as the long hot days of summer fade away and the weather turns colder and greyer with the fall and the approach of winter. Going back to work after a holiday in the sun creates its own tensions. It is more important now than ever that you eat plenty of high fibre, nutritious food to protect your skin and hair and give you the necessary energy to attack your work. If you have a house and family to look after as well, you should be extra-vigilant. Here are some tips on how to dine out in restaurants the healthy way, eat nutritious packed lunches and cook quick evening meals which taste and look wonderful.

Healthy business lunches

Although it is enjoyable to be wined and dined at the best restaurants on an expense account, you should keep a careful watch on what you eat and drink or you may find that your waistline is slowly thickening and you will no longer be able to fit into your favourite clothes. Unfortunately, many of the dishes offered in good restaurants are high in calories, saturated fat and sugar, so you must be able to study a menu with a discerning eye and identify the healthy dishes.

Realise, also, that too much wine is bad for your skin. Not only is it high in empty calories, but it also stimulates your appetite so that you eat more food than you need. It depletes your body's supply of B and C vitamins (both of which are needed for healthy skin) and causes damage to skin cells. In fact, it is one of the best ways (apart from excessive sunbathing) to age your skin prematurely. Tiny broken veins on the face are a sure sign that you may be drinking too much alcohol. Of course, a glass of wine is relaxing and enjoyable, especially with a meal in good company but in the long run, too many glasses could be harmful, especially to your looks. If you have to dine out often, order sparkling mineral water with your wine and keep watering it down in the Continental manner. This drink, known as a spritzer, tastes refreshing and delicious and is a healthier alternative to wine by itself. Keep topping up your glass with water and the waiter will not be able to fill it up with wine each time he passes. This way, you can enjoy your drink, protect your skin and not offend your companions by refusing a drink.

In order to eat out healthily, it is not necessary to suffer and exist only on grapefruit appetisers, steak and salad and black coffee. At a vegetarian restaurant serving whole-food grain, vegetable and fruit dishes, especially soups, salads and casseroles, you will have a wide choice of healthy dishes to choose from, but in most other eating places you will have to exercise a little caution. Here is a brief guide to help you make an informed choice:

Italian: for a first course, you can try the grilled sardines or king prawns, antipasto salads, *prosciutto* (parma ham) with melon or figs, risotto, *tonno con fagioli* (tuna and bean salad), tomato, mozzarella and avocado dishes or stuffed vegetables. Most pasta dishes are very healthy – choose ones in tomato, not creamy, sauces with seafood, vegetables or meat. Italian restaurants also tend to cook delicious meals with calves liver (rich in iron and folic acid), chicken and veal. Grilled fish,

Chinese leaves and orange shreds (recipe page 110)

shellfish and *spiedino* (kebabs) served with rice are also nutritious. If you really must have a dessert, opt for fresh fruit salad, sliced oranges or some mozzarella cheese.

French: this cuisine has a reputation for being deliciously rich, creamy and high in calories, but if you eat the simple cooked dishes and grills you can still enjoy a delicious healthy meal. Resist the temptation to order something in a creamy sauce – do it too often and you will soon be putting on weight. For an appetiser, try consommé or a delicious soup like *bourride* or *bouillabaisse* which are full of healthy vegetables, fish and shellfish. Most pâtés tend to be fatty, but a *nouvelle cuisine* vegetable terrine served in a fresh tomato sauce makes a good substitute. Salad and grilled fish or shellfish are also suitable. For the main course, poached fish, grilled meat or poultry with vegetables or a salad, and a sorbet, fresh fruit or low-fat goat's cheese for pudding.

Chinese: because there are no creamy sauces or saturated fats used in Chinese cookery, it is a very healthy cuisine, based on fresh vegetables, rice, noodles, meat, fish and poultry, usually steamed, poached or quickly stir-fried in the minimum of oil with spices and aromatics. Stir-fried vegetables retain their nutrients, flavour and crispness, so you have almost *carte blanche* to eat whatever you like in a Chinese restaurant.

Indian: most dishes are OK to choose as, again, they are low in saturated fats and contain very healthy ingredients. Try some of the dishes that feature yoghurt and avoid the over-sweet desserts.

Packed working lunches

Most of us are not so fortunate as to be able to eat out every day and we have to rely on a working lunch served on the desk-top. If you usually dash out and grab a greasy hamburger and chips or a white bread sandwich and a packet of crisps, you may be wondering why your skin looks oily or blotchy. Try a healthy sandwich in wholemeal bread from a whole-food sandwich bar or make your own and take it to work with you in an airtight container to keep it really fresh.

A more exciting alternative is wholemeal pitta bread pouches filled with a mixture of salad, beans, chicken or fish, or even the leftover risotto or chilli con carne from your dinner the previous evening. You can buy the pitta in specialist Greek food stores, delicatessens and even some supermarkets. Freeze them if you like until required. They are easy to hold and eat in your hand without any mess or washing-up.

Vegetables, bean, rice and lentil salads can be prepared and stored in Tupperware, taken to work and eaten with a fork or spoon. If you have a sweet tooth take a crunchy granola bar or some dried fruit to nibble. Raw vegetables (carrot strips, pepper slices, cherry tomatoes, chunks of cucumber and celery) can be dipped into low-fat quark or cottage cheese mixed with chopped fresh herbs. A pot of low-fat yoghurt or some fresh fruit makes an easily transportable dessert, while a thermos of hot home-made vegetable soup will keep you going on chilly winter days, and chilled soup is refreshing in summer.

All these recipes are suitable for taking to work. They should be stored in a refrigerator if possible to keep them cool, especially in well-heated buildings or hot weather, but it is not essential.

Sandwiches

Use 100 per cent wholemeal bread spread with only a scraping of vegetable margarine or low-fat spread. Fill with one of the following suggestions:

1 Low-fat soft cheese with chopped chives, shrimps and cress or watercress.

2 Low-fat soft cheese with sliced banana and raisins.

3 Low-fat soft cheese with smoked salmon and chopped parsley or cress.

4 Mashed avocado with lemon juice (to prevent discolouration) and sliced cooked chicken.

5 Mashed avocado with lemon juice, shredded lettuce and prawns.

6 Mashed avocado with lemon juice and yoghurt, and chunks of tuna.

7 Sliced tomatoes, mozzarella cheese and chopped basil or thinly sliced onion.
8 Watercress, sliced orange and cottage cheese.
9 Low-fat soft cheese, sliced fresh pineapple and mustard-and-cress.
10 Canned or fresh crabmeat, mashed avocado and mayonnaise.
11 Low-fat soft cheese, raisins and chopped nuts.
12 Sugarless peanut butter and mustard and cress.
13 Sliced chicken or turkey breast with lettuce and tomato.
14 Sliced raw mushrooms, lemon juice and crisp grilled bacon rashers with mayonnaise or avocado.
15 Tuna and sliced tomato with mayonnaise and beansprouts.
16 Smoked ham *prosciutto* with sliced mozzarella and tomato.
17 Brie with sliced orange and watercress.

Pitta bread parcels/pouches
Split a wholemeal pitta along the edge and gently open to form a pouch. Stuff with one of the following fillings:
1 Shredded lettuce, chopped cucumber, diced tomato, walnut, cubed apple, natural yoghurt and chopped mint or chives.
2 Cooked kidney beans, shredded carrot, sesame seeds, peanuts, chopped parsley and shredded lettuce in natural yoghurt and orange juice.
3 Peperonata (*see* recipe) with watercress.
4 Ratatouille (*see* recipe) with anchovy fillets and chopped parsley.
5 Cos lettuce, cucumber chunks, sliced tomato, chopped spring onion, feta cheese cubes and oregano in natural yoghurt.
6 Red lentils cooked to a thick purée with chopped apple, onion and spices.

Salads
Make up a salad and place in Tupperware or a similar container to keep really fresh and crisp. See also the salad recipes in the Summer Diet section.

Peperonata
1 large onion, sliced
2 cloves garlic, crushed
2 large red peppers, seeded and sliced
30ml/2 tablespoons olive or sunflower oil
salt and pepper and pinch of sugar
2 large green peppers, seeded and sliced
675g/1½lb tomatoes, skinned and chopped
few coriander seeds, crushed
chopped parsley

Gently sauté the onion, garlic and pepper strips in the oil until tender (about 15 minutes) without browning. Add the tomatoes and cook hard for about 30 minutes until the stew is thick and vividly coloured. Add the seasoning, sugar and coriander just before the end. Cool and sprinkle with parsley. This makes enough peperonata for three lunches or pitta parcels. For a hotter variation, add a little chilli or some *harissa* paste.

Ratatouille
1 large aubergine/eggplant
salt
1 large onion, chopped
1 red pepper, sliced
1 green pepper, sliced
2 cloves garlic, crushed
45ml/3 tablespoons olive oil
3 courgettes/zucchini, sliced
450g/1lb tomatoes, skinned and chopped
chopped fresh basil, marjoram or oregano
few coriander seeds, crushed
salt and pepper and pinch of sugar
small bunch parsley, chopped

Slice the aubergine and sprinkle with salt. Leave in a colander until it exudes excess moisture. Rinse well under cold running water and pat dry. Sauté the onion,

Honey chicken with mango (recipe on page 110)

Pepper and scampi kebabs (recipe on page 111)

peppers, and garlic in the oil until soft. Add the aubergine and courgettes and cook until golden. Add the tomatoes and herbs and cook hard until the sauce is thick and the vegetables very soft. Add the coriander and seasoning. Cool and sprinkle with parsley.

Fast food after work

When you get home in the evening, the last thing you will feel like is cooking a complicated meal. When you feel tired, it is tempting to heat up a convenience meal or open a can but you can whisk up a tasty nutritious meal in literally minutes. It is worth investing in good equipment and kitchen gadgetry to help you – you can stir-fry delicious quick meals in a *wok;* heat up casseroles, stews and pasta dishes and cook jacket potatoes in minutes in a microwave oven; whirl up soups in a blender or food processor; and cook delicious kebabs, fish and chicken under a good grill. And if the idea of washing-up after cooking an evening meal is too daunting a prospect, a dishwasher is the answer, either in the form of your partner or a machine. Stack the dishes from breakfast and dinner inside and then switch on, sit back and relax while the machine does all the work for you.

At this time of year when it is getting colder and you may be under additional pressures at work, it is essential to eat properly, although it is never a good idea to have a huge filling evening meal, especially just before going to bed. Try to eat not later than seven o'clock to allow time for your digestion to work and settle down, and keep the meal nutritious but light. Grilled food, salads and stir-fries are ideal in this respect. For dessert, try fresh fruit, low-fat yoghurt, a soft cheese with celery and wholemeal bread or fruit salad instead of a cloying calorie-laden pudding.

Here are some suggestions for fast food. All the dishes are easy to prepare and cook, and the maximum time involved for any recipe should not exceed 30 minutes. They are all healthy and relatively low in calories, too. Quantities given are for one person only.

Fish kebabs

175g/6oz firm white fish
1 small onion, quartered
3 chunks red pepper
3 chunks green pepper
2 cherry tomatoes
Marinade:
30ml/2 tablespoons sunflower oil
juice of ½ lemon
salt and pepper
fresh or dried oregano

Cut the fish into good-sized chunks and mix well with the marinade ingredients. Put aside while you prepare the vegetables. Thread the fish and vegetables alternately on to 1 or 2 kebab skewers. Place on a grill pan and brush with the remaining marinade. Grill for about 10 minutes, turning the kebabs occasionally. Serve with salad or puréed carrots and rice.

Spaghetti alla carbonara

100g/4oz wholewheat spaghetti
50g/2oz diced ham
15ml/1 tablespoon oil
1 egg, beaten
30ml/2 tablespoons grated Parmesan
15ml/1 tablespoon soured cream or yoghurt
salt and pepper
chopped parsley

Cook the spaghetti in boiling salted water until tender. Drain and keep warm. Sauté the ham in the oil until golden. Add the spaghetti and stir in the beaten egg. Stir in half the Parmesan and the cream. Season and sprinkle with the parsley and remaining cheese. Serve with a green salad.

Italian frittata

1 small onion, thinly sliced

15ml/1 tablespoon oil
1 courgette/zucchini, sliced thinly
1 clove garlic, crushed
1 large tomato, skinned and chopped
2 large eggs
salt and pepper
15ml/1 tablespoon grated Parmesan
few fresh basil leaves or parsley, chopped
knob of butter

Sauté the onion in the oil until soft and golden. Add the courgette and garlic and sauté until lightly browned. Add the tomato and cook until thick. Beat the eggs, seasoning, cheese and herbs together. Fold in the vegetable mixture. Heat the butter in an omelette pan and, when sizzling, pour in the egg mixture. Turn down the heat to a bare simmer and cook gently until set and golden underneath. Place under a hot grill for a few seconds to set and brown the top. Serve with salad.

Liver in orange juice
2 thin slices calves liver
15ml/1 tablespoon oil
½ small onion, chopped
2-3 apricots, stoned and halved
½ small avocado, sliced
45ml/3 tablespoons orange juice
salt and pepper
15ml/1 tablespoon chopped parsley

Sauté the liver and onion in the oil for about 2 minutes each side. Add the apricots and avocado and cook gently. Remove the liver and fruit to a warm dish. Add the orange juice and boil hard until it reduces and looks syrupy. Pour over the liver, season and sprinkle with plenty of chopped parsley.

Italian chicken breast
1 chicken breast (boned and skinned)
30ml/2 tablespoons oil or margarine
50g/2oz mushrooms, sliced
45ml/3 tablespoons Marsala or port wine
chopped parsley

Sauté the chicken breast in the oil until golden-brown. Add the mushrooms and sauté until golden. Add the Marsala and cook over high heat until the sauce is thick and syrupy. Sprinkle with parsley. Serve with a jacket baked potato or noodles and a crisp salad.

Stir-fried ginger chicken
1 chicken breast, skinned and boned
15ml/1 tablespoon oil
½ small onion, quartered and layered
½ red pepper, cut in chunks
50g/2oz beansprouts
1 spring onion, chopped
small piece root ginger, grated
10ml/2 teaspoons cornflour
75ml/3floz water
dash of sherry
5ml/1 teaspoon soya sauce
dash of oyster sauce
salt and pepper

Cut the chicken meat into chunks and stir-fry in the oil over high heat until tender. Add the vegetables and ginger and stir-fry for 4 minutes until tender but crisp. Mix the cornflour with the remaining ingredients and add to the wok. Stir until the sauce thickens. Cook for 2 minutes. Serve with rice.

Grilled sole with bananas
1 medium sole or flounder
dot of butter or oil
salt and pepper
1 banana
15ml/1 tablespoon oil
30ml/2 tablespoons mango chutney

Place the sole on a grill pan and dot with small pieces of butter or brush with oil. Season well and grill for about 5 minutes each side until golden and cooked. Meanwhile, slice the banana diagonally and sauté in the oil until golden. Heat the mango chutney without boiling. Serve the sole garnished with the banana and chutney with a crisp green salad.

Chinese leaves and orange shreds
100g/4oz Chinese leaves, shredded
salt and pepper
15ml/1 tablespoon olive oil
rind and juice of 1 orange
good pinch ground nutmeg

Blanch the Chinese leaves in boiling water for 3 minutes. Drain and sprinkle with seasoning. Mix the oil and orange juice and toss the leaves in this mixture. Shred the peel finely and scatter over the top. Add the nutmeg and serve.

Honey chicken with mango
1 chicken breast or joint
15ml/1 tablespoon melted margarine
15ml/1 tablespoon clear honey
10ml/2 teaspoons cider vinegar
2.5ml/½ teaspoon made mustard
1 small mango, sliced
salt and pepper

Smoked mackerel and courgette risotto (recipe below)

Brush the chicken with melted margarine and place in an ovenproof dish. Blend the honey, vinegar and mustard and pour over the chicken. Season and bake in a preheated oven at 190°C, 375°F, gas 5 for 25-30 minutes. Add the mango and cook for 10 minutes longer, basting well.

Pepper and scampi kebabs

2 scampi, tossed in egg and breadcrumbs
2 rashers bacon, rolled
3 button mushrooms
½ small red pepper, cut in chunks
½ small green pepper, cut in chunks
a little oil

Thread the ingredients alternately onto skewers. Lay in a grill pan and brush lightly with oil. Grill until cooked, turning occasionally. Serve with brown rice and a crisp, green salad.

Smoked mackerel and courgette risotto

5ml/1 teaspoon oil
½ small onion, chopped
1 stick celery, diced
½ small red pepper, diced
50g/2oz long-grain rice
150ml/¼pint/⅝ cup chicken stock
salt and pepper
1 small courgette, sliced
75g/3oz smoked mackerel, flaked
juice of ½ small lemon
chopped parsley

Heat the oil and fry the onion, celery and red pepper until soft and cooked without browning. Add the rice and stir well until it is opaque and glistening. Pour in the stock and seasoning and cook gently for 10 minutes. Add the courgette and cook for about 5 minutes more, or until all the stock is absorbed and the rice cooked and fluffy. Stir in the mackerel and lemon juice. Heat through gently and serve with chopped parsley.

Spaghetti Milanese

½ onion, chopped
1 bacon rasher, diced
1 small clove garlic, crushed
15ml/1 tablespoon oil
10ml/2 teaspoons flour
200g/7oz canned tomatoes
15ml/1 tablespoon tomato paste
salt and pepper
pinch sugar
pinch each nutmeg and oregano
squeeze of lemon juice
50g/2oz sliced button mushrooms
100g/4oz wholewheat spaghetti
grated Parmesan cheese

Sauté the onion, bacon and garlic in the oil until tender. Stir in the flour and cook for 2 minutes. Add the tomatoes, tomato paste, seasoning, sugar and herbs and spices with the lemon juice. Bring to the boil, stirring. Simmer gently fo 15 minutes, adding the sliced mushrooms in the last 5 minutes. Cook the spaghetti until tender. Drain and arrange on a serving dish. Spoon the sauce over the top and sprinkle with grated Parmesan cheese.

ESCAPE FROM STRESS WITH RELAXING YOGA

Autumn relaxation

We live in a fast-moving stressful world and many of us suffer intermittently from nervous tension and stress-related problems, such as migraine and insomnia. If you have a demanding job and a busy lifestyle, you need to learn the secrets of good stress-management, how to make stress work positively for you, not against you, and how to unwind and relax.

If you want to be really beautiful, fit and healthy you must look after your mind as well as your body. Learning how to relax will help you to know yourself better, enable you to deal with stress and to sleep more soundly, make you feel more energetic and full of vitality, and speed up your body's natural healing processes bringing important beauty spin-offs in its wake — healthier skin and hair. You must make time for relaxation in your campaign to get fit and beautiful. Remember that your mind and body are fused and interact – they cannot be treated independently of one another. Start by looking at stress and how you can control it.

Stress

Like a clock, if you overwind your body it will start to run down. Perhaps you overwind yourself every day if you dash around a lot, work hard to meet impossible deadlines and stay on top of your job, deal with problems at home and have a demanding schedule. Some degree of stress can be beneficial and enjoyable and enrich your life, but when it runs dangerously out of control and you can no longer cope, it may lead to physical and psychological problems. Many illnesses may be psychosomatic, triggered off by some stressful situation or our inability to cope with everyday pessures.

If this happens to you and you seek help from your doctor, he is quite likely to prescribe a course of tranquillisers to help you through this difficult time but they are rarely the answer, especially if you come to rely on them. They only treat the symptoms of nervous tension and not its root cause. Conscious relaxation, deep breathing and yoga are all more natural alternatives to drugs when it comes to dealing with stress and learning how to unwind. They are good habits to adopt anyway and will help you to monitor stress and cut it out at an early stage.

Most stress is caused by changes and upheavals in our lives – at work, at home, in our relationships with partners, friends and family, moving house or starting a new job. When your body is subjected to stress it undergoes physiological changes – adrenalin floods into your bloodstream, your blood pressure rises, your muscles flex, your heart races, you start to sweat and feel very tense indeed. Even when these symptoms subside you may be left feeling fatigued, giddy and anxious with an aching back or head.

To make stress work for you, you have to channel it into safe outlets and respond confidently and decisively to stressful situations. In this way, you can avoid some of its more unpleasant symptoms and side-effects. For many of us, anger or tears are the usual release valves, but if you are the sort of person who bottles up emotion and resentment inside, you may become very unhappy and tense. You need to find a way of releasing this nervous tension and harnessing the positive energy forces of stress to your own advantage.

You cannot spend your whole life avoiding stress. Many successful, ambitious women love their jobs and seem to thrive on a high degree of stress. It excites them, presents new challenges to be overcome and is a rewarding part of their lives which enables them to fulfil their true creative and intellectual potential. But even they have to stop sometimes, relax and unwind – escape the everyday pressures. The trouble is that they get a thrill when they feel the adrenalin being pumped through their bodies and scent a new challenge. Although we do not all have the same stress threshold, we do have the resources to cope with stress, to reduce it and switch off and relax.

Ways of managing and reducing stress

1 Treat every new stress situation as a challenge and manage it calmly. To do this you have to remove the stressful areas of your life that are not useful or fulfilling. Ask yourself whether your work satisfies you and are there areas you can change for the better? Look at your lifestyle, your relationships, your living arrangements – in other words, examine the stressful areas and cancel out the negative ones. You must be positive and realistic and not attempt to run away from stress. You are in control of your life and your body. You can decide on the quality of your life and what degree of stress you

wish to subject yourself to. You *can* handle it and make it an exciting feature of your life as long as you do not allow it to take control of you.

2 Exercise regularly to reduce stress and nervous tension. Many women have discovered that running, swimming, playing tennis, working-out in a gym or whatever sport they enjoy can help them to channel their energy into a physical outlet and add an extra dimension to their lives. Leisure interests and sport all play their part in helping you unwind and reducing tension. If you feel very wound up and tense, why not try something as simple as going for a walk or jog, doing some gardening,having a swim or attending an aerobics class. All these activities will help keep your mind off your problems and enable you to think more clearly and objectively about them. Regular physical exercise will make you feel more confident and less anxious and release negative tension. When you are more in control of your body you can manage your mind better and the negative impact of stress.

3 Eat a healthy wholefoods diet which supplies all the nutrients your body needs to combat stress and make you feel more alert and energetic. A poor diet that is high in refined food, fats and sugar may lack essential vitamins and minerals and contribute to fatigue, tension and anxiety. The B-complex vitamins are particularly important for maintaining a healthy nervous system. Vegetarians should make sure that they get adequate

B12 to protect them against insomnia, fatigue and tension. As it is found mostly in meat and animal products, they may be deficient unless they eat eggs, milk and cheese. Eating a diet that contains plenty of fresh fruit and vegetables, meat and fish, whole-grain cereals and legumes and low-fat dairy foods will supply all the nutrients you need.

4 Special relaxation techniques can induce a relaxed mental and physical state. You can train yourself to relax in this way in order to eliminate any tension from your body. Just lying down for half an hour is not necessarily relaxing if your mind is in turmoil. This tension may be transmitted through your body and you are quite likely to feel tense and stiff when you get up. You need to learn to relax and breathe correctly.

5 Many women find that yoga is an effective and enjoyable way of bringing relief from tension and exercising at the same time. Just 20 minutes' yoga a day can help you cope better with the pressures of a stressful job. Yoga's devotees claim that it makes you sleep better and feel more energetic, calm and relaxed with a clear, uncluttered mind. You can channel this new-found energy into other areas of your life – your work, family, sport, exercise and leisure interests.

Conscious relaxation techniques

These techniques help you to feel calm and restful. It is a good idea to put aside a little time every day for relaxation just to clear your mind and reduce tension and body stiffness. When you are relaxing, the way you breathe is very important. It is the key to your changing moods and energy levels. You may have noticed how you tend to breathe in shallower, quicker gasps when you are angry or upset. This restricts the flow of oxygen to your body and you may soon start to feel tired and low. However, when you are relaxed, you breathe more deeply and slowly, inhaling enough oxygen to meet your body's needs.

One of the best ways to relax is to lie flat on your back on a hard, level surface. Make sure that you are warm and wearing comfortable loose clothing so that you are not restricted in any way. Now, with your arms loosely at your sides,palms facing upwards, inhale deeply as described above. Exhale slowly and continue breathing deeply with your whole chest and abdomen until you start to feel really relaxed.

Now you can get to know the different muscle groups in your body by gently stretching and flexing them, one group at a time. Work downwards from the head in slow motion. First relax your face so that it is free of tension or any taut sensation. Continue down to your neck, shoulders, chest, arms and hands, stomach, hips, legs and feet. Do this gradually and slowly until your whole body feels totally relaxed. If someone were to pick up your arm or foot and let it drop, it should fall limply of its own accord without you tensing or controlling it – that's how relaxed you should be!

While you are in this calm, relaxed state, try to wipe your mind clean of any conflicting thoughts and emotions. Forget about the things you have to do later or what you forgot to do. Instead, concentrate on making your mind go totally blank; or think hard of a single object to the exclusion of all others. Stay like this for about 10 minutes and then gradually start regaining control of your body working upwards from your feet, to your head. Now finally stretch as far as you can go, feet in one direction, arms and head in the other. Really feel the stretch and your spine extending and then relax. If you are totally relaxed while you are in a meditative state you may even feel as though you are floating inside your body. Although it is so relaxed that it is not really within your control, you still have the power to snap back into reality whenever you wish.

Breathing exercises

You can practise these exercises regularly to feel more relaxed *and* energetic and also to increase your lung capacity and efficiency. Afterwards, you will feel fresher and less tired. There are beauty benefits to be gained from correct deep breathing, too, because it encourages more oxygen to flow to the cells and waste products and toxins to be removed from your system. If practised regularly, your hair will look more healthy and alive and your skin will glow. You should perform these exercises ideally in front of an open window or out-of-doors in order to get as much fresh air as possible, although, of course, this may not be possible in very cold or blustery weather.

1 Sit cross-legged on the floor with your back straight and arms clasped behind you. Inhale deeply and slowly through your nose and rotate your head forwards and over your right shoulder, then back behind you and over your left shoulder to form a complete circle. Exhale and repeat slowly in the other direction from left to right. These head rolls are very relaxing and help eliminate any tension in your neck and upper back. Repeat the exercise three times to each side.

2 Sit in a chair with your back straight and breathe out deeply through your mouth to completely empty your lungs. Now inhale deeply and slowly through your nose. As you do so, raise your arms above your head and push out your chest and abdomen. Hold for a count of five and exhale slowly as you lower your arms. Relax and repeat five times.

Yoga for body and mind

Yoga seeks to integrate your mind, body and spirit so that they exist in perfect balance and harmony. It is only through controlling our bodies that we can come to know ourselves and be in full control of our minds. This it can increase muscular suppleness, diminish tension and bring ultimate peace of mind. In yoga theory, there are two kinds of energy – male and female. The male branch is dynamic, creative and stimulating, whereas the female energy is gentler, restoring and calming. These different qualities and energy types are unbalanced in most people with one usually having precedence over the other. Yoga tries to release both and bring them into a harmonious union and this is reflected in the yoga postures, or *asanas.* Most of the strengthening asanas are performed standing up and these release male energy. The relaxing asanas are mostly done lying down to release female energy.

Breathing correctly right from your abdomen is important in yoga. You should breathe in through your nose and out through your mouth. It has a calming, tranquillising effect and will help blood flow to fuel your muscles as you play them gently to the edge of their stretch. If you wish to take up yoga, the best way to learn is to join an organised class and get expert guidance and tuition. But you can also practise yoga at home perhaps before you get up in the morning or go to bed at night. Stretch gently to warm up before you go into the asanas themselves. Make sure that you move slowly, gently and without straining. Never bounce into a position or move in quick jerky movements as this may damage muscles. Perform each exercise slowly and thoughtfully, stretching until you reach the desired position. Hold it until it starts to feel uncomfortable and then gently move out of the stretch.

It is important to concentrate on what you are doing and block out any other thoughts. This will make you feel calmer and more relaxed as you feel your body flowing with the movement and not fighting against it. If you start to feel any pain, don't think that you have to rise mentally above the pain barrier. Stop at once and relax. Here are three simple exercises to start you off.

The camel: this asana is great for improving posture. Kneel on the floor with your knees shoulder-width apart, back straight and arms hanging loosely at your sides. Take a deep breath and gradually arch your spine, bending slowly backwards over your legs until you can grasp your heels in your hands. Now push your stomach slowly out and forwards to increase the stretch. Hold for a count of five and gradually move out of the stretch.

Forwards stretch: stand up straight, feet together and arms extended above your head. Breathe out and slowly bend over from the waist only, keeping your legs straight and your arms extended in front of you as you lower them to the floor with your palms touching. Bring them in to touch your toes, and raise your head and neck to push them forwards towards the ceiling. All this time your back and legs should be perfectly straight. Hold the pose for a small count, breathing deeply all the while, and then gradually come out of the stretch and relax. Repeat.

The plough: this is a good relaxing stretch to finish a yoga session or a hard work-out. Lie flat on your back on the floor with your arms at your sides, palms facing upwards. Slowly raise your legs off the floor and above your head. Support your body with your hands and lower your legs over your head until they are extended perfectly straight behind you and with toes touching the floor. Hold this stretch for as long as you can.

Overcoming sleeping problems

We all need daily sleep if we are to function properly and be really healthy. It is healing, calming, restorative, restful and vital for your physical and mental health. The amount of sleep we need varies, although eight hours is usually considered an ideal amount for any one night. Some people seem to need more while others function perfectly well on less. As a general rule, the more demanding and stressful your schedule the more sleep you will need, although sleeping too long can sap your energy and vitality. While you sleep, your body is still hard at work, renewing cells, healing tissue, pumping blood and nutrients around your system. If you want to be beautiful, you need sufficient sleep to keep your skin looking healthy and fresh and to avoid dark rings under the eyes.

Many people who worry about being insomniac and get only four or five hours' sleep a night, may be needlessly anxious. Perhaps this is your body's way of telling you that this is all it needs to renew itself. Here are some hints on getting a good night's sleep:

1 Don't take stimulants before bedtime: strong coffee, alcohol and even tea can keep you awake. It is a fallacy to think that having a few drinks will calm your nerves and send you to sleep. Even if you do drop off, you are likely to wake up several times in the night feeling dehydrated and may have a groggy head in the morning. Alcohol tends to make you sleep lightly anyway as it destroys the deep-sleep REM phases.

2 Establish a regular sleeping pattern: go to bed at around the same time every night so that your body clock will find its own rhythm. You will come to subconsciously associate a certain time with sleep and drift off automatically.

3 Do not go to bed until you feel sleepy: you won't sleep if you are wide awake. Stay up a little longer and read a book or watch television, but do nothing that is too stimulating.

4 Have a bath and a hot milky drink: a lukewarm bath will make you feel rested, warm and relaxed. It will soothe your body and ease out any muscular tension. And a hot milky bedtime drink or herbal tea will also be relaxing.

SELF DEFENCE TO PROTECT YOUR WINTER BEAUTY

Now is the time to keep out the winter cold and shelter your skin behind a shield of protective hard-working creams to keep it moist and smooth. The drying effects of cold winter winds and air are cumulative and inescapable, so don't think that you are immune. Good skincare and beauty routines are more important now than ever before.

You can adapt your make-up to winter living by making the most of a pale skin and using more dramatic colours on eyes and lips. Learn how to transform your daytime look into a glamorous party face for evenings just by applying more make-up on top. It is easy to do and you can achieve several different effects building on the same basic make-up. To complement your make-up you will need to give your hair a treat, too. Put long hair up in an elaborate or a simple style, or spray it with colour or glitter. Parties give you the ideal opportunity to express yourself more freely and really experiment with new looks and colours.

Don't let your figure go to fat or develop a winter bulge through neglect. Exercise regularly and wage war on cellulite every night in the bath. You can enjoy warming, nutritious foods without putting on unwanted weight if you are careful about what you eat and how you cook it. You need them for your body's self-defence system – to ward off colds and infections and to stay beautiful. By eating sensibly you can keep your figure throughout the cold winter months.

Damson **Burgundy** **Dove Grey** **Sand** **Mushroom**

WINTER SKINCARE

RESTORE YOUR SKIN'S NATURAL MOISTURE

Winter is the time when we are most aware of our 'ageing' skin. Drying winds and cold visibly affect the skin and rawness, chapping and cracks appear on ill-protected skin. Even well-cared-for skin can show fine lines, wrinkles and drying tautness at this time of the year and these are reminders of encroaching age as far as the skin is concerned. Now is the time to remind yourself that constant nourishment is the only way to keep the skin young and supple and if you have not already done so to take positive steps to slow down the ageing process.

How the skin ages

Most of the body's organs age and deteriorate without us being particularly aware of them. The skin's ageing process is really no different from other parts of the body but it is more obvious and can be much quicker. Women in their twenties can have ageing skin if they have neglected it, and by the thirties and forties almost every woman has some fine lines and wrinkles which are virtually impossible to eradicate. Just how fast the skin ages depends on a number of factors, one of which is heredity. If your mother's skin aged gracefully, it is likely that yours will too. But equally important, if not more so, is how you look after your skin. Regular moisturising and nourishing from an early age can help slow down the ageing process although it cannot, of course, prevent it.

As we grow older, cell growth slows down. This leads to a build-up of dead cells on the skin's surface which causes roughness and dryness. At the same time there is an increase in skin pigmentation so that discolouration begins to develop in the form of freckle-like patches called liver spots. In middle age, hormonal levels also alter, reducing secretions from the sebaceous glands and so causing further dryness on the skin's surface. Wrinkles and crêpey skin appear because of loss of elasticity in the inner layers of the skin, and later as the skin's connective tissues lose their firmness, the skin itself literally ages.

Sunlight and ageing

These inevitable physiological changes can be hastened by a number of environmental factors, the most important of which are the sun and drying winds. The way in which sunlight affects the skin can result in harder, thicker skin, forming in a tough outer layer. The sun is also responsible for permanent changes in the elastic fibres of the dermis. These results are cumulative and not immediately visible. Although over exposure to the sun causes premature ageing, if you confine your sunbathing to a few weeks a year – and always use an effective sunscreen – you are unlikely to suffer too much damage. Those who spend more time in the sun must pay the inevitable price as many women from South Africa, Australia and parts of North America have learnt.

Protecting your winter skin with moisturisers and nourishing creams

It cannot be stressed too strongly that regular moisturising is the best preventative measure for ageing skin. The earlier you start this routine the better, but even a neglected skin will begin to show improvement after frequent moisturising. For dry and ageing skins, the best moisturisers are water-in-oil emulsions. These contain oils, fats and waxes specially formulated to nourish dry and ageing skins. As well as helping to prevent the development of wrinkles, these rich moisturisers are an excellent way to protect the skin from the weathering effects of sun, wind and cold and also from the ever-increasing number of pollutants in the air.

Dealing with wrinkles and lines

Preventing the development of wrinkles, although in the end, impossible, is obviously easier than trying to deal with existing lines, wrinkles and crêpey skin. However, there are many preparations available that claim to get rid of these and generally they do so on a temporary basis by plumping up the skin and getting rid of superficial lines and wrinkles.

Face masks are marvellous short-term rejuvenators. Use them before a special occasion to give the skin a plump, rosier look. The gentle peel-off masks which harden like transparent skin across the face are specially suitable. When the mask is peeled off, the blood vessels expand, giving the skin a glowing look temporarily free of fine lines and wrinkles. All masks increase skin circulation, including the very effective cream ones that are available.

Exfoliation is another technique which removes dead cells and waste matter from the surface of the skin. It can give life to a dull, dry skin and older women should practise it regularly to stimulate new cell growth. Because it surface-peels the skin, one of its by-products is the removal of some, but by no means all, of the superficial lines and wrinkles on the face. It certainly softens them and makes them look less obvious.

Treating with skin creams

Rich nourishing creams, especially formulated for ageing skins, should be used regularly by all women with a dry skin, especially as they get older. These help to prevent the formation of wrinkles but when smoothed into the skin, they can soften any stress and fatigue lines which could become permanent. These creams are applied at night after cleansing and toning the skin. Some are especially designed for busy women and you can choose one that aims to relax tense facial muscles and soothe away strain. Others will revitalise dull, lethargic skin, impoverished by late nights, exhaustion or a demanding lifestyle. These treatments can also be used to good effect before a special night out to soothe or stimulate the skin, as desired.

Facial massage step-by-step

1 After cleansing and toning the skin in the usual way, smooth the cream generously all over the face except for the area around the eyes.
2 Start with the neck and chin as this helps blood supply to the face. Massage upwards with both hands from the base of the neck towards the chin. Repeat four times. Remember at no stage while massaging the face must the skin be dragged or pulled.
3 Jawbone: begin with the fingertips of both hands under the chin and smooth back to the ears in continuous, upward spiralling movements. This helps to release tension lines around the mouth. Repeat four times as before.
4 Cheeks: place fingertips of both hands on each side of the nose and stroke upwards towards the cheekbones with gentle, circular movements. Take care not to drag the very delicate skin around the eyes.
5 Nose: gently tap each side of the nose with the ring finger of both hands. Repeat four times.
6 Forehead: with fingertips of both hands, use circular motions to smooth from the centre of the forehead outwards to the temples. This helps to iron out frown wrinkles. Repeat four times.
7 Eyes: glide the tip of the ring finger of both hands from the outer corner of the eyes towards the inner corner along the lower lid and then outwards over the upper lid. Be very gentle when massaging around the eyes. Repeat four times.
8 After massaging the face, leave the cream for about 10 minutes before gently dabbing off with tissues. For an intensive treatment, leave on overnight.

Biologically-active treatments

'Energising' or biologically-active treatments are among the most exciting and revolutionary developments in cosmetic chemistry. Advances in biological research and the use of sophisticated electronic measuring systems have meant that scientists now know a great deal more about the complex life of skin cells, and so have been able to isolate the active ingredients of youthful skin. One factor, the rate of cell renewal, is of particular importance.

In normal, young skin the continuous process by which young cells are renewed takes approximately 21 days. In the deeper layers of the skin, the cells are nourished by a moisturising fluid which is essential for cell regeneration and reproduction. Daily stress, the damaging effects of the environment and the ageing process all cause a decrease in richness of this essential fluid. Cells take longer to reproduce and moisture loss increases. The result is that skin shows a tendency to dry out, lose vitality and the first signs of ageing – wrinkles – appear.

The downward path usually starts in the early thirties. You can tell if your skin is losing vitality by examining it under a magnifying glass. If your skin appears smooth and even, it is still youthful. If, however, it is finely furrowed with numerous criss-cross lines similar to parchment, the ageing process has begun.

Cosmetic scientists have now been able to produce a biological complex which closely resembles the essential moisturising fluid from which skin cells draw the nourishing regenerative elements essential for healthy life. This substance has been incorporated into nourishing emulsions intended to be worn during the day and into richer creams for night use. Intensive or concentrated treatments are also available. These come in individual tiny phials, one of which is used daily for a set period of time.

Scientists claim that with regular use of those biologically-active products, wrinkles can be improved in some cases by up to 50 per cent. Added benefits are that the surface skin becomes smoother, softer and more resilient. Because biologically-active treatments are in their infancy, it is too early to judge whether they can significantly slow down the ageing process. However, they certainly have immediate and beneficial effects on most skins which are longer-lasting than most other short-term rejuvenating teatments.

Skin peeling

Another method of getting rid of lines, wrinkles and pigment spots associated with ageing skin is skin peeling. This is a drastic treatment mainly used for removing severe acne scars. Known as dermabrasion, it involves taking off one layer of skin and growing another one. There are two methods of skin peeling. The safest is where the skin surface is planed by an electrically-operated abrasive disc or brush – the depth of planing depends on the severity of the case and the process may take an hour or just a few minutes. A scab quickly forms which is treated with ointments until it comes off (the time varies from about 10 to 20 days) and although the skin looks red and sunburnt for some time, it does resume its normal colour. Protection from sunlight is essential for six months otherwise the skin will get an uneven, mottled look. The treatment certainly reduces scars, blemishes and fine wrinkles and makes the skin finer and more resilient, but it can take up to six months before the complete visual improvement is obvious and, depending on how well you look after it, your skin can 'relapse' after a couple of years. It should only be performed by people with proper medical training so do make sure that it is carried out by a qualified dermatologist or surgeon.

The alternative operation to dermabrasion, achieving the same effects, is chemical peeling. This involves the use of a caustic agent which gives the skin a second-degree burn. This is as potentially dangerous as it sounds and many cosmetic surgeons disapprove of it because of the side effects it can cause when the chemical is absorbed through the skin.An alternative treatment offered by some beauty salons is a much gentler, safer form of peeling which is similar to exfoliation.

Cosmetic surgery

This really is the only treatment that can take up to 10 years off your age, but there are many physical, psychological and financial complications that go with it. If you are seriously contemplating plastic surgery, examine your motives. Plastic surgery cannot work miracles and turn you into someone different, nor can it solve emotional problems like a failed marriage or love affair. Simple vanity – the desire to look a little better for your age – is one of the healthiest motives for cosmetic surgery – if you can afford it. Whatever form of plastic surgery you choose, it is absolutely essential that you go to a qualified, reputable practitioner; cosmetic surgery is a branch of medical, not beauty, therapy.

Eyelid surgery

Blepheroplasty, or eyelid surgery, is one of the most popular and effective ways of combating ageing; it heals very quickly and has long-lasting results. Hooded eyes, eye bags and deep lines and wrinkles around the eyes can be removed by taking out a section of skin and fat. Because the incisions are made very close to the edge of the eyes just below or above the lashes, or in the creases of the eye, the scar is virtually invisible. The operation takes about one and a half hours under local or general anaesthetic, the stitches come out after 3 to 4 days, and slight bruising and swelling may remain for 10 days, or more. Beneficial effects last up to 10 years if you are fortunate.

Face lift

The improvements achieved in all full face lifts are in smoothing cheeks, getting rid of deep creases, firming the jaw line and ironing out a flabby neck. It is a major surgical operation which can take up to three or four hours and the patient must be fit and in good health. Incisions are made in the hair above the temples, going down in front of the ears, under the lobes and behind the ears. The surgeon cuts the skin free from the face and simply lifts it tight before cutting off excess skin. Most patients spend two or three days in hospital and stitches come out after about a week. Bruising, swelling and numbness usually disappear within three weeks. The effects of the operation last from 5 to 10 years and a face lift is not generally recommended for women under forty, largely because their skin and face contours are not sufficiently wrinkled or sagging for a face lift to work and show real benefits.

Hints for ageing skin

1 Use a moisturising cream every day to protect and preserve the texture of your skin.

2 If you are in the sun a lot, wear a hat, sunglasses and a sunscreen if you want to avoid wrinkles later.

3 Treat the skin every night with a rich nourishing cream or a biologically-active cream.

4 Before a special occasion, give the skin a stimulating treatment – either a face mask, or facial – to produce a youthful, glowing look.

5 Once skin has wrinkled, try using biologically-active creams or serums. They are effective for many skins in reducing wrinkles and making skin more resilient.

6 The only sure treatment for badly-lined and wrinkled skin is plastic surgery but consider its advantages and drawbacks and your own motivations very carefully before you rush into it. It is not permanent.

7 Do not stay in the bath for long periods – just as long as you need to relax and cleanse your skin. And be sure to use some bath oil – a few drops will be sufficient to keep your skin really moist. Cheap bath foams and salts can very drying to skin and should never be used if your skin tends to be on the dry side anyway.

8 If you live or work in a centrally heated or air-conditioned environment, make sure that the air does not become too drying to your skin. You could install a humidifier to add moisture to the atmosphere, or even install a lot of houseplants which will also help. Be sure to reapply your moisturiser regularly.

DAYTIME BEAUTY AND EVENING GLAMOUR

Winter is the season when women can be at their most experimental with make-up. This is the party season and there is a whole range of effects you can achieve to match your mood and clothes from the purely dramatic look, to the Oriental style and the fun face decorated with glitter. But even your daytime face can take on a new look in winter. Your skin is paler in tone and winter light is less harsh than at other times of the year. Now is the time when you can be a little more adventurous with colour and go for brighter reds and strong blues, for instead of looking brash, it can light up your face and your morale on dull, wintry days.

Your winter daytime face

First of all, make sure that your foundation matches the tone of your winter skin. Your autumn foundation, which likely as not covered a fading tan, may well be a shade too dark now. You may also need one different in type and texture. Shiny gel foundations which look fine on almost all skins in summer are inappropriate on all but the youngest skins at this time of the year. Foundation evens out the colour of your skin and makes the rest of your make-up stand out, so it really is important that you get the tone and texture right. Remember that foundation should never look cakey and masklike. Always wear the lightest-textured foundation you can get away with.

Classic look

If you live or work in a city you could go for a sophisticated, classic look in winter. This admirably suits a pale, matt skin and although seemingly formal, it can be wonderfully glamorous. Try an amber-toned blusher which will add mellow warmth to the face, and colour the eyes in soft shades of mauve, taupe and golden beige for a subtle but rich effect. Charcoal grey eyeliner and mascara will add a flattering smoky look. For the all-important classical contrast, colour the lips in crystal red or rosewood. This elegant style is perfect with chic or well-tailored winter suits and warm woollen knits and dresses. It is perfect for the businesswoman or career girl.

Ethnic style

Many fashion-conscious younger women prefer a more earthy, ethnic style for winter and indeed this is admirably suited to the rough-textured tweeds and woollens and naturally coloured silks and leathers that many women find so easy to wear. This can be an extension of your autumn look but intensified to be more vibrant for dull winter months. Choose a cool beige foundation if this suits your skin tone; it can help lift a dull complexion and is an ideal base for an earthy brick blusher, stroked lightly over the cheekbones. For a more glowing effect, apply on either side of the forehead, as this helps to frame the face. Use spicy shades such as cinnamon and suede on the eyelids with perhaps a soft grey or brown in the creaseline. Smudge deep smoky blue eyeliner on the upper and lower lids and finish off with a deep violet mascara. Choose a brick or berry-coloured lipstick and accent it with lip gloss. The overall effect is warm and glowing with colour.

Day into night

Busy, working women don't usually have the time to create exotic party or fun faces. So how can your make-up look good in the evening when going straight from the office to a party or when you have a mere half-hour to prepare for a special evening out?

There is a quick and clever way of changing a day look to one for night by doing little more than adding highlights, shaders and shine in the right places. Usually this simply means emphasising the eyes, lips and cheekbones with shiny cosmetics. Whatever your daytime shade of blusher, touch it up in the evening; colour should always be more intense in the evening to counteract the draining effect of artificial light. Choose a silvery or gold-toned highlighter that echoes your blusher shade and stroke it across the top of the cheekbone. Emphasise the eyes by adding a darker shadow in the eye socket and around the outer corner. Make sure it is in the same colour family as your day eyeshadow. Highlight the centre of the eyelid with a silvery, gold or pearlised shadow and brush a little of the same sheen just under the browbone. Touch up your mascara and eyeliner if necessary and wear a lipstick which tones with but does not overpower your eye colour. Add shiny lip gloss or choose a lipstick with its own built-in shine. To see how to do this and transform your daytime face, turn over the page to the special step-by-step guide.

Winter evening faces

For your evening face, let your imagination run riot and use make-up in an inventive way to match your mood and the occasion. In the dimly-lit atmosphere of a restaurant, theatre or party you can choose to look smouldering and mysterious, dramatically glamorous, exotic or glittering and fantastical. You can achieve any of these effects — or whatever you want – once you have mastered the basic art of make-up. Whatever your age and way of life, it really is a good idea to experiment with different make-up styles not only because it prevents you from getting in a rut, but also because it is the best way to explore the potential of your own face. Of course, you do need time – never try a new make-up just before going somewhere special; it must be practised before the big occasion and be sure to test the results in the right light conditions. If you are going out, be sure to make-up in artificial light as this will be the light that you will be seen in later on.

Dramatic evening face

For this look, the emphasis is on the eyes. Choose a sienna or coral-toned blusher, according to your skin tone and brush directly onto the cheekbones with just a light touch on the temples. Use a deep iridescent bronze on the lid and give the eyes a lift by taking it up to the brow at the inner corner only and lightly under the lower lashes. Use a thin, black or soft brown pencil to line the lower and upper lashes, and to dot the creases of the eyes. Smudge the creaseline and blend with the lower lash line into a cat's eye shape. Highlight the top of the cheekbones and under the brow with gold iridescent powder. Finish off with two coats of dark brown or black mascara. Possible lip colours are fiery orange or deep red. For an interesting and truly dramatic effect, outline the lips with your bronze lip pencil before filling in with a russet-red transparent lipstick. Or choose your own favourite strong, dramatic colours and experiment with them to obtain the right effect.

Pink party looks

Shades of pink and especially fuchsia look wonderful on pale-skinned blondes. For a really stunning effect, try a light ivory base and use a pearl-pink or bluey-pink blusher on the cheekbones. For this look, the eyes are dramatically emphasised with lots of mascara or even with false eyelashes. These can be rather fiddly to put on — you need a steady hand and, for individual lashes, plenty of time.

False eyelashes

A full strip of lashes is the easiest to apply. Check the strip for length and cut with a razor if necessary. The lashes should not extend beyond the outside corner of the eyes. Apply glue to the base of the strip with a toothpick; be generous enough with the glue so that it will stick firmly but not ooze out too much on your eyelid. Then press onto your eyelid as close as possible to your natural lash line and cover the fixing strip with eyeliner.

Small strips can be used to create special effects. Applied to the centre of your lashes, they can give your eyes a wide, open look; attached to the outer edge, they elongate the eyes.

The most natural-looking effect is achieved by the lash by lash method. You need to be really dedicated – and patient – to use this technique since each false lash is attached to one of your own, and the process takes at least half-an-hour per eye. The aim is to double the thickness of your own lashes. You will need to cut individual lashes from a strip and use tweezers to attach each to the base of a lash. If it is for a very special occasion, it may be worth the trouble. If you don't have the time or patience to cope with false eyelashes, try curling the lashes – they look thicker when swept upwards rather than in a straight line.

For the pink party style, use pearl-pink shadow on the lid and under the brow – or if you prefer a more subtle smoky effect, use a matt grey shadow and blend it away towards the brow. Black kohl pencil should be smudged and blended all around the eye shape and the eyes then re-defined with black eyeliner. Finally stroke silver or silver-grey iridescent powder on the arc of the brow. Add black mascara to your own or false lashes and colour the mouth with a fuchsia pink or pale pink lipstick topped with lip gloss for a wonderfully shiny effect.

Riches of the Orient

Exotic silks, brocades and velvets demand a richly sensual look hinting at the mysteries of the orient. These rich, dark fabrics look stunning in winter, especially for evening wear. Choose a silky beige base and use a frosted blusher in honey-brown or russet swept strongly up to the temples. The eyes can be a dramatic contrast of greens and browns. Shade the upper eyelids with pearly sage green, blending up and beyond the outer corners of the eye. Stroke and blend a warm matt brown into the socket of the eye to create depth and mystery. Use a shiny sea-green pencil, smudged and blended to define the eyes above and below the lashes into a subtle doe-shape. For a really opulent look, add gold leaf highlights to the browbone. A dusky brown or black mascara completes the exotic eye look. Colour the lips in a warm rose-brown finished with lip gloss, or for a truly theatrical effect, wear a shimmering bright gold lipstick if you feel sufficiently daring and confident to carry it off in style.

Glitter with style

For a really sophisticated, dressy party when you may

be wearing sequinned, lamé or other shimmering fabrics, try using glitter as part of your make-up to pick up or contrast with the shades and shimmers of your dress. Glitter now comes not only in silver and gold but in all the colours of the rainbow, so you can be really adventurous in your choice of colours.

Glitter needs a cream base to adhere to and it should be carefully dabbed in place with a sponge-tipped applicator. However, it does come off quite easily – and onto other people's clothes if you are dancing cheek to cheek – so be careful. Glitter is not for the faint-hearted. You do need a vibrant or dramatic face and the right dress to carry it off. Use iridescent blushers and eye colours and use glitter as you would highlighters – across the cheekbones and under the brows. Do remove all traces of glitter before you go to bed. It has a nasty habit of clinging relentlessly to bed linen, face cloths and other materials.

Fun face

A style which the young and brave can adopt is the 'painted' face. This looks good with bright multi-coloured, zany clothes either with lots of frills or in geometric patterns. The aim is not necessarily to beautify the face, although young women with good features can look marvellous, but rather to create a startling effect. Use a warm beige as a base and blend a triangle of colour across and just under the cheekbones. Use a reddish-orange and highlight the top of the cheekbones with shiny yellow or bright gold. Use iridescent purple or violet on the eyelids, blending right up to the edge of the browbone. Dot and smudge black eyeliner or pencil in the creases of the eyes and outline the eyes firmly with black eyeliner. Brush yellow or gold on the browbone and define the eyebrows quite heavily with black pencil. Use a frosted lip colour in pale pink or fuchsia and paint your nails in a matching shade or in a shiny yellow, gold or even a bright purple.

Ski make-up

Not all women realise that sun reflected on snow is more burning than direct sunlight. This, combined with cold weather and chilling winds, means that the skin needs maximum protection. Use non-cloying moisturisers which refresh as they protect and always wear a sunblock. When you are out all day on the slopes use creams with a high sun protection factor number; off the slopes you need just a little less protection. Do pay particular attention to the nose which easily catches the sun and can burn badly. The lips too need maximum protection, since wind and sun can cause cracking and burning. Use a lip cream or lipstick which contains a sun filter and is richly moisturised to smooth and soothe away lines and chaps. Use day and night alone or under colour and, since lipsticks and cream wear off easily, reapply regularly.

Apres-ski beauty

The make-up you choose off the slopes obviously depends on how deep your tan is. White snow can drain colour from your face so for outdoors choose warm colours depending on your skin tone. If you are fairly well-tanned, choose warm brick or russet blushers and use shiny, burnished highlighters across the top of the cheekbones in the evening. Use shiny muted colours on the eyes and highlight the brows. Both soft and bright reds and shiny burgundies or bronzes can look good on the lips. If you have retained your fair skin, warm up your winter face with rosy blushers and use blues, mahogany and mauves for the eyes, using shiny highlights in the same tones for the evening. Pale pinks and corals, iridescent for evening, can look marvellous on fair-skinned faces. For more detailed information on Ski beauty, turn to the section on page 150.

Pale perfection for winter

Your skin tends to be paler in winter than at any other time of the year and it is a good idea sometimes to make the most of a pale skin rather than darkening it with dark-tinted foundation and bronzers. The general perception of a beautiful woman for many years has been someone with healthy-looking tanned skin, but pale can be beautiful, too, especially in the colder winter months. For daytime or evening wear, a pale, delicate complexion can look very sophisticated and attractive.

Choose a foundation shade which is similar to your natural skin tone and smooth it evenly over the skin so that the effect is matt and porcelain-like for day. A dampened cosmetic sponge will give the smoothest finish. If you have very oily skin, you might consider using some sort of blotting base product beneath your foundation to stop the skin's natural shine creeping through and spoiling the matt effect. If you have very fair skin, you can choose an ivory shade, but if you have naturally dark skin, you should not go more than two shades lighter than your natural colouring or the end result may look strange.

You can use powder to give your skin a velvet-smooth finish. Don't worry that it will look unnatural on your skin. It can be very luminous and fine. Use loose or compact powder and dust over the face. You can brush off any excess so that the powder itself is almost invisible.

Using a bright blusher will spoil the pale effect but even so you need to add definition to cheekbones. So opt for the merest hint of colour in rose or honey tones so that it does not stand out unnaturally against your skin. You can use a powder, gel or creamy blusher, although a powder will lend itself best to the overall matt effect of the make-up.

Eye make-up needs to be in tune with your skin and should be bright but not over so. Choose just two or three complementary shades and use with a bright mascara, applied thickly for maximum impact and longer-looking lashes. For greater depth, use two coats. You can accentuate your eyes with a soft pencil, outlining them perhaps in blue, violet or brown. Apply a thin line close to the lashes and smudge it softly at the corners if the effect seems a little too harsh.

A bright or dark lipstick will stand out unnaturally against your pale skin and give you an unhealthy pallor, so keep lips soft and subtle in peach, pink or coral. Outline with a lip pencil and then fill in with matt or faintly shining colour. Do not use a lip gloss as this will create a gleaming mouth which will not be in keeping with the rest of your make-up.

Make-up for older women

More mature women should take special care wih their make-up during the winter as well as their skincare system. It may well need a total re-think and a different approach to that of the past. Rather than slavishly adhere to the latest fashions, find a make-up that suits you and feels comfortable. It should be neither too light nor too heavy as both can be ageing. It is best to opt for a foundation that matches your skin tone and will cover any blemishes and variation in colour. Add a touch of pink or peachy blusher to add colour and to prevent your skin looking too matt and lifeless. Translucent powder fluffed on lightly will give a finished look and should not be allowed to settle in any facial lines to make them more noticeable. Dark eyeliner thickly applied can look very harsh, so try a soft pencil and gently smudge it in perhaps a grey or blue shade instead of dark brown or black. Some women find that bright, iridescent eye colours are best avoided in favour of softer, smoky shades of blue, green, brown, grey, violet and pink.

Lip colours in creamy soft pinks, corals and oranges look effective but you could use brighter colours for evenings out. Be sure to outline your lips with a brush or pencil before filling in with colour – this will prevent any 'bleeding' and smudging which will spoil the effect, especially if it settles in any tiny creases.

Just because you have used the same make-up perfectly well for years does not mean that this look will last you for ever. It may look dated and no longer suit the new fashions or your changed lifestyle. Analyse your present beauty potential and whether a change would be for the better.

Your winter scent

Just like your make-up or hairstyle, you may wish to change your scent, too, as a new season approaches. There are trends in fragrances and you should be aware of the latest fashionable perfumes. The fragrance you wear reflects your mood to some extent and makes a statement to other people about your personality and the way you perceive yourself. You can change your mood just as significantly with a dab of scent as you can with make-up. Do not be a stick-in-the mud and always wear the same perfume come what may – to the office, to a party or to a friend's home right through the year. Now is the time for a change especially as the party season draws nearer.

You can choose from classic, floral, oriental, savoury and lemony scents. Whereas lemony and light floral scents are particularly good in summer, heavier fragrances and the classics that always endure may be more suitable for winter. Try a softer, more sophisticated approach now with sensual, lingering overtones, perhaps with a base of wood and spices rather than flowers. Many beauty houses have their own special scent in this sort of mood. You may enjoy wearing this for going out in the evening but prefer something lighter and more classic for daytime, especially if you work in an office or meeting people.

Some fragrances are quite powerful and last all day while others need to be reapplied for maximum impact. The best places to dab them are the pulse points – on the insides of the wrists, on the temples and around the hairline, in the crooks of elbows and on either side of the ankles. Although most women tend to spray them onto their necks and behind the ears, this can be drying to skin. The important thing is to place the scent where it will gradually diffuse its fragrance in the warmth of your skin.

If you are buying a new scent, don't buy an enormous bottle. Apart from the risk that you may grow tired of it (although this is unlikely) it will not stay 'true' for a long time. Smaller bottles are more economical in the long run as they will be used more quickly and the perfume within will not lose its essential character. Changes of light and temperature affect a perfume, too, so store it in a box in a dark, cool place rather than on show on a sunny windowsill or dressing table. Some women prefer to use a spray atomiser to bottle scents. These are handy to carry about in your bag and there is no danger of them leaking and everything reeking strongly of perfume. Once you have opened a new bottle, use it frequently and don't be tempted to keep it just for special occasions.

You should not mix different fragrances as each one may take anything up to six hours to fade away. For the fragrance to stay true to itself, if you must add more perfume make sure that it is the same as the one you used earlier. And if you wash or have a bath, use bathroom accessories to match your scent – talcum powder, bath oil and soap.

Day make-up routine

1 *Cleanse, tone and moisturise before you apply the make-up. Apply concealer under the eyes, round the nose and over any blemishes and spots. Don't exert too much pressure and drag skin around eyes.* **2** *Dab on the foundation and blend upwards,* **3** *Gently roll powder onto the skin and dust off any excess.* **4** *Outline your eyes with eye liner, applying along the edge of the upper and lower lids. Do this before using eye shadow as it will soften the hard line.* **5** *Apply pale gold on the lids and brown in the sockets. Then mascara the eyelashes.* **6** *Gently brush your cheekbones with a little blusher, stroking upwards towards the hairline.* **7** *Outline your lips with a dark shade of lipstick, using a lipbrush. Carefully fill in the lips with a lighter lipstick.* **8** *Apply another coat of lipstick and some shiny lipgloss. Check your make-up in mirror to see if it needs any touching up or last-minute adjustments.* **9** *Let down your hair and brush into usual style. The finished daytime look.*

Day into night beauty routine

The step-by-step photographs on page 127 and these pages show you how to transform your daytime look into sparkling evening glamour with the minimum of fuss and effort. A beautiful night-time face is not difficult to achieve if you have got the daytime basics right. You need not even remove your day make-up in most cases – just apply more colour over the top for a truly stunning effect. This is possible no matter whether you are lightening or darkening your eye make-up. The most important thing is to add shine. You can do this by using iridescent eye shadows and pencils, highlighters, a soft shimmering shade of blusher, and a shiny lipstick or a slick of lip gloss over your chosen lip colour. Whereas your colouring was more subtle by day, you can really go to town at night and opt for brighter, more dazzling shades of blue, silver, plum and gold for eyes, and scarlets and bright pinks for lips. In fact, evening make-up can be as flamboyant and dramatic as the occasion demands and can complement your party mood, your clothes and even your personality.

This is the time for free expression and some experimentation with colours and contrasts. Even if you have to maintain a sophisticated, cool daytime image, you can still sparkle at night. As you can see from the pictures, it is not difficult and with a little flair and a steady hand you can quickly achieve a transformation. You need not even go home to do it. The 'looks' shown here could be achieved in the office, for example, with the aid of a make-up mirror. Remember that your hair should be suitably dressed for the occasion, too. Therefore if you have long hair, you may wish to put it up or pin it back from your face with pretty diamanté combs so that the loose tresses fall on either side to drape and frame your face.

Don't forget your fashion accessories – if you have a short hair cut or a piled-up evening style, you may need to wear some extra-large earrings for a really dramatic effect, or perhaps a colourful necklace to show off your long neck. Obviously your hands are important, too, and you should be sure to manicure them and paint your nails in an appropriate shade of polish – perhaps the same colour as your lipstick. Your dress should match your make-up, too, and should complement the colours you wear on your face. For example, if you wear a glittering silver lamé dress, you will need some sparkling make-up to complete the overall effect; but if you choose a more elegant little number in black velvet, you can wear a slightly more matt party face. Heavy, dark glossy satins and sumptuous velvets look good for winter evenings, worn with sparkling jewellery and exotic make-up colour in deep blues, red, gold, emerald green, violet and cinnamon. Invest in a wide range of colours and products so that you can mix and match your winter make-up to your mood and situation.

1

2

3

4

6

5

7

Night-time make-up

1 *Using the basic daytime look on page 127, you can transform your evening make-up. No need to strip it off and start again—just apply more make-up on top. For an informal dinner, add more gold eye shadow to eye lids and smooth a darker shadow into the corners outside. Apply more frosted glossy lipstick and sweep up your hair and pin in place.*
2 *For a more sophisticated look, add some copper/bronze shadow, and intensify your blusher and lipstick.* **3** *The finished look.*
4 *Change make-up completely by applying a silvery blue eye shadow on top of your basic eye colour and darkening the outer corners. Apply a pale silvery pink lipstick.*
5 *The finished look.* **6** *For evening glamour, apply more grey shadow to the eye lids with a light plum shade above on the brows. Brush cheeks with a dusty pink blusher and fill in your lips with a darker shade of lipstick such as bright red.*
7 *The finished look: ultra-sophisticated for evenings.*

WINTER HAIRCARE

MAKE WAVES WITH YOUR PARTYTIME HAIR

Winter is the time to perfect the art of looking good. Traditionally the season for party-going and evenings out, you should aim to be at your most glamorous and attractive. You now have the opportunity to dress your hair in elaborate styles, if you so wish, and to use pretty accessories such as diamanté combs and clips and shiny bows, ribbons and headbands. To really look your best you should, perhaps, have your party hair styled by your hairdresser, but this is simply impractical – or too expensive – for many women. Keep such visits for a very special occasion, like a grand ball, and acquire the art of setting and styling yourself. With so many do-it-yourself hairdressing aids on the market, this is relatively easy once you have learned the knack of using your appliances correctly, and without damaging your hair.

Art of blow-drying

Nowadays with casual, unstructured hairstyles in vogue, blow-drying is the most popular way of creating bouncy, natural-looking styles for both day and evening. Some styles do not need heat at all. If your hair has been permed to give you tight, squiggly curls, run your fingers through your hair and leave it to dry on its own. If your hair has been well-cut and falls naturally in a wavy or straight style, comb or brush it into shape and leave it. For a good blow-dry result, however, a precision haircut is essential. When this is the case, blow-drying can give long-lasting shape and volume to virtually all lengths of hair.

Tips for blow-drying

1 Towel-dry hair and comb it through gently to remove any knots or tangles. Hair is more prone to damage when wet, so do this carefully. Do not pull wet hair from the roots. If your hair is long, start combing it from the bottom and work upwards towards the scalp.

2 If your hair is exceptionally fine, straight or unruly, or prone to static electricity, use a little blow-dry lotion which adds body and strength to the hair as you dry it. It can also help to hold the style. The tendency today is not to use setting lotions, especially alcohol-based ones which dry out the hair. However, there are occasions, mostly on cold, damp evenings, when a light setting agent can help to hold your hair's shape and bounce longer than usual.

3 Hold the hair dryer at least 15cm/6 inches away from your head and move the dryer around all the time so that the heat is not concentrated on too small an area for too long.

4 Use warm, not hot, air otherwise you will burn your hair causing the ends to be dry, brittle and split.

5 Divide your hair into four sections – crown, back and two sides – and pin up each section separately on top of the head.

6 Start at the back of the head and begin with the bottom of the back. Place a circular or semi-circular brush under the hair at the roots and blow-dry over it, swirling the hair into position.

7 Dry the middle and then the upper strands of the back section in the same way. Then dry the sides and finally the front section, working up from the undermost layer to the top layers.

8 Once the hair is dry, you can use several styling tricks as described below.

Styling tips for blow-drying

Turning the hair under: wrap the dried hair around your brush and direct the heat along the top of the brush for a moment or two. Hold in place until the hair has cooled and then gently unwind, taking care not to tear the hair.

To flick up hair: wrap the hair over the brush, blow with hot air. Hold the brush in place until the hair has cooled and then gently unwind.

Full curls: use a circular 'jumbo' brush. Wrap each section of hair around the brush and blow-dry until the curl has taken. Hold until the hair has cooled and then unwind the hair gently.

Tighter curls: use a circular brush with a small circumference and proceed as for full curls.

Straight hair: grip the hair underneath with a broad flat brush and stretch it tightly as you dry it.

To give hair lift and height: lift the hair up from the scalp and dry underneath each layer before winding into a curl or shape.

For extra bounce: blow the hair in the opposite way to the direction you eventually want it to go. Then switch direction and shape as desired.

Fringe: brush away from the face first, then bring forwards, twirling around the brush. Direct the heat from the dryer onto the brush and then let the hair cool before removing the brush.

Brushes: use natural bristle brushes if your hair is very fine or frizzy, and a nylon/bristle brush if your hair is thicker or coarser. If you like to vary your style between tighter and fuller curls, use two to three circular brushes of different circumferences.

Setting hair in rollers

Roller setting is a bit outmoded in these days of natural, easy-to-manage hair, yet there are times when a slightly more formal 'set' look is required. Rollers are particularly useful for shaping curly, wavy or very thick hair. Roller setting and drying is a relatively lengthy business if you are doing it at home, so allow yourself plenty of time. Above all, don't try to rush the drying process or you will ruin all your efforts.

The size of rollers you use depends on the type of curl you want. Big rollers will provide large, loose curls; small rollers hold only a little hair and result in small, tight curls. If your hair is very coarse or curly you need large rollers. Depending on the style you want and your haircut, you can use a combination of both, possibly some rolling forwards and some rolling back. Do try to avoid rollers with brushes in them; these can tangle and tear the hair.

Tips for roller setting

1 Squeeze excess moisture out of the hair with a towel and gently comb a little setting lotion or gel (preferably alcohol-free) through the hair.
2 Brush the hair back from the face and divide into neat sections as for blow-drying.
3 Work from the top of the front and gradually move down and around the bottom of the back.
4 Generally rollers are set downwards at the back and sides. You can vary this by rolling upwards if you really know what style you are hoping to achieve and have a natural professional touch. However, with roller setting, the cut and brushing out usually determine the finished look and style.
5 Comb the section of hair you are going to roll, hold it straight up from the roots and wind it carefully and smoothly with your fingers around the roller. Make sure all loose ends are neatly tucked in.
6 Do not put too much hair in one roller or it will not curl properly and do not wind the hair so tightly that it pulls at the roots.
7 Secure with a wide hairpin making sure that the pin does not hurt or scratch your scalp.
8 For hair too short to wind around a roller – usually at the nape of the neck and sides – make a pincurl, winding hair from the tips in the direction you want and secure with a flat metal clip or hairgrip.
9 Tie a loose net around your hair before you dry it. This helps to prevent any rollers falling out and also helps to dry the hair without ruffling it too much with the hot air from your dryer.
10 Dry the hair naturally if you can, although this takes time and usually is not very practical; or use a hood or blow-dryer.
11 Allow the hair to dry completely before removing your rollers. If the slightest dampness remains, roll up again and dry for a bit longer.
12 Once you have taken the rollers out, brush the hair straight back and up, and underneath at the nape of the neck. This helps to evenly distribute the curl and gets rid of demarcation lines left by your curlers. Put into final shape using a comb or brush as needed.

Heated rollers

These are simply marvellous party aids which can give you a mane of fluffy curls in twenty minutes. However, they should only be used on dry hair to shape or set styles between shampoos – and they should not be used every day. They can dry out the hair and cause it to lose shine, and they can also alter the colour of tinted or bleached hair. They really should only be used for special evenings out to transform your hair quickly and easily into a glamorous party style. If you find you are relying too heavily on these rollers over a longish period, think about restyling your hair, or having a soft perm, both of which are better for the health of your hair. Of course, if you are using heated rollers more regularly for winter party-going, be sensible and give your hair extra conditioning. Some manufacturers recommend special conditioning agents to use while setting so read the instructions carefully when you buy heated rollers.

Hints for heated rollers

1 Heated rollers can be used over the whole head or simply on certain sections to give curls or waves.
2 As with ordinary rollers, small sizes produce tight curls or ringlets, medium rollers bouncy curls or waves and large rollers, looser curls or waves.
3 When putting in rollers, start at the top of the head and work back. Hold the hair vertically from the scalp and make sure all ends are neatly tucked in.
4 Rollers remain hot for about 15 minutes after you have taken them from their heating rods.
5 Allow the hair to cool completely before taking the rollers out. Usually by the time you have finished rolling the back and sides, the top sections are cool, so this sort of setting really is quick.

Curling tongs:

These are very useful for smooth, gentle, wavy styles or loose curls and as a quick way to repair a drooping style. Avoid uneven bends and kinks by making sure that the end of each section of hair is firmly secured around the tongs and that you wind hair firmly and smoothly. However, heated tongs can easily scorch the hair so do use them with caution – they should never be

so hot as to burn the hand. Curl in the same direction as you would for rollers.

Curling brushes:
These are easier to use than tongs since the brush makes winding the hair simpler. They are also more versatile because they can be used to straighten as well as curl hair. Be careful, though, not to tangle the hair on the brushes or else it will break easily.

Crimpers:
These are rather like an electric sandwich-maker but with a corrugated interior to turn the hair into a series of tiny, even waves. They can give a marvellous, crinkly Pre-Raphaelite look to medium or long hair and are great fun for special occasions, but should never be used to achieve this effect on a regular basis. They are especially damaging since heat combined with the crimping ridges will quickly dry out and break even the healthiest hair.

Hairspray:
A good haircut and style shouldn't need hairspray, and unless you have really fine, unmanageable hair, avoid using it for your natural everyday style. More complex party styles can often be helped by a light hairspray, particularly on damp, cold evenings when a style into which you have put a lot of effort can go lank. Modern hairsprays are light in texture, do not dull the hair and aim to gently hold it in shape and not 'lacquer' it. Buy a kind that suits your hair type and make sure you brush it out at night before you go to bed. Hairspray does attract grime and dirt, so you may need to wash your hair more frequently.

Perming the hair
If you are bored with your straight hair, or find you are spending a lot of time using rollers to curl your hair, think about a perm. Perms are soft and less damaging than ever before and they are extremely versatile. They can be used to give lift and body but no curl to fine hair; you can have a mass of tight curls; or a soft wave; or you can confine your perm to one section of the hair such as stubborn ends or particular layers. As your hair grows, your perm will flatten out near the roots but even so a good perm will be effective for about six months.

There are many home perms available but unless you really do have the professional touch, it is advisable to go to your hairdresser for a good perm. Not everybody's hair can take a perm successfully and home efforts can sometimes end disastrously. Moreover, home perming is complicated and extremely time-consuming. A good hairdresser will not only advise whether your shape and cut is suitable for the perm you want but will also get the solution strength and roller size right for your hair type and style of curl or wave.

However, some ultra-modern perms, thanks to new beauty technology, actually leave your hair in superb condition – shiny, silky, soft and full of body. They can be used to perm even the most difficult hair and incorporate conditioning agents both in the neutraliser and in the perm itself. Some even contain a special combination of lactic acid and emollients to counteract the effect of humidity on your hair. In hot discotheques and centrally heated environments, your permed hair may sometimes flop, but these new special perms can prevent this and keep it looking full and natural.

The degree of porosity of the hair is also an important factor when considering which type of perm to have. Healthy hair is less porous than damaged hair. The state of the cuticle is the crucial factor in determining porosity. If it lies flat, reflects the light and gives the hair a healthy sheen your hair will be less porous. But if the cuticle scales are broken and protruding due to over-strong shampoos, too much sun, chlorine or salt water, or harsh colourants and perming solutions, then it will be very porous indeed and this will affect the perm, resulting in an uneven curl, especially if some areas of hair are more porous than others. Now there are substances which can even out the hair's porosity and fill in the eroded scales on the cuticles themselves. These products are often offered as a special pre-perming treatment for very damaged hair, and could be very valuable if your hair falls into this category.

However, many women still worry needlessly about having a perm – especially about the final look of it and whether it will suit them. Will it go frizzy? Will it be easy-to-manage? Will it require meticulous setting? These are frequent questions to hairdressers. A good experienced hairdresser who knows your hair and the way you like it to look will be able to advise you. Some top salons even use a computer to help them decide the best products to use, the ideal processing time, what size curlers, rollers, rags or tissue paper to get the required effect. Talk to your hairdresser and see what she advises – she is the best judge. After the perm, your hair should look healthy and natural, and feel silky and soft — a great pick-me-up in the middle of winter when you need a boost.

Straightening the hair:
This is a far more drastic procedure than perming and cannot be done at home. And unlike perming it can only be carried out once a year. Special chemicals are used which can be particularly damaging, causing severe hair breakage, and you will need to carefully protect the hair from the harmful effects of sun and sea water. Straightened hair can also react unfavourably to the chlorine in many swimming pools. If you have very curly hair, it is far wiser to take advantage of your hair type – ask your hairdresser's advice about styles – than to straighten it.

Long hair can be piled up on top of the head or left sleek and loose for a party or special occasion.

Party hair styles
For short and medium length hair, the quickest and easiest way to achieve a party hair style is with heated rollers and tongs. Within half-an-hour you can transform a casual day style into a riot of waves or curls, perhaps swept off the face with combs, hairclips or headbands covered with glitter or sparkling colours. Long hair swept back with a shiny ribbon can also cascade into instant curls or be crimped into a romantic Pre-Raphaelite look. Even without the use of appliances, long hair can be swathed into a myriad of elegant styles, the hair fastened with decorative pins, clips and bows. See below for ideas.

Instant colour
An even quicker way to 'dress' your hair for an evening out is to use instant colour spray. This is ideal for busy women who may be going straight to a party from work and have no time to restyle their hair. There is a wonderful range of colours now available from simple silver and gold to a glittering range of exotic fantasy colours such as vivid magenta, royal blue and saffron if you are feeling particularly adventurous. Be daring and choose brilliant or pearlised colours. Magenta streaks can look wonderful on layered brown hair, and gold, saffron or shiny copper on fairer hair. You can choose colours that match your eye make-up or clothes – or spray only sections of the hair like tips or layer lines. Use colour spray on long styles to single out a plait or to highlight a coil or knot on the top of the head. Do remember to brush out all traces of colour before you go to bed, otherwise stains may be left on your bedlinen.

Party styles for longer hair
Edwardian style: the hair is drawn back high and evenly from the face and caught in a circular knot on the crown; a few strands should curl onto the cheeks. Use instant colour to highlight or streak as you wish.
Straight plaits: start two thin plaits, one on either side of the head. Take to the centre back and unite to form one wider plait. Secure at the tip with a covered elasticated band and a tiny glittering bow.
French pleat: brush the hair back off the face and to one side. Roll over the hand in a wide pleat and secure top and bottom and along the sides with hairgrips. You can add interest by using a glitter-tipped comb to secure the sides or by adding a decorative rosette or flower at the top of the pleat.
Alice look: for long curly hair. Brush the hair straight back from the face and hold back from the ears with a gilt-ornamented band.

FIGHT CELLULITE AND BE A BATHTIME BEAUTY

It takes more discipline to be beautiful in the winter when there is less pressure on you to stay slim and to keep your skin smooth and moist especially when it is probably concealed between several layers of bulky warm clothing. The only way to acquire self-discipline is to make an effort to practise it regularly and incorporate your new beauty routines within your way of life. You need dedication, energy and enthusiasm to look after your looks and body at this time of year. You can start off by waging war on cellulite and developing a bathtime routine which incorporates bath exercises and beauty treatments. Learn also how to give yourself a soothing massage that will stimulate tired circulation and relax you all over.

You should also watch your figure to check that no winter bulges develop on hips, thighs and stomach – this is all too easy in cold weather when you may be eating more than usual. If you belong to a gym or exercise studio, make sure that you continue to attend classes regularly and are not tempted to skip any. This winter exercise will prove beneficial when the spring comes round again and you are in good shape with clear, moist skin and strong, supple muscles.

Get rid of cellulite

Many people think that cellulite is just another fashionable word for fat, but it is a special problem which seems to affect the majority of women, even very slim ones. Basically, it is an internal pollution problem which manifests itself in the form of deadened areas of skin. You can discover whether you have cellulite by performing this simple test: pinch the skin on your inner thigh or upper arm. If it looks puckered and dimpled rather like orange skin, then you have a cellulite problem and it needs treating fast to prevent it spreading and getting worse.

If you want to stay free of cellulite, you will have to make the effort to work on it every day – two or three times a week is not enough. So what is cellulite? Well, it occurs when toxic wastes and metabolic by-products build up in the body and form a sort of 'tissue sludge' in areas where circulation is poor or muscles are in spasm. These areas gradually become deadened to the touch and even when you pinch, pummel or knead them there is little feeling.

Eating an unhealthy highly refined diet that lacks fibre and may make you constipated creates the ideal conditions for cellulite to form, especially if you lead a sedentary lifestyle and seldom exercise. Toxic wastes will gradually build up in your body as they are not eliminated in the normal way, or through the skin. If you are under stress and tend to eat a lot of processed foods, then you are even more susceptible to cellulite formation, while smoking and drinking alcohol can exacerbate the problem. Smoking, in particular, steals vitamin C from your body which is urgently needed for the formation of healthy skin collagen. In addition, nicotine interferes with normal circulation of blood,

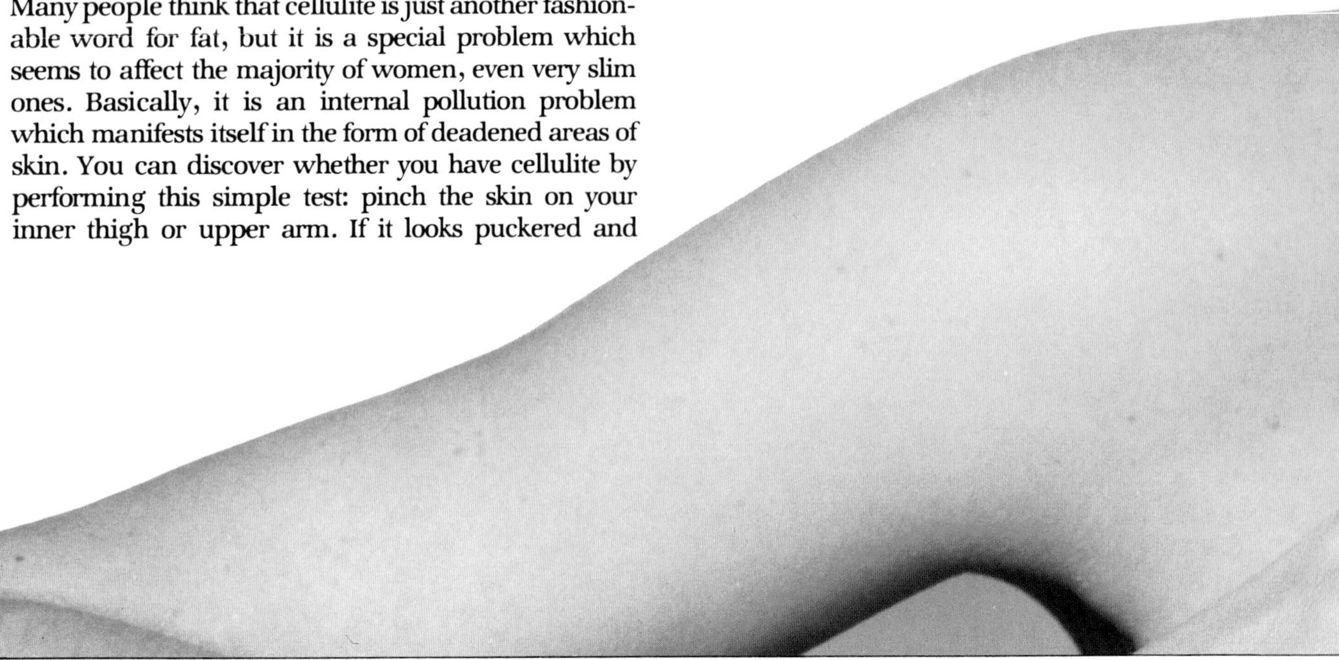

creating an environment which is just right for cellulite. If you have a cellulite problem you will have to check your lifestyle and improve it immediately. Here's how to go about it:

1 Improve your diet

Eat lots of fresh fruit and vegetables, whole-grain cereals and other high-fibre foods. Cut out highly refined products and sugar, tea, coffee and alcohol. Instead, drink fresh fruit and vegetable juices. These will help cleanse your system and eliminate wastes. Try to drink at least two glasses a day – choose from carrot, celery, cucumber, watercress, apple and orange. The best ones are freshly squeezed in a juice extractor and drunk immediately, before any vitamin C oxidises. You should also drink plenty of natural spring or mineral water. Following the special spring-cleaning regime outlined in the Spring diet section will prove beneficial.

2 Take regular exercise

Physical activity, especially the aerobic sports which improve cardiovascular efficiency, will improve your circulation, help get rid of deadened areas, tone up muscles and burn up fat. It will certainly help prevent the formation of further cellulite even if it cannot totally cure an existing problem.

3 Take care at special times

Most women seem to get a cellulite problem when their bodies are undergoing great hormonal changes; for example, when they first start taking the contraceptive pill, get pregnant or go through the menopause. At times like these, you must take special care to eat a good diet, take regular exercise (specially designed antenatal ones if you are pregnant) and to gently massage yourself regularly along the guidelines laid down below.

4 Make use of massage

Deep massage, especially Rolfing, can help break down tissues and encourage and restore normal circulation in areas of cellulite. A powerful electric massager will also break up these awkward pockets, but it is better to seek professional help from the experts at a beauty salon and enrol for a course of either Rolfing or connective tissue treatment than to try and do it yourself. In the wrong hands, deep massage can be damaging and you should ensure that the beautician or physiotherapist is properly trained or you may end up with disfiguring broken veins.

A gentle hand massage can only be beneficial, however, and you can learn to do it yourself, preferably after a bath or shower while your skin is warm and receptive. It is also soothing and relaxing after a busy day and a useful skill to acquire. It is important to start off lightly and gradually build up the pressure as the blood begins to flow better through the area – after about five minutes of stroking. Always start stroking above the area of cellulite and away from it to draw away any toxins and eliminate them. You will build up a steady rhythm as you go along.

Massage routine: Use some oil or a figure-firming gel so that your hands can move across the skin's surface more easily and smoothly. Otherwise they may get hot and sticky and will not move freely as your circulation is enlivened and the skin gets warmer. While you massage any areas of stubborn cellulite, make sure that you are dry and warm and comfortable. Lie on the bed or on a rug or towel on the floor and cover any bare parts of your body with a blanket or towel so that you do not catch cold after a warm, bath.

1 Start off by stroking the skin very gently, hand over hand, gradually increasing the pressure until your skin is warm and starts to tingle, always working away from the heart.

2 Knead lightly but firmly to boost the circulation and break down any adhesions. You can very gently twist the cellulite with your thumbs and knuckles as long as it is not painful. Do not pummel your skin as this may be potentially harmful. Just apply firm pressure.

3 When your hands and arms start to ache and grow tired, ease down and stroke and gently coax the skin again, getting progressively slower.

4 Rub in some moisturising cream or a specially formulated product for fighting cellulite and softening the skin.

5 Invest in a massage glove

You can buy a specially designed massage 'glove' which is made of rubber and encloses a bar of soap, usually made with extract of ivy. It fits snugly around your hand and is easy to use in the bath or shower on wet skin as you work up a soapy lather. You can rub very hard indeed and if you use it regularly, at least once every day for a month or more, you will notice the difference. You will feel slimmer and firmer and your cellulite should look better. The gloves are refillable – you just buy another bar of soap when the old one runs out. Don't be alarmed if your skin looks very red and sore after using the glove – it will soon fade and resume its normal colour.

You can also use an ordinary hemp glove or massage mit to boost the circulation and encourage the elimination of skin toxins. These are available from most chemists and department stores. For maximum effect, rub briskly every time you bathe or take a shower.

Bathtime beauty

It is not enough just to cleanse and moisturise your face – your body needs your attention and loving care, too. Regular bathing will keep your skin feeling really soft and fresh and smelling sweetly. However, you must take care to bathe correctly or the water can be drying and ageing to your skin. After a busy day, one of the most relaxing, calming things you can do is to lie back in a warm bath; and early in the morning when you need waking up, or before you go out on a date in the evening, a shower can be very invigorating. Generally, baths are soothing whereas showers are brisk and stimulate the skin, leaving you tingling and glowing.

It is important to develop a bathtime routine from which you never waver. This should be: bathe or shower, dry, massage and moisturise. Never look on bathing as a waste of valuable time – it is amazingly therapeutic and a great way of recharging your batteries, relieving tension, muscular stiffness and headaches. If you feel like a bath, have one and enjoy it. You know that you will feel better and more beautiful afterwards.

Choosing the right temperature

When you run a bath or shower your choice of water temperature is crucial. A combination of factors will influence your decision, including the time of day, how you feel and the benefits you wish to receive. Most of us choose a sensible middle path and avoid scalding heat and Spartan ice-cold water but, nevertheless, we do tend to choose too high a temperature which, when the cumulative effect of literally hundreds of baths is taken into account, is potentially damaging to skin. Here is a brief guide to bathing temperatures from the very cold to the extremely hot:

Cold: at a temperatue of 55-65°F/13-18°C, you are more likely to want a bracing shower than an icy soak in the tub. As a morning pick-me-up under a powerful jet of water to stimulate circulation and get your muscles moving, it may be acceptable, but it certainly isn't relaxing and you should not stay in there long.

Tepid: in hot weather, this is the perfect water temperature at 75-85°F/24-29°C for cooling you down, especially after a day outside in the sun or beside the sea. Reviving and refreshing, it helps boost tired circulation, too. If taken immediately before going to bed and not languished in for too long, it will also help you to sleep better.

Warm: for most people, this is the best all-year-round temperature at 85-95°F/29-34°C. Soothing and relaxing, it is a most enjoyable wallow and will help you sleep at the end of a tiring day. It is also ideal for easing out tired, aching muscles, relieving pain and helping to avoid stiffness after strenuous activity. If you like to take a bath after a run, cycle or work-out, this is the best temperature range for you. Just lie back and gently massage your sore legs to ease out tension.

Hot: there is no excuse for taking a bath above 95°F/34°C although it is surprising how many people do this. There are no benefits whatsoever and you will probably feel lethargic and sagging afterwards. Hot baths loosen your muscles, dehydrate the skin and cause it to get slack and age more rapidly if taken regularly over a large period of time. They also encourage the formation of tiny broken veins on the surface of the skin which look ugly and cannot be removed in most cases.

Of course, it is difficult to measure the temperature of your bath and you will get to know what is right instinctively as soon as you dip a toe or finger into the water. You can use a thermometer if wished but it is a fiddly business and not necessary.

Fragrant baths

Baths are even more enjoyable and relaxing when they smell pleasantly of your favourite scent. Adding a few drops of sweetly smelling bath oil to the water will help keep your skin moist and prevent it drying. It is also very soothing and afterwards you will feel suitably perfumed and relaxed. You can add a foaming bath gel if you like to languish in a luxurious bubble bath but beware of some of the cheaper brands which can be dehydrating to skin. There are some products, however, which leave your skin moist and silky smooth. They cleanse your skin, boost circulation and encourage the elimination of toxins. Or you can add some specially formulated bath salts or powder to the water which have a restful effect on your body and will help you recover from stress and tension. They smell lovely and come in a wide range of fragrances to recreate the smell of the sea or various flowers, herbs and fruits. Use a good-quality soap but only sparingly as it may be drying – the milder pH-balanced bars are best as they will not strip away too much of your skin's natural protective acid mantle.

Bathtime exfoliating

Like your face, your body can also benefit from regular exfoliating treatments to remove dead cells, and smooth and soften the skin. You can purchase special creams which contain coarse granules for this purpose. They rid the skin of impurities and excess sebum by thoroughly cleansing blocked pores to give it a satiny sheen. You should pay particular attention to any areas of rough skin – for example, on knees, elbows and heels. Rub briskly all over your body and then rinse off under the shower, or with the shower attachment before bathing. Practise this ritual two or three times a week while you have rough skin and then at least once a week thereafter.

Bathtime activity

Unless you are very tired and in need of some peace and quiet and a rest, don't just lie there in the bath –

after an initial soak, get to work on any neglected areas of your body. Remove any dead patches of skin on the soles of your feet with a pumice stone or liquid hard skin remover if it is very stubborn. Invest in a massage mit or glove to attack cellulite and condition your skin. It will also help remove toxic wastes near the surface. A loofah is also useful. This rather bizarre-looking coarse-textured sea gourd is useful for rubbing away dead cells and stimulating circulation. A word of caution, however; if your skin tends to be sensitive, massage only gently at first – vigorous rubbing and scrubbing may irritate it and even produce tiny broken veins.

You could try applying a special figure firming gel to your waist, hips, thighs and any other areas which are inclined to run to fat. Rub in lightly into your damp skin in circular movements to accelerate blood circulation and activate the cutaneous liquid masses. It will soon become saturated with waste matter and should be rinsed off thoroughly.

Special bathtime exercises will help tone up muscles. Practise them if you have a largish bath. Lie on your back and do alternate leg kicks, as high as you can, 20 times each side. Then try gripping a sponge between your feet and slowly raising your legs above the water without bending your knees. Keep them straight and hold for a count of five and then lower. Repeat the exercise 10 times.

After-bath beauty

Rubbing yourself briskly dry with a soft towel will make you feel tingly and warm. When you are thoroughly dry (and don't forget to wipe between your toes and any other areas that most people miss) you should moisturise your skin. Too many hot baths can be very drying to skin, especially in winter. Many women labour under the misapprehension that bath water will actually replace lost moisture in their skin but this is not true. In fact, it has the opposite effect, so you must not skimp on the moisturising part of your bathing routine. It should be second nature to keep a jar or bottle beside the bath and automatically smooth it into your skin while it is still warm and pink.

You can buy special body lotions which are designed to restore the skin's natural balance and suppleness. Lightly smooth them over your body in circular movements. They will quickly be absorbed by the skin to leave it feeling really satiny and soft.

Before you get dressed or ready for bed, you will need to apply some deodorant or antiperspirant under your arms to prevent body odour. You can choose from roll-ons, lotions, creams and aerosol sprays, either unperfumed or in a wide range of fragrances. Wait until you are cooler, and all dampness has disappeared and your skin is completely dry before applying. They are more effective used on hairless skin so be sure to shave your underarms regularly. However, you should never apply one of these products immediately after hair removal as it might irritate the area and cause a sharp, stinging sensation and even a nasty rash. Wait a few hours and then apply.

Daily bathing, using an antiperspirant and wearing clothes made only from natural fibres (cotton, linens, wools and silks) will cut down on perspiration and keep you smelling fresh. Although there is nothing unpleasant about perspiration itself (it is your body's natural cooling system), it quickly develops an offensive odour when small bacteria get to work on the wet skin. If you have a problem and tend to perspire a lot, you may have to use an extra-dry antiperpsirant with a special long-lasting formula to keep you dry and odour-free throughout the day.

Last of all, after your bath, spray yourself with some cool scent or eau-de-cologne to freshen you up, or dust all over with talcum powder to dry away any dampness and leave your skin feeling really fragrant and soft. If you want to massage yourself, now is the time to do it (*see* cellulite and massage on page 138).

Skipping to make you glow

You may be surprised to learn that skipping is a good

The backwards skip

The cross-over skip

form of aerobic exercise – it helps condition your muscles as well as your cardiovascular system. Boxers have long used skipping to get fit and trim, build up stamina and lose weight before a big fight, so why don't you try it, too. In many ways, it is the ideal form of exercise for winter because you can do it indoors in your own home and the only special equipment you need is a skipping rope. It is easy to do and you can control the speed and time you spend – add more repetitions and skip faster as you get fitter and more proficient. You can even try some complicated fancy skipping as you progress.

How effective skipping is as an aerobic exercise depends on the heartbeat rate you reach. To work out your ideal level of aerobic activity and the best training rate for you, all you have to do is subtract your age from the figure 200 and then subtract another 30. For example, if you are 30 years old, subtract 30 from 200 to find your maximum pulse rate of 170. Now subtract 30 to find your minimum training level of 140. To benefit aerobically from skipping your pulse rate should fall in this range of 140-170 beats per minute.It is easy to take your pulse before and after exercising and halfway through as well to measure your resting rate and training rates. If it is higher than 170 you are overdoing it; lower than 140 and you are not skipping hard enough.

One of the problems about skipping is that it is not so exciting or interesting as, say, running or cycling which entail a change of scenery and can be a social activity if you exercise with friends. Skipping is more solitary and monotonous in nature. You probably won't be able to take more than 10 minutes or so at a time, and if so you should supplement your skipping with another form of aerobic activity as well. However, just 10 minutes of skipping three or four times a week will bring health and fitness benefits.

How to skip: this may seem obvious but if you haven't skipped since you were a child you may have forgotten some of the skips such as backwards and even cross-over skips. However, you should start off by skipping forwards, just twirling the rope forwards over your head and jumping over it. The length of rope is very important if you are to skip safely and correctly. It should be long enough that if you stand on the middle of it, the handles should reach up to your armpits. If it is too short, buy another longer one; but a long rope can be shortened by winding the ends round the handles to reach the required length.

Start off by learning the skipping rhythm. You can do this by holding both ends of the rope in one hand and swinging it from behind your back down in front of you so that the middle hits the floor. Repeat this several times, trying to keep the rhythm steady and listening to the sound it makes as it hits the ground. Change hands and repeat the other side.

Now you are ready to start skipping over the rope keeping the same rhythm. Just before you hear the rope hit the ground all you have to do is to hop over it – not too high but just enough to clear the rope. You can make just one hop per revolution or two hops if you turn it more slowly. You will soon build up a steady pace and rhythm and be skipping quite fast.

The running skip: this should not be attempted until you are a proficient skipper with good natural rhythm. Practise by skipping slowly and holding one foot off the ground in front of you each time you skip. You should be bouncing on the balls of your feet as though you are running on the spot very slowly. When you are quite proficient at this speed, you can try skipping faster. An even more difficult variation is to cross your arms in front of your waist as you skip. After the rope passes over your head, cross your arms, jump through the loop and uncross your arms. Don't be surprised if you end up in an untidy heat on the floor the first time you try this cross-over skip.

The backwards skip: as a variation on the forwards skip, twirl the rope backwards over your head instead of forwards and jump over it each time. Build up the rhythm until you get faster. You could even try the running skips in a backwards motion.

WINTER DIET

KEEP OUT THE COLD WITH WARMING FOOD

During the winter, you tend to eat more and when you over-indulge, you tell yourself by way of compensation that you can always diet when the spring comes to lose the unwanted weight that you have put on. But to keep warm and healthy, you don't have to fill up on high-calorie puddings and cream sauces – you can enjoy thick, warming vegetable soups and stews, hot fresh fruit desserts and even nutritious winter salads. This healthy food is nourishing, delicious and not too calorie-laden either.

Winter is not a good time for dieting, and the last thing you will feel like on a cold, dull day is cutting down on your food. Learn how to keep your figure through the winter months and how to eat well. A combination of healthy diet and regular exercise at this time of year will prevent any worries about unwanted fat, heavier hips and thighs and a growing spare tyre. Make good use of low-fat and high-fibre ingredients to keep your weight stable; and be careful about the cooking methods you choose – for example, you should always grill food in preference to frying.

Winter salads

Salads deserve a special mention as many people seem to think that they should forgo them during winter. Lettuce, cucumber and traditional salad vegetables are expensive and scarce at this time of year and, anyway, are seldom at their best. However, you should try to make a salad an integral part of your daily diet to supply vitamins and minerals to keep your hair and skin looking good – glossy and healthy. They will also help protect you against coughs and colds and other seasonal infections.

You have to be imaginative to create delicious salads in winter, and make more use of unusual ingredients. The best salad greens are watercress, Chinese leaves, chicory/Belgian endive, radicchio (Italian red chicory which has a slightly bitter taste but adds a marvellous touch of colour to salads) and crisp iceberg lettuce. You can mix all these with chopped or grated winter vegetables such as baby turnips, crisp celery, fennel, mushrooms, carrot, raw cauliflower florets and even cooked parsnips, potatoes and Jerusalem artichokes. Fresh fruit will add sweetness and colour – try diced or sliced red-skinned apple, tangerine, orange or grapefruit segments, seedless grapes, sliced pear, lychees and avocado. You can even add dates and raisins. For a more crunchy texture, you can scatter some cashews, peanuts or hazelnuts over the top. Add a faint mist of chopped parsley or chives and toss in your preferred dressing – a lemony, garlic or curry flavoured mayonnaise; a yoghurt and fresh herb mixture; or olive oil with garlic, mustard, lemon juice or herb vinegar. To make the salad more substantial and a main course meal, add some chopped chicken, diced cheese, flaked fish or cubes of cooked ham, or mix with cooked beans, lentils or brown rice.

You can also experiment with warm and hot salads – very popular at the moment with exponents of *Nouvelle cuisine.* For simpler versions, try a hot potato salad – cubes of cooked potato tossed in a warm oil dressing with a sprinkling of fresh herbs, crumbled crispy bacon, chopped onions and anchovies. Spinach, bacon and mushrooms are also delicious served in a warm dressing, as are Chinese leaves.

Here are some main course recipes for you to try which are filling and warming but not too high in calories. All the recipes given serve two people. Include them in your daily wholefoods regime.

Soups

Fish chowder

15ml/1 tablespoon oil
1 small onion, chopped
2 rashers streaky bacon, chopped
15ml/1 tablespoon flour
300ml/½ pint skimmed milk
200ml/8floz fish stock or water
225g/8oz cod or firm white fish
50g/2oz shelled shrimps
2 medium potatoes, peeled and diced
salt and pepper
pinch nutmeg
juice of ½ small lemon
chopped parsley

In the oil, sauté the onion and bacon and stir in the flour. Add the milk and stock gradually and bring to

Opposite: Chicken noodle moussaka (recipe page 147)

the boil. Reduce the heat, add the fish, potato and seasoning and simmer for 20 minutes (until the potatoes are tender). Add the lemon juice and parsley. Simmer for 5 minutes and serve.

Pea and ham soup
150g/5oz split peas
1 small onion, chopped
1 carrot, diced
1 leek or stick celery, chopped
1 parsnip, chopped
15ml/1 tablespoon oil
570ml/1¼pints chicken or ham stock
small piece smoked bacon or gammon
salt and pepper
sprig fresh thyme (or dried)

Soak the split peas for about 1 hour, and drain. Sauté all the vegetables in the oil until tender. Add the stock, split peas and gammon. Bring to the boil, skimming the surface, season and simmer very gently for 2 hours until thick and smooth. Remove the gammon, discard any fat and then cut up the meat into small pieces. Return to the soup and serve.

Spicy carrot soup
225g/8oz carrots, diced
1 large parsnip, diced
1 leek, chopped (optional)
1 onion, chopped
1 clove garlic, crushed
15ml/1 tablespoon oil
550ml/1pint chicken stock
75ml/3floz skimmed milk
good pinch turmeric and nutmeg
salt and pepper
squeeze lemon juice
pinch brown sugar
chopped parsley

Sauté the chopped vegetables in the oil until soft. Add the stock, bring to the boil and then simmer for about 20 minutes. Liquidise the soup until smooth. Reheat with the milk, seasoning, lemon juice and sugar. Garnish with the chopped parsley and serve.

Bean and bacon soup
50g/2oz dried kidney beans (or 175g/6oz canned beans)
1 onion, chopped
1 carrot, diced
1 clove garlic, crushed
small piece swede or turnip, diced
15ml/1 tablespoon oil
3 lean rashers streaky bacon, chopped
10ml/2 teaspoons mixed dried herbs
good pinch turmeric
2 tomatoes, skinned and chopped
juice of ½ small lemon
salt and pepper

Soak the beans overnight if using dried ones. Rinse and place in a pan of fresh water. Bring to the boil for 10 minutes, then rinse and replace in the pan with fresh water. Boil and simmer for 1 hour. Sauté the vegetables in the oil until soft. Add the bacon, herbs, turmeric and 450ml/¾ pint water. Boil, then simmer for 15 minutes. Add the beans, tomato, lemon juice and seasoning. Simmer for 10 minutes and serve with grated cheese.

Goulash soup
1 small onion, chopped
½ green pepper, chopped
1 small carrot, diced
15ml/1 tablespoon oil
225g/8oz stewing beef, diced
15ml/1 tablespoon paprika
good pinch caraway seeds
450ml/¾pint beef stock
2 tomatoes, skinned and chopped
2 potatoes, peeled and diced
salt and pepper
natural yoghurt and chives to garnish

Sauté the onion, pepper and carrot in the oil until soft. Add the beef and spices and fry gently until brown. Add half the stock and simmer for 60 minutes. Add the tomato, potato and seasoning and the remaining stock. Simmer for about 45 minutes or until the meat and vegetables are really tender.

Potato and watercress soup
1 small onion, chopped
1 clove garlic, crushed
15ml/1 tablespoon oil
1 large potato, diced
100g/4oz watercress
400ml/14floz chicken or vegetable stock
salt and pepper
15ml/1 tablespoon cream or yoghurt
squeeze of lemon juice

Sauté the onion and garlic in the oil until tender with the diced potato. Add the watercress and stock and bring to the boil. Reduce to a simmer and cook gently for about 20 minutes. Liquidise until smooth. Return to the pan and stir in the seasoning, cream and lemon juice. Season to taste and reheat.

Opposite: Somerset supper (recipe page 148).

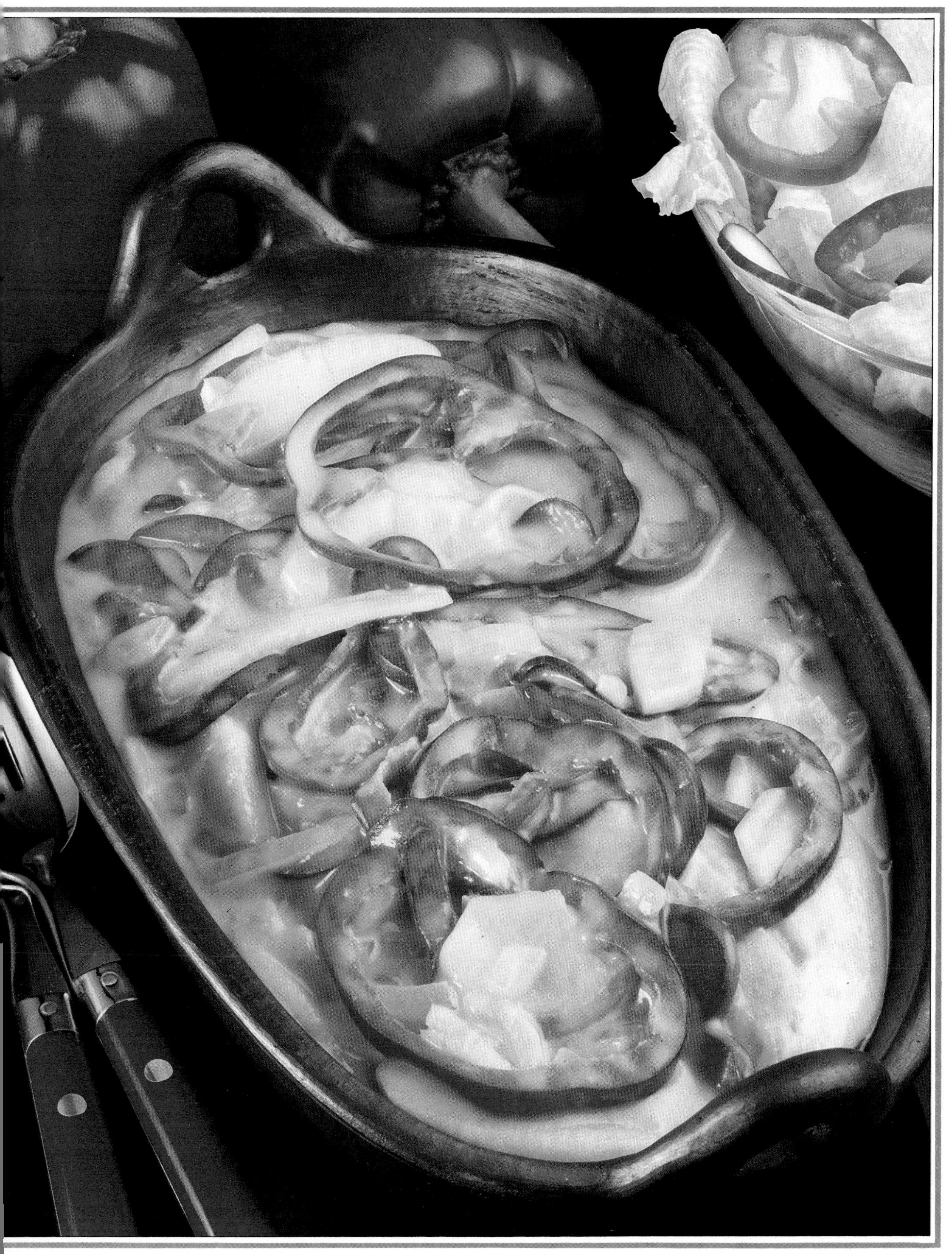

Swede and bacon soup
1 small onion, chopped
1 clove garlic, crushed
225g/8oz chopped swede
50g/2oz diced lean bacon
15ml/1 tablespoon flour
400ml/14floz stock
15ml/1 tablespoon cream
salt and pepper
chopped parsley
crumbled crisp bacon rashers

Sauté the onion, garlic, swede and bacon in the oil until tender. Stir in the flour and cook for 1 minute. Add the stock and bring to the boil. Simmer for about 20 minutes. Liquidise and return to the pan. Reheat with the cream, seasoning and parsley. Garnish with crisp bacon if wished.

Celery and blue cheese soup
1 small onion, chopped
5 sticks celery, chopped
15ml/1 tablespoon oil
15ml/1 tablespoon flour
400ml/14floz stock
50g/2oz mashed blue cheese
50ml/2floz milk
squeeze lemon juice
salt and pepper
chopper parsley

Sauté the onion and celery in the oil until tender. Stir in the flour, cook for 1 minute and add the stock. Bring to the boil, stirring, and simmer for 45 minutes. Liquidise, return to the pan and whisk in the blue cheese and milk. Add a squeeze of lemon juice and seasoning. Heat through and sprinkle with parsley.

Hot dishes

Liver and tomato casserole
275g/10oz sliced lamb's liver
seasoned flour
15ml/1 tablespoon oil
2 rashers streaky bacon, chopped
1 onion, chopped
15ml/1 tablespoon flour
300ml/½pint stock
3 large tomatoes, skinned and chopped
15ml/1 tablespoon tomato paste
juice of 1 orange
strip orange rind
salt and pepper
pinch oregano and sage
50g/2oz sliced mushrooms
6 black olives
chopped parsley

Dust the liver with seasoned flour and sauté in the oil in a flameproof dish until browned. Do not overcook — about 2 minutes each side. Remove and keep warm. Sauté the bacon and onion and stir in the flour. Cook for 2 minutes and add the stock, tomatoes. tomato paste, orange juice and rind, seasoning and oregano. Bring to the boil and stir until the sauce thickens. Replace the liver and cover the dish. Cook in a preheated oven at 180°C, 350°F, gas 4 for 45 minutes. Add the mushrooms and olives, remove the lid and cook for another 10 minutes. Sprinkle with parsley.

Spicy beef tajine
1 onion, chopped
1 clove garlic, chopped
1 large carrot sliced
15ml/1 tablespoon oil
275g/10oz stewing steak
15ml/1 tablespoon flour
300ml/½pint stock or water
15ml/1 tablespoon tomato paste
good pinch cumin, coriander and cinnamon
pinch cardamom seeds
25g/1oz soaked prunes
50g/2oz soaked apricots

Sauté the onion, garlic and carrot in the oil until tender. Add the meat and brown. Stir in the flour. Cook for 1 minute and add the stock. Bring to the boil and then add the tomato paste and spices. Bake in a preheated oven at 150°C, 300°F, gas 2 for 2½ hours. About 45 minutes before the end, add the soaked dried fruit. Serve with wholewheat pasta.

Vegetable couscous
1 small onion, chopped
1 carrot, diced
1 leek, sliced
½ small green pepper, chopped
½ small red pepper, chopped
15ml/1 tablespoon oil
good pinch each cinnamon and ginger
small packet saffron powder
400ml/14floz water
15ml/1 tablespoon tomato paste
100g/4oz couscous
1 courgette/zucchini, sliced
2 tomatoes, skinned and chopped
50g/2oz French beans
75g/3oz cooked chick peas
15ml/1 tablespoon raisins
1 pear, peeled, cored and diced

few sprigs chopped parsley
Hot sauce:
30ml/2 tablespoons tomato paste
2.5ml/½ teaspoon harissa paste
pinch paprika

Sauté the onion, carrot, leek and peppers in the oil until tender. Add the spices, saffron, water and tomato paste. Bring to the boil and reduce the heat to a simmer for 30 minutes. Soak the couscous in cold water for 10 minutes. Drain and put in a steamer above the vegetable stew. Leave open to steam. After 20 minutes, add the courgette, tomatoes, beans, chick peas, raisins, pear and parsley. Cook gently for 20 minutes. Season the couscous and gently separate the grains. Just before serving, remove a ladleful of cooking liquid and blend in a bowl with the hot sauce ingredients. Arrange the couscous in a ring and pour the stew into the centre. Serve with the hot sauce.

Baked fish Greek-style
1 small onion, cut in rings
¼ bulb fennel, sliced
1 clove garlic, crushed
2 white fish steaks or 1 small fish, gutted and cleaned
juice of 1 lemon
strip lemon rind
4 large tomatoes, skinned and chopped
½ small red or green pepper, thinly sliced
few black olives
salt and pepper
150ml/¼ pint red wine or fish stock
chopped parsley

Arrange the onion, fennel and garlic in the base of an ovenproof dish. Place the fish on top and add the lemon juice and rind, tomato, pepper, olives and seasoning. Pour in the liquid, cover with a lid or oiled paper and bake in a preheated oven at 190°C, 375°F, gas 5 for 20-25 minutes. Sprinkle with parsley.

Brown rice risotto
1 onion, chopped
1 clove garlic, crushed
1 leek, sliced
15ml/1 tablespoon oil
175g/6oz long-grain brown rice
75ml/3floz white wine or Marsala
450ml/¾pint chicken stock
1 packet saffron
salt and pepper
175g/6oz cooked chicken, chopped
50g/2oz sliced button mushrooms
30ml/2 tablespoons grated Parmesan

Sauté the onion, garlic and leek in the oil in a large flat pan until soft. Add the rice and stir until glistening. Add the wine and stock, together with the saffron and seasoning, and bring to the boil. Reduce to a bare simmer and cook gently until all the liquid is absorbed and the rice plump and cooked. Add more liquid if necessary (about 45 minutes). Just before serving, add the chicken and mushrooms and heat through. Serve with Parmesan and a green salad.

French bean cassoulet
225g/8oz cooked haricot or aduki beans
1 small onion, chopped
1 clove garlic, crushed
15ml/1 tablespoon tomato paste
good pinch each basil, oregano and parsley
45ml/3 tablespoons red wine
2 tomatoes, skinned and chopped
pinch brown sugar
salt and pepper
few drops Worcestershire sauce
15ml/1 tablespoon lemon juice
Topping:
15ml/1 tablespoon wheatgerm
15ml/1 tablespoon chopped nuts
30ml/2 tablespoons grated Parmesan

Sauté the onion and garlic in the oil until tender. Add the tomato paste, herbs, wine, tomato, sugar and seasoning. Bring to the boil, reduce the heat and add 100ml/4floz water or stock, together with the beans and remaining ingredients. Cover and leave in a preheated oven at 180°C, 350°F, gas 4 for 1 hour. Add more liquid if necessary and sprinkle with the topping. Bake uncovered for 15 minutes until crisp and golden. Serve with green salad.

Chicken noodle moussaka
50g/2oz macaroni or noodles
1 small aubergine or ½ large one
1 small red or green pepper, diced
2 skinned tomatoes
1 onion, chopped
1 clove garlic, crushed
15ml/1 tablespoon oil
100g/4oz chicken, cooked and cut in chunks
salt and pepper
200ml/8floz white sauce or velouté sauce
15ml/1 tablespoon breadcrumbs
chopped parsley
knob margarine

Cook the noodles until tender. Drain and set aside. Meanwhile, slice and salt the aubergine and leave to drain for 30 minutes. Wash well. Sauté the pepper, tomatoes, onion and garlic in the oil until tender. Fry the aubergine until golden. In a deep ovenproof dish, layer up the aubergine, chicken, vegetables and noodles. Season well and pour over the sauce. Bake in a preheated oven at 180°C, 350°F, gas 4 for about 20 minutes. Sprinkle with breadcrumbs and parsley and dot with margarine. Replace in the oven for 5-10 minutes until crisp and golden.

Somerset supper

15ml/1 tablespoon oil
1 small onion, sliced
2 pork chops or steaks
15ml/1 tablespoon flour
200ml/8floz apple juice
salt and pepper
1 red pepper, sliced
1 dessert apple, peeled, cored and sliced
15ml/1 tablespoon natural yoghurt

Heat the oil and fry the onion until tender. Toss the pork in the flour and fry for 5 minutes each side. Remove and keep warm. Gradually add the apple juice. to the pan juices, stirring well and bring to the boil. When it thickens, turn down the heat and add the chops, seasoning, pepper and apple. Simmer for 30 minutes or until the pork is tender. Remember from the heat, add the yoghurt and serve.

Winter salads

Chicken and chicory salad

225g/8oz cooked chicken, cut in strips
1 large head chicory, washed and sliced
1 radicchio, washed and separated in leaves (optional)
1 red-skinned apple, cored and diced
50g/2oz Swiss cheese, diced
25g/1oz walnuts, chopped
small bunch watercress, washed and trimmed
1 small red pepper, thinly sliced
30ml/2 tablespoons mayonnaise
50ml/2floz natural yoghurt
juice of ½ lemon
salt and pepper
chopped parsley

Place the chicken, chicory, radicchio, apple, cheese, nuts, cress and red pepper in a salad bowl. Blend the mayonnaise, yoghurt and lemon together. Season and toss the salad gently. Sprinkle with chopped parsley.

Hot dill potato salad

275g/10oz small or new potatoes
3 spring onions, chopped
2 rashers crisp-grilled streaky bacon

Avocado winter salad (recipe on page 149)

10ml/2 teaspoons dill
few anchovy fillets
75ml/3floz natural yoghurt
squeeze lemon juice
salt and pepper
chopped dill or chives to garnish

Boil the potatoes until tender but still firm. Cut into chunks and place in a bowl with the crumbled bacon, dill and anchovies. Toss gently in the yoghurt and lemon juice. Season and sprinkle with herbs. Serve the salad while it is still warm.

Italian tuna and pasta salad

225g/8oz cooked or canned butter beans
1 small onion, sliced in rings
200g/7oz canned tuna in brine, in chunks
30ml/2 tablespoons chopped parsley
Dressing:
30ml/2 tablespoons olive oil
10ml/2 teaspoons herb vinegar
juice of ½ small lemon
pinch sugar
salt and pepper

Mix the salad ingredients together in a bowl. Make the dressing and toss gently. Scatter over the parsley.

Chinese bacon and avocado cups (see recipe below)

Chinese bacon and avocado cups

4 large Chinese leaves
1 avocado, peeled and diced
squeeze of lemon juice
15ml/1 tablespoon oil
50g/2oz streaky bacon, chopped
1 onion, sliced
3-4 button mushrooms, sliced
1 hard-boiled egg, sliced thinly
salt and pepper

This makes a good winter salad-type snack meal. Arrange the leaves to form double 'cups' on a serving dish. Add the avocado and squeeze over some lemon juice. Heat the oil and sauté the bacon, onion and mushroom unil cooked. Mix with the avocado in the cups and garnish with egg. Serve warm.

Avocado winter salad

1 avocado, peeled and sliced
few crisp lettuce leaves
few sprigs watercress
1 small onion, thinly sliced
1 small red pepper, sliced
2 tomatoes, quartered or sliced
50ml/2floz French dressing

Mix the salad ingredients together and toss well in the dressing. Serve immediately. If wished, use Chinese leaves instead of lettuce for a more crunchy texture.

Puddings

Winter fruit salad

1 red apple, cored and sliced
1 pear, cored and sliced
1 tangerine, segmented
few seedless grapes
1 small kiwi fruit, sliced
4 peeled lychees
1 small banana, sliced
juice of 1 small lemon
100ml/4floz unsweetened orange juice

Put all the prepared fruit in a serving dish. Sprinkle with lemon juice to prevent the apple and banana discolouring. Pour in the orange juice and serve with a dollop of natural yoghurt.

Cider baked pears

2 large hard pears
2 thin strips lemon peel
small cinnamon stick
150ml/¼pint cider
50ml/2floz water
15ml/1 tablespoon honey
15ml/1 tablespoon chopped nuts

Peel the pears and flatten their bases, leaving the stems intact. Stand in an ovenproof dish with the lemon peel and cinnamon. Pour the cider over the top with the water and finally drizzle with honey. Bake at 170°C, 325°F, gas 3 for 1¼ hours, until the pears are tender but firm. Leave to cool, remove to a serving dish and boil up the pan juices until they are thick and syrupy. Pour over the pears and sprinkle with nuts. Serve still warm with a spoonful of thick yoghurt.

Dried apricot fool

50g/2oz dried apricots
juice of ½ small lemon
10ml/2 teaspoons honey
100ml/4floz thick yoghurt (eg. Greek)
toasted almonds

Soak the apricots overnight, then simmer gently until tender. Strain and liquidise. Leave the purée to cool, then stir in the lemon, honey and yoghurt. Top with the toasted almonds and chill.

WINTER SKI BEAUTY

GET FIT AND BEAUTIFUL FOR THE SKI SLOPES

More women than ever before are discovering the excitement and pleasure of skiing and winter-sports holidays but many are ill-equipped to care for their skin and hair which may need special treatment on the cold, sunny, snow-covered slopes of high mountains. You must adapt your make-up, too, to the bright sunlight and wintry conditions. Here is some practical advice on how to stay beautiful and keep fit in the snow, as well as tips on après ski looks and diet.

Skiing suncare

The sun's ultraviolet rays are reflected off the white snow and can give you a nasty burn unless you protect your skin with a powerful sunscreen. For advice on choosing the right product and sun protection factor number for your skin type, turn to Summer Suncare. On a really sunny day, a snowfield can double the winter sun's intensity. Apply the sunscreen to your face and all exposed areas of your body. Unless it is very warm, you will probably be quite well covered up to protect you from the cold and wind. But even the wind can burn your skin and give it a weather-beaten look. If you want your skin to stay fresh and smooth and not like old leather, wear that sunscreen and reapply often. Carry it around in your pocket while you are skiing. If you do get burnt, treat the affected parts by cooling them down with cold water and moisturising with soothing after-sun preparations and oils.

You should also protect your lips with a zinc oxide paint for extra-protection, a thick coat of glossy lipstick or a specially designed lip sunblock which moisturises as well. If your lips tend to chap easily, you could apply an under-coat of lip repair cream to 'fix' them, seal in their natural moisture, strengthen fragile membranes of skin and soothe away cracks and lines. Worn underneath a lipstick (a pale silvery shade of pink looks good with colourful skiwear against a white snowy backdrop), it will give long-lasting protection and prevent your lipstick smudging and bleeding.

Under your foundation, you should wear a moisturiser to form an effective barrier between your skin and the drying effects of the cold air. The trick of good skincare is not to let winter penetrate and test your skin's strength. It can shelter behind a weatherproof moisturiser and foundation with built-in sunscreen.

Skiing make-up

Don't wear bright, dramatic make-up in the snow. Cold, alpine beauty is pale with subtle silvers and pinks, or tanned and natural. Although you can make-up your eyes beautifully they will be concealed for much of the day behind dark or mirror-coated ski goggles to protect them from the harsh sunlight. However, you can emphasise them at night when it's time for *après-ski* entertainment. Whatever make-up you choose, the stress should be on protection and prevention of moisture loss at all times.

Skiing is hard work and involves a lot of physical effort so you should wear waterproof mascara as you are bound to get hot and sticky at times and the dazzling sunshine may make your eyes water. To avoid streaking, you can 'set' your make-up with a dab of translucent powder. Of course, if you want to cultivate a tan and wear a lighter tinted moisturiser with built-in sunscreen, this won't be necessary.

Your ski wardrobe

Part of the fun of skiing is showing off your glamorous skiwear. You can hire an anorak jacket and salopettes at one of the big ski retailers which has its own hire department before you depart for your holiday, but if you intend to take skiing seriously and go several years running, it is less expensive in the long run to buy yourself a new outfit. You can even wear your jacket at home as a car-coat so the money will not be wasted. Whether you opt for a two-piece salopettes and jacket or a one-piece suit, you should look for a non-slip material which is warm and cosy to wear. The trouser bottoms should be the right length and fit around your boots. There is a whole range of fashionable skiwear in the shops in very attractive colours and styles – make sure the suit you buy is waterproof and comfortable to wear with enough room to allow freedom of movement.

You will also need a ski hat to keep your head warm. It should fit securely and not fly off if you take a tumble or gather speed going down a slope. Gloves or mittens in bright colours can match your ski-suit and should be really waterproof and warm. Allow plenty of room for your fingers to move inside them. When you're not skiing but tramping about in the snow you will need some special *après-ski* boots with non-slip soles so that

you can walk safely on impacted snow and ice. They will keep your feet warm and dry, and come in shaggy fur or so-called 'moon boots'.

Goggles are a 'must' to protect your eyes and reduce the risk of snowblindness. They are also useful when it is snowing or the surface is very powdery and sends up a shower of snow as you ski across it. They are preferable to sunglasses as you can slide them up and down when necessary, or you can even wear them on your arm when they are not required. Buy a quality pair with lenses in neutral colours to cut out glare and reduce eye strain. Brown lenses are best for bright sunlight; yellow for misty conditions. You can wear sunglasses instead, but it is a nuisance to push them back onto your forehead and hold them in place when they aren't needed – goggles are easier to wear. However, pack a pair of sunglasses into your 'bum-bag' for walking in the sun or dining out and sunbathing on mountain tops.

Your ski equipment

The three indispensable items for all skiers are skis, boots and bindings. You can hire or buy these, but it is vital that you get the right ones for you. Boots, in particular, must fit snugly and be comfortable to wear – many a winter holiday has been ruined by ill-fitting ones which cause soreness and blisters.

Skis: these are wonders of modern technology and come in many lengths and types. They may be competition skis, grand sport skis, sports skis or compact skis. Ask the experts in the shop which type you need and what length they should be. Length of skis is correlated to your weight and height. Most beginners should start off with sports skis, and you should make sure that they are sharpened and waxed regularly to keep them in good condition.

Ski boots: although these look clumsy and uncomfortable to wear, they can make all the difference when it comes to successful, enjoyable skiing. You can choose between front-opening and rear-entry boots in many styles and colours. When trying on boots for comfort, consider the following points:

1 They should not constrict the top of your foot.
2 Your toes should feel comfortable – not tightly packed or squashed.
3 Your ankles should be comfortable – not crammed into the boot.
4 The boots should be waterproof and leakproof.
5 There should be no uncomfortable edges or joins, especially at the top.
6 They should be well lined for insulation and warmth as well as comfort.

These factors will not only affect the way you feel in the boots but the way you ski in them, too. In fact, the boots should have certain basic design features which make them efficient:

1 The side supports at the front of the boots should be firm and well-supported for steering the skis.
2 They should hold your heels down securely or you will not be in control of your skis and your steering will be affected.
3 There should be side flex adjustments at the tops with a choice of positions to give good snow contact.

Bindings: never cheat on your safety bindings or adjust them wrongly. Always follow the manufacturer's instructions and they should protect you in a fall. Most consist of a heel-piece, toe-piece and ski-stopper which are multi-directional. Whichever way you happen to fall, and even the most experienced skiers do from time to time, your bindings will help you to avoid injury.

Prepare for your ski holiday

You can take measures to get ready for your wintersports holiday by learning the basics on a dry ski slope if there is one near your home. There should be a qualified instructor who will coach you through a course of lessons. It will probably feel very strange at first and you will not be able just to zoom off down the slope. Your skis may feel odd, long and cumbersome; your boots heavy and stiff; and even your trusty sense of balance may desert you. Don't worry — everybody feels like this in the beginning. You will soon learn to move on the artificial slope and perform various simple manoeuvres. At first, just concentrate on getting your balance right and learning how to get up if you fall down. Armed with the knowledge of a few lessons you will be ready to try out the real thing – a nursery slope well-covered with genuine snow.

Get fit for your ski holiday

Skiing, like running and cycling, is an aerobic sport and you need to be reasonably fit if you are to really enjoy and master it. While you ski, you will use most of the muscles in your body, and it is a help to be slim and supple. Endurance and stamina are important, too, as you may be out for several hours skimming across the snow. You cannot expect to slide effortlessly across the surface – you have to work at it, bending and stretching as you weave your way down the slopes.

Coordination and strength are important and the fitter you are, the better prepared you will be, and the more likely you are to enjoy your holiday. If you have been following an aerobic programme throughout the year, working-out regularly in a gym or with weights, then you are probably quite firm anyway. But skiing puts additional strain on your leg muscles, especially thighs, and you should try to strengthen them in anticipation of what is to come. Ankles and knees also take a lot of the strain in flexing and turning, so they should be ultra-flexible and strong.

You may be surprised to know that you need powerful shoulders and arms for pushing on the poles as you propel yourself across the snow. Weight-training under supervision in a gym is an excellent way of building up strength in your muscles and joints. You can start off gradually with light weights and gradually build up the repetitions as you get fitter. If you are unfit, you are quite likely to feel stiff and tired at the end of your first day and ready for a hot bath and bed. If you want to enjoy the nightlife (in moderation!) and be fresh and ready to face another day's skiing, you must build up some aerobic stamina. Jogging and skipping are useful ways of doing this.

Some health clubs and gyms even run special pre-ski fitness courses to help you get into shape and build up stamina, strength and suppleness. If you want to perform well on the piste you must work on strengthening not only your upper and inner thighs but your abdominal muscles, too. These help you to improve your posture and support you during skiing. General stretching exercises will increase joint and muscle flexibility. Exercising before you go away will also improve your figure so that you look more dashing and glamorous in your skisuit and full of vitality.

Just concentrate on building up your stamina so that you are well-armed for hours and hours of skiing without becoming over-tired. Here are some exercises that you can try out at home. Practise them every day for at least one month leading up to your holiday departure date. Wear something loose and comfortable such as a tracksuit and allow yourself plenty of space for all-round movement.

Thigh strengtheners and toners

1 Lie on your left side, supported by your left elbow with the other arm bent in front of you, palms flat on the floor. Bend your left leg inwards slightly and extend your right leg above it. Lift it off the floor and lower it again without touching down. Be careful not to roll backwards. Do this 10 times with your foot flexed and then 10 times with toes pointed. Turn over and repeat on the other side.

2 Now to make it more difficult, lie on your side, supported in the same manner, and try to lift *both* legs off the floor together. Repeat 10 times.

3 Lie on your left side in the same way and bend your right knee over your left leg. Try to lift the extended left leg off the floor 10 times with toes flexed and repeat with toes pointed. This is marvellous for reducing and strengthening the inner thighs.

Abdominal firmers and strengtheners

1 Lie on your back with your arms extended at your sides, palms upwards and your knees bent. Wedge your feet under a chair or chest or ask a friend to sit on them or hold them down. Slowly raise your body off the floor into a sitting position and then gently lower yourself to the floor. Your head and shoulders should not touch down. Repeat 15 times, gradually building up the repetitions. Feel the 'pull' on your stomach muscles. If they feel tight and sore the next day and it hurts to laugh, you have overdone these sit-ups. Rest for a day or two and then try again with fewer repetitions.

2 Lie on your back, hands behind your raised head, and lift your legs off the floor. Hold them vertically above you and support your body with your hands. Now cross your legs in a scissor-like movement, backwards and forwards 20 times. Then lower your legs to the floor and relax.

3 Lie on your back, hands behind your raised head and elbows well back. Lift your legs and hold them at a 45° angle to the floor. Lift your head and shoulders up and exhale. Lower again without touching down and inhale. Repeat 20 times.

Calf stretchers and strengtheners

1 Stand with feet shoulder width apart, knees slightly bent and back straight. Extend your arms straight out in front of you and clench your fists. Press down hard on the floor with your heels, then release and relax your hands. Repeat 20 times to stretch out calf muscles.

2 Standing, with hands resting on your hips, bend your left knee and push it forwards in front of your body, and extend your right leg behind you, keeping both feet flat on the ground. Keep your back straight and feel the stretch in your calves. Hold for about 20 seconds and then repeat five times.

3 Stand about four feet away from a wall and lean towards it, resting your bent elbows and forearms against it. Keep your heels on the ground, tuck your bottom well in and concentrate on keeping your whole body in a straight line. Hold for 10 seconds and then repeat three times.

Quadriceps stretch and firmers

1 Kneel down on the floor in an upright position. Then supporting yourself with your arms, elbows bent and forearms on the floor, lean as far backwards as you can go without experiencing any discomfort. Hold for 10 seconds, relax and repeat.

2 Stand with your back against a wall, knees together. Now gradually slide down the wall, keeping your back flat against it, into a sitting position so that your thighs are perpendicular to your body. Hold this posture for as long as you are able – you will feel the stretch in your quads. This is an excellent strengthener for skiing.

3 Kneel down on all fours – knees squarely under hips and hands under shoulders. Raise your left leg backwards and bend your knee. Hold the stretch for 10 seconds and then repeat with the right leg.

Aerobic exercises
These will help you develop strength and stamina. Try room-running or jogging on the spot for at least five minutes, preferably 10. Then do some jumping jacks, jumping up in the air and twisting your body at the waist from side to side. Or you can run, cycle or swim. Do these exercises at least three times a week for 30 minutes each session.

Ski slope exercises
These can be performed on a dry slope or snow-covered piste to warm-up muscles and stretch them out before you start skiing. Wear your skis throughout. They may help you avoid muscle tears and strains.
1 Ski stretch: standing with skis parallel, about 30cm/12 inches apart, bend over from the waist to touch the toe of your left boot with both hands. Straighten up and twist round. Bend over to the right and repeat. Try this exercise 10 times. It will increase suppleness and mobility, especially around the waist and hips, and will stand you in good stead for when you are performing tricky manoeuvres and turns.
2 Ski flex: bend down over your skis with knees bent and extend your left leg out to the side with knee bent at a slight angle so that the side of your foot and ski are lying along the ground. Push downwards, relax and then repeat with the other leg.

Après-ski beauty routine
After several hours' hard skiing or even practising the basics on the nursery slopes, you are bound to feel tired, stiff and a little sore, especially if you took one too many tumbles. The best way to relax and ease out stiff, aching muscles is to run a warm bath when you return to your hotel or chalet and add a few drops of soothing oil. Lie back in it and have a good wallow, letting your muscles soak luxuriously and feeling the tension flowing away out of your body. Make use of this time before you get ready and changed to go out for dinner or dancing, to massage aching muscles gently, stroking and kneading them in the warm water. This will help prevent any stiffness the following day when you hit the ski slopes again.

Towel yourself dry and moisturise liberally to counteract dry skin. Use a good antiperspirant and lie down and relax for 10 minutes with a cotton wool pad soaked in soothing skin freshener placed over each eye. Enjoy these few quiet moments to yourself in a busy, energetic day. You will feel fresher after skiing if you remove all your daytime make-up and sunscreen and start again. After cleansing, toning and moisturising thoroughly, make-up your evening face to suit the occasion. Some resorts are informal and you should achieve a casual look which is beautiful but understated. Other resorts, however, are very smart and jet-setting indeed and you may have to look suitably glamorous, especially if you are dining out at a notable restaurant or going night-clubbing.

If you have started to tan, complement your golden skin with glossy silvers, golds, bronzes and honey shades. You can use iridescent eye shadows and glosses and just concentrate on adding some evening sparkle. Cover your lipstick with some shiny lip gloss. Silvery-pink highlights and lipsticks are very flattering, but you could opt for more extravagant colours like fuchsia lips and deep blue eye shadow. Be sure to emphasise your cheekbones and give your face shape and definition with a shimmering blusher, and add some soft highlights to your brows.

Just because you are on holiday, don't forget your hands. They may have been covered up all day under warm gloves, but in a party dress, your hands and arms are on show. For a special occasion, give yourself a manicure and varnish your nails in brilliant colours to match your lipstick and make-up.

Check for hairy or stubbly legs if you are wearing a short dress and don't forget to dab some perfume behind your ears and on wrists, neck, hands and chest so that you smell irresistible. Before you get changed into evening clothes, wash your hair. It will probably be a bit worse for wear after being covered or pinned up under a ski-hat or hood all day. Shampoo and condition thoroughly and set in your favourite style. You can take a handy dual voltage travel hairdryer with you which folds up neatly inside your case. A gas-energised styling brush is also useful when travelling.

Your ski diet
A skiing holiday is not a good time to slim. By all means go on a sensible diet before you leave home to lose a few excess kilos (pounds) but you should eat regular hot meals when you are out in the cold all day. Remember that skiing is an aerobic exercise and actually increases your metabolic rate. Even at the end of the day when you finish skiing your metabolism will stay at a higher level than normal and will help you burn up calories fast. This does not mean that you can make a pig of yourself and eat over-large portions of rich, fattening food. Try to make sensible choices on the menu, giving yourself the occasional treat.

If you are skiing in the Alpine resorts of Austria, Switzerland, France and Italy this can be difficult. Food is often filling and calorie-laden with delicious-looking gâteaux, steaming hot chocolate topped with a swirl of whipped cream and wafer-light fruit strudel and more fresh cream as local specialities. You will obviously succumb to some of these temptations. Pasta dishes, hot stews, goulash, vegetables and fruit will all be healthy. Eat sensibly along the guidelines laid down for a wholefoods diet – you will need the benefit of these

nutrients to keep you warm, give you energy and feel really fit and healthy. You could take some vitamin supplements with you if you suspect that the food may not be very nourishing or rich in nutrients.

Always eat a filling breakfast before you go out into the cold for a day's skiing. This will supply much-needed calories to keep you going and give you energy. Muesli, eggs, bacon, wholemeal toast and orange juice are all good food choices. Never skip lunch, even if it is only a nutritious snack – don't fill up on creamy cakes and pastries instead. A bowl of hot vegetable or goulash soup with crusty bread is more nourishing. And eat a good dinner, but not too late – about seven o'clock is the best time so that your digestion will have plenty of time to do its work before you go to bed and you can burn off some of the calories going for a walk, dancing or a toboggan ride. If you eat really late, you are more likely to store these calories as fat and to have a restless night, as your heart will be pumping faster to aid the digestive process. Wine is tempting and refreshing as an accompaniment to your dinner but don't over-indulge. You won't feel like skiing the following day if you are slightly jaded with an aching head. Drink it in moderation and top up your glass with mineral water – perfectly acceptable in Europe.

If you stick to these general diet rules and eating guidelines, you will be able to enjoy your skiing holiday and not have to keep worrying about your figure, whenever you eat a delicious meal out in a restaurant or in the hotel dining room. Just apply your normal healthy eating principles to whatever is on offer and have fun experimenting with the new dishes and exciting flavours of a foreign cuisine. Who knows? You may get some interesting ideas.

INDEX

Numbers in *italics* refer to illustrations

Recipe index

Picture credits

We would like to thank and acknowledge everybody who provided pictures for this book. All the photographs were supplied by Helena Rubinstein with the exception of the following:

British Iceberg Growers' Association: page 79
California Raisin Advisory Board: page 83
C & A Ski-wear: pages 151, 155
Carmel: pages 43, 45, 49, 107, 108, 109, 111, 143, 145, 148, 149
Clairol: pages 31 (top right), 69 (top right), 131
Club Mediterranée: page 71
L'Oréal: pages 31 (top left), 69 (top left), 135 (top left)
Speedo (Europe) Ltd: page 53
U.S. Rice Council: page 81